Murph

The Sports Entrepreneur Man and His Leagues:

The American Basketball Association, the World Hockey Association, World Team Tennis, the International Basketball Association, Roller Hockey International, Bobby Sox Softball and Professional Women's Softball

By Dennis Murphy

Fullerton, California

Edited by Richard Neil Graham

Published by Inline Hockey Central

Cover photos:
(*Top right and down, in color*)
Gordie Howe,
Larry Brown,
Wilt Chamberlain,
Wayne Gretzky.
(*Bottom left to right, in black and white*)
Billie Jean King, Bobby Hull, Julius Erving, Chris Evert.

Back Cover:
Photo by Peter Young

Murphy, Dennis Arthur, 1926-
Murph: The Sports Entrepreneur Man and His Leagues

Printed in the U.S.A. by CreateSpace

ISBN-13: 978-0-9834060-4-4
ISBN-10: 0983406049
LCCN: 2013931155

Table of Contents

SECTION I: The Early Days (1926-1962)

Page 1: *The China Days and My Early Years, My Love of Sports, USC Days, My Mayoral Days, A City Hall Memory*

SECTION II: The ABA (1967-1976)

Page 10: *The American Basketball Association and its Beginning, A Spin-Off League, Our New York Press Conference, Organizing the ABA, Pat Boone, Rick Barry, Bob Bass, The Best Sports Transaction, Slam Dunk, The Great Dr. J, Hubie Brown, Lee Meade, George Mikan, Bob Cousy, The Indiana Connection, Wilt the Stilt, Reuben "Ruby" Richman – A Canadian Basketball Man, The Miami Floridians, Hal Blitman, My Stay in Denver, The Denver Rockets, The Dallas Chaparrals, Jerry Saperstein,*

Earl Foreman, Larry Brown, Doug Moe, Bill Sharman, The New Orleans Buccaneers, The New York Nets, Lou Carnesecca, Charley Finley, A Signing Nightmare, Spencer Haywood and his Hardship Case, Arthur Kim, The Referees, The Three-Point Shot, The Troubled Stars, The ABA All-Stars, Great Pride

SECTION III: WHA (1972-1979)

Page 71: *A Piece of Cake, Larry Pleau and the New England Whalers, Visionary Thinking, Bobby Hull, Gordie Howe, The Birth of the Los Angeles Sharks, Celebrity City, California Governor Pat Brown, Dr. Leonard Bloom, Wild Bill Hunter, Walter and Jordan Kaiser, New England Whalers' Owner Howard Baldwin, First-Year Playoffs, Ben Hatskin, The European Connection, The Greatest Hockey Line, Ulf Nilsson, Nick Mileti, The 1974 WHA Season, The 1974 Summit Series, John Bassett, A Good Stepping Stone, Ice Capades, Fighting Alphabetically, Quick Change, Big Thrill, True Pressure, WHA General Managers and Coaches, Terry Slater, John Kanel, Jacques Demers, Jack Kelley, Whitey Stapleton, Glen Sonmor, Bill Dineen, Glen Sather, Jack Stanfield, Rejean Houle, How to Tell a Winner, The WHA Teams, Gordie Howe and His Best Seller, Wayne Gretzky, Ralph Backstrom, Frank Mahovlich, André Lacroix, Scotty Bowman, The Lawyers, Gary Davidson, Donald Regan, Telly Mercury, Larry Gordon, Max Muhleman, Walt Marlow, The Minnesota Fighting Saints, The Phoenix Roadrunners, The New York Raiders, Paul Racine, The Ottawa Nationals, Jim Pattison,*

Author's Note

One morning my wife and I were discussing the naming of this book. Elaine envisioned the title "Sports Entrepreneur Man." She suggested that we put the pictures and list the names of the sports legends that performed in the leagues detailed in the book I told her it sounded like a good idea – and away we went.

I want to dedicate this book to my family, who helped me, stood by me, and who will always be my greatest joy and happiness. They, and my God, are what life is all about. I give special thanks to my wife of 58 years, Elaine; our son Dennis, Jr.; our two daughters, Dawn Mee and Doreen Haarlammert; our granddaughters Melissa, Denise, Mindy, Debbie, Dina, Michelle and Danielle; our grandson Sean; my late brothers, John and Bob; and to my deceased parents, Adele and Arthur Murphy. In addition, I want to thank my sons and daughters who have joined the family through marriage; namely Guy Haarlammert, David Mee and Nanci Murphy. To all the family I bequeath my happiness and love forever. I hope I did you all proud.

Sarah Chisick is my Shanghai, China, cousin. She is a classy and terrific relative. She and her husband Brian have been there for me all my life. When I had any financial or personal problems, I always got help and advice from them. Thanks, Chisicks.

I have always believed in the credo that in order to win, one must think positive, act positive, and be ready to tackle something new. One must also be willing to change directions when things are not going well. One must be willing to admit his mistakes. One must think like a winner, act like a winner, and before you know it – you will be a winner.

I hope that this book will be fun to read and bring back some memories of days gone by. Together with Richard Neil Graham, Don Anderson, my daughter, Dawn, and my wife, Elaine, we assembled these materials and facts for your reading pleasure.

Thank You

Jerry Dovin

For your advice in making the RHI section successful.

Richard Neil Graham

For reorganizing and editing the manuscript.

Loretta Creelman

For the endless hours of typing that you did.

Dawn Mee

Thanks, daughter, for your help and support.

Elaine Murphy

For your support and guidance in assembling the book materials, and for being there for me.

Walt Marlow

For providing many of the pictures for the book.

Randy Friend

For helping with the legal work and for producing the wonderful documentary on my life in sports.

Elliott Haimoff

For creating the documentary on my life in sports.

Denise Krakover-Lyons

A USC Trojan who copy edited this book.

Ron Brothers

Friend of 70 years and a Trojan.

Mike Lee

Wrote the proposal for this book.

Joanne Fox & Jose Sanchez

For the aid in my documentary.

My Special Thanks

Larry King of CNN
Rocky Kalish, producer, director, writer
Richard Neil Graham, editor
Tom Carney, owner of the Miami Floridians and banker
Jerry Dovin, accountant
Ralph Backstrom, owner of Colorado Eagles, "Mr. Class Act"
Gordie Howe, "Mr. Hockey"
Colleen Howe, "Mrs. Hockey"
Del Reddy, business manager of the Howes
Jerry Saperstein, former owner of the Harlem Globetrotters
Don Marshall, longtime friend
Gary Davidson, founder and president of the WHA and ABA
Tom Adams, president of Tiodize Corporation
Wayne Gretzky, "Mr. 99"
Don Regan, attorney
Ruby Richman, member, Canadian Basketball Hall of Fame
Patrick Mulcahy, president Team China (USA)
Bill Dannemeyer, former congressman
Ron Mix, attorney and member of Football Hall of Fame
Ted McCaskill, president "Top Hatter Inc."
Brian Kennedy, president, Regency Outdoor Advertising
Howard & Karen Baldwin, Crusader Entertainment
Ed Pilot, attorney
Bobby Hull, "Mr. WHA" (The Golden Jet)
George Mikan, former commissioner, ABA
Billie Jean King, commissioner of World Team Tennis
Jerry Buss, owner, Los Angeles Lakers
Jeanie Buss, executive VP, Los Angeles Lakers
Pierre Nicholas, businessman
Steve Arnold, attorney
Lee Meade, former sports editor, Denver Post
James Lilley, former U.S. ambassador to Korea and China
Dick Tinkham, attorney
Pat Boone, entertainer and owner of Oakland Oaks
Pat Lynch, L.A. Coliseum Commission and executive director
Dale Roos, business executive
Dianne Carlson, friend of USC

Frank Michelena, government relations
Norton Herrick, president of the Herrick Company
Joe Cerrell, public relations in Los Angeles
Norm Drucker, chief of referees, ABA
Bill Stumpus, high school double-play partner of Murph's
Walter and Jordan Kaiser, developers of fitness centers
Aaron Howard, business executive
Lenny Bloom, president of the Marquee Corporation
Bobby Yee, president of Windsor, Ontario, casino
Otis Bell, president of BAF Industries
Tom Gilmore, former L.A. Sharks player
Patsi Marshall, mayor of Buena Park
Jack Stanfield, player for WHA's Houston Aeros
Bob Erhlich, attorney
Sandy Mattie, member of St. Julian's Men's Club
Merv Bodnarchuk, securities executive
Marty Bauer, family member
Marvin and Mary Ellen Bauer
Julius Erving, "Mr. ABA"
Ed Litwak, securities company president
Larry and Rocky, Minuteman Press, Brea, California
Mike Carroll, ABA 2000 team owner
Mike Storen, former ABA general manager in Indiana
Phil Chirella, friend and benefactor of RHI
Ed Horne, director of properties, NHL
Bob Barger, my brother-in-law
Telly Mercury, lawyer
Maury Silver, owner of Anaheim Bullfrogs, RHI
Elliott Haimoff, producer
Randy Friend, president, Eagle Productions
Pat Brown, former governor of California
Jesse Unruh, speaker of the house, California legislature
Bill Sharman, coach of the Los Angeles Lakers

Editor's Note

by Richard Neil Graham

In early 2004, when I was an editor at Sports Afield magazine, Dennis Arthur Murphy asked me to edit his self-published 2002 autobiography. I took a red pencil to its 435 pages and gave it back to him some weeks later. Murph paid me for my work and I didn't see the manuscript again until 2011, when he dug it out of storage and asked if I would turn it into a new edition that we could publish on Amazon.com as both a print book and an eventual e-book version.

I'd known Murph since about 1993 when I was the editor of Roller Hockey magazine and he was the president of Roller Hockey International, a new professional league that rode on the back of the inline skating craze of the 1990s. Murph became enamored with the idea of a professional roller hockey league after seeing children playing the sport in the street. "That could be a pro sport!" Murph said to himself. If anyone could turn that seeming pipe dream into a reality, it was Murph.

Known as the "Sports Entrepreneur Man," Murph helped create the American Basketball Association (ABA), the World Hockey Association (WHA), World Team Tennis (WTT), and Roller Hockey International (RHI). He was also an integral part of many other leagues, including the 6′4″ & Under International Basketball Association (IBA), the Women's Professional Softball League (WPSL) and others.

A who's who of professional sports legends competed and starred in Murphy's leagues, including Gordie Howe, Wayne Gretzky, Bobby Hull and Ralph Backstrom in hockey; Julius Erving, Rick Barry, Connie Hawkins and George Gervin in basketball; and Billie Jean King, Martina Navratilova, Chris Evert, Rod Laver and John Newcombe in tennis. Thanks to the vision and spirit of sports entrepreneurs like Dennis Murphy, we now have NHL and ABA teams in cities that would not have had them under the old systems.

As I wrote in "Wheelers, Dealers, Pucks & Bucks: A Rocking History of Roller Hockey International," my own book about one of Murph's leagues, "Dennis Arthur Murphy might be the most unlikely, least known and most influential visionary in North American professional sports history."

Despite all of his successes, Murphy was often "thrown out on his ear" by businessmen he approached to support his leagues, but he got back up on his feet and beat the odds. What's Murph's secret? How did he convince people in all walks of life to change their way of thinking; to help them to see what he saw? How did he get people to jump in with both feet and play ball? This book, in Murph's own words, tells how.

Foreword

by Ralph Backstrom

Two men are largely responsible for my becoming the commissioner of Roller Hockey International in 1992 – Maury Silver and Dennis Murphy.

I first heard of "Murph" when the World Hockey Association began raiding the National Hockey League for players, back in 1972, but I didn't meet him until I began playing for the WHA's Colorado Cougars in 1974. I'll always remember his catch phrases: "Hey, big guy, don't do anything I wouldn't do," "You turkey!" "Can you imagine that," and "He *thinks* he's a goaltender."

I met Maury Silver shortly after I was traded to the Los Angeles Kings from the Montreal Canadiens in 1971 and he showed me his ideas for an inline skate. We took the blades off of an old pair of L.A. Kings skates and added wheels. I suggested rockering the skate – raising the heel and toe wheels to better simulate an ice-skate blade – and I still have that first pair of "Super Street Skates." I'd skate around my Los Angeles neighborhood and I could see neighbors peering around corners wondering, "Who is this crazy Canadian?"

Twenty years later, Murphy called me. He knew that I had been involved in inline skating during the 1970s, so when he was contemplating starting a new league, I was one of the first persons that he contacted. He asked if I would be interested in getting involved in roller hockey. I said, "Dennis, I've been expecting your call."

The days of Roller Hockey International were pretty exciting, and there were always a lot of things happening. We had a lot of former NHL players involved in the league besides me. Dave "Tiger" Williams was a co-owner of the Vancouver VooDoo, Bernie Federko was an owner and coach of the St. Louis Vipers, and my old teammate Yvan Cournoyer from the Montreal Canadiens coached the Montreal Roadrunners in RHI. There were many others, including Terry Harper, Mark Howe, Nicky Fotiu, Garry Unger, Mark Messier, Perry Turnbull and Dave "The Hammer" Schultz.

With my background in the inline skate, it really appealed to me – I could live my dream all over again. As commissioner of RHI, it was my job to write the rules. Dennis wanted to make it a really creative game, so I eliminated all of the ice hockey rules I didn't like. I got rid of the blue line, and with four-on-four play, I knew that it would open the game up. We created a wide-open game that averaged between 90 to 100 shots and 10 to 12 goals a game. With fewer players, there was less overhead and travel expenses. We finished games in less than two hours and instituted a shootout from the very beginning to eliminate tie games. Now the NHL has four-on-four overtime periods and shootouts to eliminate ties. In many ways, we were ahead of our time.

Roller hockey could be played just about anywhere – in parking lots, tennis courts and in the street. Anybody with a street address can play inline hockey. It was a great sport and Dennis Murphy is a great visionary in sports. At age 86, he's still working on new leagues today, and he hopes to create a new 6′4″-and-under pro basketball league, a Women's Sports Walk of Fame at Knott's Berry Farm in Buena Park, California, and a 4-on-4 ice hockey league. Oh, and he has dreams of bringing back Roller Hockey International.

As Dennis himself might say, "Can you imagine that?"

Thanks, Dad,
for all the memories.
Love you,

Guy & Doreen Haarlammert
and family

Life moves on and love stays
in our hearts for you.
Love you, Dad,

Nanci & Denny Murphy Jr.

SECTION I: THE EARLY DAYS

The China Days and My Early Years

I was very lucky; I had a great early life. I was born in Shanghai, China. The Standard Oil Company employed my dad, and my mom was a housewife who cared for her children. I had two wonderful brothers, Bob and John.

We lived very well. Each of us boys had our own room and we were spoiled. We had a lot of love from our parents. Our family belonged to the American Club in Shanghai, a club for Americans only, and we were members of the famous Shanghai Race Association. This was membership in the racing fraternity in Shanghai; my grandfather owned horses, thus the membership.

My father was the catcher on the Shanghai American baseball team and he was very proud of that fact. I attended my grammar school days at the Shanghai American School, which catered to the hundreds of missionary kids we had throughout the Orient. I had two special friends who did themselves proud. My friend Brayton Meyer became a vice president of the Standard Oil Company, and my friend James Lilley became the United States ambassador to Korea and later to China. These achievements were special and I am extremely proud of them.

We loved the Shanghai ice cream shop, the Bund, the International Settlement, and the Garden Bridge and, of course, the American Club and the racetrack.

My Love of Sports

It started early for me. When the visiting American vessels made their stops in Shanghai to refuel their ships, they would usually play the Shanghai American All-Stars. I was the batboy of the team. I loved the spirited action, and after the games, we would all make our way to the Shanghai Chocolate Shop and have our chocolate sundaes. This became a ritual and I loved it.

This love for sports continued for me all my life. While in Shanghai, together with my boyhood friends Brayton Meyer and Jim Lilley, we played a game where we would throw a tennis ball against the garage. We would make believe that we were Johnny Pesky or Phil Rizzuto, and had their excellence as ballplayers. I was a Red Sox supporter and the other two "turkeys" were New York Yankee supporters.

After my Shanghai days, I played varsity baseball at University High School in Westwood, California. I was the second baseman and my double-play partner at shortstop was Bill Stumpus, who later signed with the New York Yankees organization. He was a great player, and throughout our lives, we have always kidded each other over the fact that he carried me at the high school games. The truth is, he did!

It is ironic that later in life I was in other sports like basketball, football, hockey, tennis, softball and roller hockey, but never baseball. Our grandson, Sean Murphy, plays baseball. He has a great arm, speed, and a loving desire for the game. His dad, Denny Jr., takes him to many ball games, and he loves it too.

Genes do have a place; as in our case, they have been paramount in four generations.

Those were great early years and they all got uprooted in 1941 when America was attacked at Pearl Harbor. Prior to that attack, however, the U.S. government ordered all the women and children out of China. We left Shanghai prior to the attack. Fortunately for me, my father was on the high seas when December 7 happened, and he thus came home to the United States mainland and joined the family in Long Beach, California.

Our family lived in Long Beach for two years and then moved to Westwood, California, where I attended University High School. Those were wonderful years and I enjoyed my high school days. I was picked by my fellow students as Student Body President and in the winter of 1945 was called into the service. I served the United States Army by being drafted and trained in Camp Roberts, California.

After my basic training, I served 18 months in the Asian theater, specifically the Philippines. I then attended the University of Southern California where I met my wife Elaine. My cousin Sarah Chisick and her husband Brian live in Orange County and are now my only ties to my China days.

USC Days

I loved the cardinal and gold, and especially, Trojan football. My departed brother John was Notre Dame and blue and gold. Boy, did we have some good debates. I loved John McKay; he loved Ara Parseghian. I loved Craig Fertig; he was a Johnny Lujack man all the way. When it was the big football week, we conjured tricks to play on each other. One year when we played the Irish in South Bend, our Trojan Train Special was rolling into South Bend and John and his two cronies got the conductor to say, "Now, folks, we are entering the Mecca of college football, the University of Notre Dame." This precipitated in a major debate and caused me untold embarrassment with my Trojan buddies. As the years have rolled by the Irish-Trojan battles have become more epic. I have tried not to miss this game each year, as it is the majesty of college football.

All of my life, I enjoyed the crowds and excitement of the L.A. Coliseum. I usually had pregame lunch with my fellow Trojan Football Club members. Not that I played for the Trojans, but I did serve as student manager and loved every minute of it. My friend Jimmy Lewis, a fellow student manager, got me to join and I will be forever grateful to him for that honor.

I was an economics major and I found that education came in handy as I moved ahead with my career. I agree with those who say education is the key to financial security. I always provided for my family and I credit my education process for that. I urge all of you to follow that path. At USC, we had in addition to our academic studies a lot of student activities. I was chairman of the Homecoming Parade one year and we had a big parade. I was such a Phi Beta Kappa that I got one of the floats stuck in the Coliseum tunnel.

Our coach Jeff Crawath was furious at me because it delayed the football game for 15 minutes while we got the float free. Luckily we tied the Irish that year, as they were a 13-point favorite, or I might not be writing this. Crawath had a terrific temper, and I'm sure I would have gotten it. Thank you, Mr. Upstairs, for helping me out.

The game was always played with spirit and pride. The names of Knute Rockne and Howard Jones will always mean Trojan-Irish times. I loved going to South Bend and throwing down a few with my pal, of TV fame, Tom Kelly, and my brother John. I was not a drinker, but this game we all enjoyed and we had a few. As the echoes of this historic matchup keep coming, all blue and gold fans will rally, and so will the cardinal and gold's.

I met my wife at USC. She was a "10" in every way. After 58 years of marriage, we're now unfortunately separated. We were blessed with three kids, Denny Jr., Dawn Adele and Doreen Avis. Elaine did a marvelous job bringing them up. I was on the road a lot and she took good care of them. I wish her all the best.

USC will always be special to me. The cardinal and gold will always be in my heart. "Fight On" will be my motto until the Good Lord takes me.

I returned from the service and went to USC. I was on the GI Bill and I stayed in the Army Reserves until I was called back in because of the Korean War. I enlisted as a private and came out as a first lieutenant. It's a period of my life that I really enjoyed, and it was eventful.

The USC-Notre Dame game always brings out the goose bumps when you're either at South Bend or at the Coliseum. The cardinal and gold and the blue and gold always bring excitement and pride to all of us attending that ritual each year With all of my sports-related activities and the thousands of sport events, I have been honored to watch the "premiere" game and event each year when the Irish play the Trojans. To my dying day, it will always be that way. My kids and friends, other than Trojans, never have understood that feeling, and I have had to withstand a lot of kidding about it all of my life. What they don't understand is the happiness it brings when we beat those Irish. It's like having a "little bit of heaven" as a teaser.

My Mayoral Days

After college, I was called back into the Korean War as an officer, serving my time at Fort Huachuca, Arizona. Elaine was with me. Our son Denny came into this world in 1953 when I was a district representative for the Sego Milk Company. We moved to Buena Park in 1955, and our oldest daughter Dawn was born in Long Beach, California. Two years later, our second daughter, Doreen, was born in Lakewood, California. We lived in Buena Park for nine years and then moved to Fullerton, where we have been ever since.

When Elaine and I moved to Orange County in 1955, we bought our first home on the GI Bill in Buena Park. Then it was a city of roughly 30,000 people. I had no idea at the time that I would be elected to the city council, nor did I dream that my fellow councilmen would later select me as their mayor. I had just completed my education, served as an officer during the Korean War, and was recently married. I was 28 years old. We started a family and did all the things a new homeowner should do. We first put in a new lawn, and the bought furniture, followed by building a fence. We later got a dog and then settled in as a family. Our son, Denny, was just two years old, our two girls were "still in the oven," getting ready to enter the world. getting ready to enter the world. Elaine and I were making a lot of new friends and our life together was beautiful. While at USC, I was interested in politics. I became good friends with Jesse Unruh, who later coined the famous phrase, "Money is the milk of politics." I was a "Roosevelt and Truman conservative" in the Democratic Party. Jesse Unruh urged me to run for city council. He helped me with financial and advertising support. Much to my surprise, I was elected. Buena Park was a new, young city. In my four years as mayor, we became a city of 60,000, mainly through annexation.

Elaine and I quickly became totally involved in Little League, Pony League, the Chamber of Commerce and other related organizations. It was a great honor being involved. However, it did set a pattern of becoming separated from my family. I was so busy that I wasn't home often enough to be involved with my family. This was a case of "misguided ego" at its worst. Although I made the "important family functions," I wasn't considerate to my wife and family. I now realize just how important family is, and how much I missed out on. I enjoyed being of service to my community and was honored to be selected as mayor, but in doing so, I greatly neglected my family. That is something I have always been sorry for.

After serving my four-year term on the city council, I ran for the California state legislature. I lost. That decision and subsequent defeat led me away from politics and directed me right into the sporting arena. It definitely changed my direction in life. I was defeated by Bill Dannemeyer, who subsequently became a congressman from Orange County, California. Bill was a city attorney from Fullerton who had great credentials, and who turned out to be my friend in later years and traveling partner on our tour to Asia.

A City Hall Memory

It was a beautiful California winter's afternoon. The temperature was in the 70s and it was February 26, 2002. Two weeks prior, I had received an invitation to attend a groundbreaking ceremony for the new city hall that was going to be built in the city of Buena Park. I then reflected back 44 years to when we built our first city hall in Buena Park. I was a young man at the time and was so very proud that we had built a beautiful new facility for the residents of our city. As city councilmen, we wanted to give our citizens and city employees a place that we could be proud of. My friend Jack Armstrong, who is now a city commissioner of Buena Park, was with me, and he said, "We grew out of that old building. We now have 70,000-plus residents in the city and must keep up with the demands."

I reflected that this was what it was all about. Progress and time were moving on. The city had only 40,000 residents when I was mayor. Mayor Patsy Marshall, Buena Park's chief official today, took a white spade, and with it, the groundbreaking of a new facility began. She said they would tear down the old building and a new one would take its place. I sat there thinking that 21 mayors had come and gone, and reflected that time moves on and does not turn back. Our children grew up in Buena Park. Our son played Little League baseball, our daughters were Girl Scouts, and we all enjoyed California living. Now our kids, too, will see their kids grown. Time does move on.

SECTION II: THE ABA

The American Basketball Association
(1967-1976)

"The will to win comes from within. There is an attitude about winning that makes an individual reach their potential."
– Dale Brown

Davidson and Murphy: A Good Team

By Veteran Los Angeles Sportswriter, John Hall

Dennis Murphy has dreams. Gary Davidson turns them into reality. Together, the two enterprising Southern Californians built major leagues. First it was the American Basketball Association, which Murphy founded in 1967. The ABA was Murphy's idea; Davidson was its first president. The two collaborated on the World Hockey Association and the format has been the same. Murphy had been thinking about a "second" major hockey league since the infancy of the ABA. In fact, he told Lee Meade, then sports editor of the Denver Post, about his idea over breakfast one morning. The plan was shelved for a few years. Both Murphy and Meade became heavily involved in the ABA. League founder Murphy served in executive capacities with, at various times, the Oakland Oaks, Denver Rockets, Minnesota Muskies and Miami Floridians. Meade became the ABA's public relations director.

Midway through the ABA's 1970-71 season, Murphy started thinking about his own future. Although he was born in Shang-

hai, China, where his father was employed by the Standard Oil Company, Murphy is first, last and foremost a California. He moved to Los Angeles with his parents as a teenager in 1940, he attended and was a second team all-city second baseman on the University High School baseball team, and he then attended the University of Southern California. He was elected mayor of Buena Park, where Knott's Berry Farm is the big tourist attraction, and became a marketing executive for one of California's largest civil engineering firms.

Davidson's migration to Southern California had been very similar. Born in Missoula, Montana, Davidson moved to Los Angeles with his mother as a first grader following his parents' separation. Davidson attended UCLA, then passed his bar exam and went into partnership with Donald Regan, a fellow UCLA Bruin. Together with Ray Nagle, they formed the Orange County firm of Nagle, Davidson and Regan. Davidson was introduced to Murphy by a mutual friend, Roland Speth, and together they made a good team. Murphy was an organizer; Davidson was the administrator and leader.

The ABA and Its Beginning

The ABA was a tremendous success. It brought the fans the slam-dunk, the red, white and blue ball, the 30-second clock, and the three-point shot. The NBA today has adopted two of the four innovations – the slam-dunk and the three-point shot. Both innovations have greatly increased the level of excitement in the

NBA. It also elevated to the forefront players like Julius Erving, Billy Cunningham, George McGinnis, George Gervin, Artis Gilmore, Moses Malone, Dan Issel, Mel Daniels, Roger Brown, Rick Barry, Larry Brown, Mack Calvin, Doug Moe, the exciting Connie Hawkins, and many more great basketball stars.

The spirited dunk-contest went straight to the heart of the ABA and was important to the league, as it became a full-blown show during the team's warm ups. Many ABA fans arrived at arenas early just to watch the likes of Artis Gilmore, Willie Taylor, George Gervin, David Thompson, and of course, the great "Doctor J," Julius perform their acrobatic aerial shows.

The Denver Nuggets, New Jersey Nets, Indiana Pacers, and San Antonio Spurs are current NBA teams that merged from the ABA. In addition, Miami, Salt Lake City, Anaheim, Memphis, Birmingham, Cincinnati, New Orleans and Louisville had teams in the ABA. Those cities enjoyed basketball at its best. The "Big Three" included teams in Los Angeles, New York and Chicago.

I've been given the honor of being known as the "Patron Saint" of the American Basketball Association. Cleveland sports writer Terry Pluto bestowed this honor upon me. He wrote a best-seller, "Loose Balls," a book that depicts the highs and lows of the ABA and its glorious nine years of existence. John Vanak, an official who worked both in the NBA and ABA, also complimented me by saying that if there were a league on the moon, it most probably would have been started by "yours truly." This is genuinely a nice sentiment coming from someone whom I admire as a man, as well as a basketball official.

The ABA was my first professional sports league. Prior to its launching, I had helped organize the Bobby Sox girls' softball program in Buena Park. Bobby Sox is a youth program similar in scope to Little League baseball, National Junior Basketball and Pop Warner Football. I am proud that the program is still alive and flourishing.

A Spin-Off League

The ABA actually began as a spin-off of the American Football League. In 1965, I had previously completed a stint as the mayor of Buena Park, when the AFL and NFL were embattled in a major war. That war changed my entire life. While attending the University of Southern California in the 1950s, I fell in love with the USC football tradition. I was also a fraternity brother of former USC and St. Louis Cardinals quarterback, Jim Hardy. Jim became the director of the Los Angeles Coliseum in the middle '60s, and one of his friends, Al Davis, was the commissioner of the AFL.

One evening Jim called me at home and asked if I could put a group of Orange County, California, businessmen together and attempt to secure an AFL franchise for Orange County. Since the city of Anaheim had just built Anaheim Stadium, now called Edison International Field, it seemed like a perfect fit. I took the challenge and gathered a strong group of potential owners that included Russell Knott and Ken Arnsburger of Knott's Berry Farm, Dr. Lou Cella of Anaheim, and Larry Shields, a home-builder with the firm of Doyle and Shields. Jim Hardy also brought to the table his friend, Jim Thompson, owner of the radio station KEZY.

That year, 1965, led by Hardy, Thompson, Joe Ingalls, Ken Carlson and Jim Trindle, we spent a lot of time preparing a presentation to the AFL's Board of Governors.

We then put on the first double-header football game ever held at Anaheim Stadium. It was highly successful and Orange County was then declared as a leading candidate to receive an AFL franchise. Unfortunately for all of us, the AFL and NFL merged, and Dan Reeves, the owner of the Los Angeles Rams, refused to let us in the Los Angeles/Orange County territory. He made his position clear that as a part of the merger agreement there would be no team in Orange County. This was a huge and disappointing setback for our group.

The businessmen we had gathered together commissioned me to explore the possibility of starting a new major league in either the basketball or hockey fields. They reasoned that we had a vibrant group of men and that we should look around for other sports ventures. Given this mandate, I did some research and concluded that while there were already two football leagues that were now merging, basketball and hockey leagues were dominated by a group of cities and greedy individuals, making those areas of influence limited.

I felt that if the NFL had merged with the upstart AFL, then maybe we could do the same in pro basketball and pro hockey. At the time, I knew more about basketball and knew more people involved with that sport, so that's where I concentrated my efforts. Bill Sharman, who was coaching Cal State Los Angeles at the time, was an acquaintance at USC. He was a natural source for the beginning of the ABA.

Together with my brother John Murphy and my longtime friend Joe Ingalls, we arranged a meeting with Sharman at the Olympia Hotel, a sports hangout in downtown Los Angeles. Sharman had been involved with Abe Saperstein's American Basketball League, which had existed for six months and closed up shop during the Christmas break of 1964.

Sharman said our idea of a new basketball league had merit, and he urged us to use the three-point shot and the 30-second clock. Since he was being considered at the time to be the head coach of the NBA San Francisco Warriors, he told us that he needed to concentrate on that effort because he needed a job in basketball. He recommended that we contact former NBA great George Mikan instead.

As it turned out, my next-door neighbor in Fullerton, California, had a passing acquaintance with Mikan. Mikan had a travel agency in Minneapolis, Minnesota, and Fred Goff was a client. Goff said that he would contact Mikan and set up a meeting. A few days later, Mikan called and said that Connie Seredin, who was in the advertising business out of New York, was also trying to organize a competitive league with the NBA. Mikan suggested that I call Seredin and find out the status on his league. Connie Seredin was a "carny," although a really nice person. He was the consummate salesman and talked his way, at times, into oblivion. I called him. He made it sound like his league was all in place and that he would consider us to join him. I fell for his blarney and set up a meeting in New York.

Our first meeting in New York was a complete fiasco. Seredin said that he would have some of his people there, and I brought along John McShane, Roland Speth and Joe Ingalls. Seredin's friend, Mark J. Binstein, was also there. It became obvious during the meeting that Seredin had some great ideas, but very little substance. The conversations reminded me of a resolution that I have tried to follow ever since:

"Resolve to listen more and talk less. No one ever learns anything by talking. Be wary of giving advice. Wise men don't need it and fools won't heed it." – Lloyd Shearer

I was also reminded that some people are darn right unreasonable, illogical and self-centered. One must be reminded that one should love those people, anyway. It's the right thing to do.

The second meeting to organize the ABA took place in California at the Beverly Wilshire Hotel in Beverly Hills. We had more than 40 people at the meeting, including Seredin, Binstein and Rubin. Together with my friend John McShane, a popular disc jockey at KMPC, it was agreed that we would advance $10,000 each to the project and move forward. We asked Seredin to do likewise and he demurred, offering to put up just $3,000.

McShane and I agreed that since we wanted a united front, we would include Seredin and his group in the formal merger. We were on a mission and moved forward together to make our project a success. Over the next six months, we traveled the length and breadth of the United States, visiting hundreds of prospective owners. Don Regan and Dick Ackerman, our California lawyers, organized the legal part of the project. We then opened up our office in Anaheim. We were now finally on our way.

We continued to have meetings to formulate our structure. We had two important people, Gabe Rubin and Art Kim, who lent us their basketball experience. Rubin was in the entertainment field and would become the owner of the Pittsburgh Pipers of the ABA. Kim owned the Washington Generals, a professional basketball team that played against the Harlem Globetrotters. These two men were invaluable to our group, as they had the acumen and background as owners of previous professional basketball teams.

We visited with an extremely cooperative George Mikan during this period; however, it was decided by all that he would wait until the league solidified before he joined us. George had a well-respected basketball reputation and he did not want to be out front until we had our act together, which certainly was understandable.

After the shaking-out period, it was apparent that we were moving forward with 12 markets which had potentially strong financial partners. We had truck owner Arthur Brown for New York; the business-oriented De Voe family in Indiana; Gabe Rubin and his entertainment company were in place in Pittsburgh; oil man T.C. Morrow committed to Houston; Joe Gregory and his wife, who owned the Hope Jewels, became the owners of Kentucky; businessman Bob Folsom, who later became mayor of Dallas, became the Dallas owner; Larry Shields, a major California builder, spoke for Minneapolis; Ken Davidson and Pat Boone grabbed the Oakland team; legislator Charlie Smithers and entertainer Mort Downey took charge of the New Orleans franchise; Jim Trindle and Ken Carlson, a pair of engineers, along with trucker Bill Ringsby, moved on Denver; and Washington Generals owner Art Kim became the owner of the Anaheim club.

Our league was ready for the next step – a press conference in New York City.

Our New York Press Conference

We initially agreed upon to hire the foremost New York public relations executive, Joe Goldstein, to put on the initial press conference. Connie Seredin, however, suggested that we allow his public relations firm to conduct the conference instead. Reluctantly, we agreed. It was truly a bizarre, exciting and costly press conference. Connie hired girls in hot pants to serve the booze and food, which were both in plentiful supply. We gave away red, white and blue basketballs, which the media loved. The press conference wound up costing us $35,000. But it did get us a great send off. The day began with a major confrontation between some of the owners and George Mikan, who was to be our commissioner. He stood tough on his dollar figure, and he made it clear that he would announce the introduction of the three-point shot and the red, white and blue basketball to the press that afternoon. He insisted upon this. If not, he would not become commissioner.

The morning shakedown produced a six-to-six vote. Both sides were in a deadlock. It was important to have George Mikan as our commissioner. I felt that without his impeccable credibility, we would become the laughing stock of the sports world. I lobbied hard for George and finally persuaded my friend, Mike Storen of Indiana, to change his vote. Without Mike's vote, I hate to think what might have happened. Luckily, the change of Storen's vote was made just 10 minutes before the start of the press conference.

The red, white and blue ball carried by a 7-5 vote. It became the ABA hallmark over the years and was highly accepted by the fans. It was George Mikan's baby and he fought for it all the way. I stood with him on it because I thought it would develop into a successful gimmick that kids would especially like.

I usually sided with Gary on issues, but this time I went with "Big George." It was a beauty of a fight, but on this issue, I broke ranks and we prevailed. Now, 30 years later, I'm happy that I did. More than 30 million red, white and blue balls were sold in just four years. It was a ball that had character and heritage attached to it.

Commissioner George Mikan then took charge. With the combination of his business stature, his impressive 6'10" frame, and the fact that he was regarded as the best basketball player of the first half century, when George spoke, people listened. The ABA's first press conference transformed from a potential disaster to a level of stability and integrity. Hence, the ABA was born. The opening act of the ABA reminded me that failure will never overtake you if your determination is strong enough to prevail. In my life, I have always felt that way when I was ready to tackle something new. A losing position is one that proclaims, "It cannot be done."

Organizing the ABA

I knew that we were going to make the ABA happen after our organizational meetings when Gary Davidson and Don Regan joined us. At that time, I was working with Ken Carlson and his engineering company. I had a family of five and didn't have much money saved. I realized that after we paid our bills for travel, hotels, legal fees, brochures and press conferences while starting the ABA that there would be no financial bonanza left for anyone. Gary Davidson and Don Regan volunteered to help with our expenses by advancing $10,000 to the cause without requiring any collateral. I liked Gary and Don from the very beginning. They are both good people and were gracious to take chances with their own money. Both men have always been there for me and I am proud to have been associated with them through the years.

Before we finalized details of the configuration of our league, I decided that the only way the founders could make any remuneration for ourselves would be to take a franchise and then sell it to one of the potential investors. Looking back I now realize that our price for a franchise compared to today's prices was very weak. However, this was back in 1967, not 2013. Professional sports were in their early days of development and can't be compared on the same terms as today's crazy sports world.

I decided to take Oakland because it was closest to Los Angeles and had not already been taken. My brother, John and I would oversee the Oakland team. I didn't want to leave my job because I had my loved ones to take care of. My bosses, Ken Carlson and Jim Trindle, were also involved in the league and had money invested. I wanted to protect their interests as well. They initially had taken Kansas City and then moved to Denver.

Pat Boone, Singer and Team Owner

This is when Ken Davidson came into my life. Ken is one of the few people in this world who wasn't always straightforward with me. We didn't share a mutual trust with one another. Davidson came into the scene when he called me cold to tell me that he had a very high-profile entertainer as a partner who wanted a franchise in our league. I asked him who it was and he responded, "Pat Boone."

Needless to say, this caught my attention. Pat Boone was a star in everyone's eyes and I felt his profile as a league owner would immediately lend credibility to our league. I asked Ken to have lunch and invite Pat Boone so that we could pursue the matter. We had lunch in Beverly Hills but only Davidson showed up. We talked about our league, where we stood with our franchises and what we thought a franchise could be operated for. Davidson said that the only city that made sense for Pat Boone and himself was Oakland. I told him that I was already in progress putting some people together for Oakland, and I wanted to be part of it.

Davidson said, "Dennis, I am sure Pat and I would not want any partners in our franchise. We'd like you to help us get started and then we would pay you a fee and operate it ourselves."

I asked him why Pat didn't come to our meeting as he originally indicated. Davidson said that he was going to be the decision maker and that Pat was going to be the passive investor. This sounded all right to me and we moved on. Ken also told me that he had a banking relationship with Bank of America; for loan purposes, they requested that only he and Pat be involved in the ownership package.

The first time I met Pat Boone is when we had our press conference in Oakland when we were announcing the team, its ownership and structure. Being a founder, I conducted the meeting together with George Mikan, our commissioner. I found Pat Boone to be a class act in every aspect. During his ownership in Oakland he conducted himself with dignity and decency. He completely trusted Ken Davidson.

In the period between our lunch in Beverly Hills and the press conference in Oakland, about three months, I often asked to meet Pat but was always told by Davidson that Pat was too busy. Also during that time frame I sold my rights in Oakland to Ken Davidson for $15,000. This was a lesser amount than what a franchise would have cost, but I wanted Pat Boone in the league because of his credibility. Davidson later told Pat that it was because of his negotiations that he was able to get the franchise for a lesser amount. I'm sure that Davidson thought that this would earn him some Brownie points.

My brother John and I helped Davidson and Pat Boone get things started in Oakland. We then moved on to help my bosses Jim Trindle and Ken Carlson develop the Denver franchise. Pat said that he knew Ken Davidson for years since they attended the same church in Inglewood, California. Davidson knew that Pat loved basketball and that Pat was a good amateur player as well. Ken Davidson convinced Pat that by using Pat's name, Ken could get the necessary funds from the Bank of America. He told Pat that his family, especially his mother-in-law, was going to put up the collateral and that Pat would only have to lend his name to the venture. This wasn't true. And, Pat, in order to protect his good name and integrity, was nailed for a huge amount of money.

The ABA was fortunate to have a high-profile entertainer as the owner of the Oakland Oaks. Boone gave the league credibility and substance. In the late 1960s, he was already a legend in the music industry. Boone loved his basketball. He was a good amateur player in his own right, and he could shoot the ball with the best. He, together with Davidson, built a sound team under the direction of Bruce Hale. Hale was the father-in-law of Rick Barry, the famous player for the San Francisco Warriors. Hale, a successful coach at the University of Miami, had a strong personality and good contacts in the basketball world. He brought respectability to the new league. The trio of Boone, Davidson and Hale developed a strong squad, and together they secured the services of Barry, the leading scorer in the National Basketball Association.

The courts ruled that Barry had to sit out a full season before his contract could go into effect, but Pat Boone stepped up to the plate and guaranteed Barry's salary. Barry became a radio commentator for the initial year until he was able to play. Pat Boone was a terrific owner. He let Bruce Hale operate the team and Ken Davidson run the front office. He lost a lot of money, but always with dignity and grace. After a few years as the owner of the Oaks, he sold the team to Washington attorney Earl Foreman, who then moved the club to Washington, D.C., and subsequently, to Virginia. In the first years of the league, Pat Boone gave the league substance, dedication and integrity. Today he is active in his church. Boone is a man of God and is an entertainment legend of whom we can all be proud.

Rick Barry, Sharpshooter

Pat Boone was appearing at the Golden Nugget in Reno when he and Ken Davidson had their first meeting with Rick Barry, hoping to persuade Barry to jump leagues. Barry had just finished his second season with the NBA's San Francisco Warriors and was the leading scorer in the NBA. Barry wasn't happy playing for the Warriors. He felt that his contract with the Warriors was up and he could negotiate a contract with the Oaks of the ABA. He also had some misgivings about playing for Warriors Coach Bill Sharman, because he was very set in his particular style of basketball. Rick found that basketball in this situation wasn't fun anymore. He respected Sharman as a coach, but he wasn't comfortable playing in the system that Sharman had installed.

At the meeting in Reno, Barry insisted that the contract offer be substantial in order for him to jump leagues, because he would be severing ties with an established league to jump to a league that was new and unestablished. The American Basketball League had folded just two years earlier, and Barry had to have something solid. The negotiations seemed to bog down until Davidson promised Barry that the Oaks would acquire big men and dominant centers to compliment his skills. The offer broke down the barriers and Barry consented to join the Oaks.

Another reason that Barry was persuaded to jump leagues was being able to play again for his father-in-law, Bruce Hale. Hale had been his college basketball coach, and Barry loved playing for Hale. Naturally, when the Oaks hired Hale to be their coach this appealed to Barry.

After talking to some of our ABA lawyers, Barry felt that the NBA reserve clause wouldn't stand up in court. The NBA reserve clause made it mandatory for a player to play another season with the same club, before allowing the player to jump leagues and become a free agent. However, the courts ruled that Barry had to sit out a full season before his contract could go into effect, and Pat Boone took on the challenge and guaranteed Barry's salary. Barry became a radio commentator for the 1967-68 season until he was able to play. George Mikan was instantly happy with the signing – he knew that Barry would bring credibility to the new league.

Barry had led the NBA in scoring during the 1966 season, averaging 37 points a game. When he jumped leagues, a Miami Floridian stat crew member, Pat Mitchell, asked Barry if he felt he could do the same in the ABA. Mitchell and Barry both felt that he could. Imagine the coup in getting the NBA's leading scorer to join our new league.

"Yesterday has forever passed beyond our control... we cannot undo a single act we performed. We cannot erase a single word we said. Yesterday is gone... Tomorrow's sun will rise, either in splendor or behind a mask of clouds, but it will rise."

– Jennifer Kritsch

Coach Bob Bass

The phone rang and an unfamiliar voice on the other end said, "This is Coach Bob Bass and I would like to be the coach for your ABA team in Denver. I have coached in college and I would like a chance to coach in your new league. I would love the challenge of coaching professional basketball."

This was the beginning of a friendship that has lasted for more than 40 years. Bass, who is now vice president of the Charlotte Hornets, is a short and dynamic "Okie" with one of the most experienced and knowledgeable minds in the game of basketball. Bass coached in Denver, Memphis and Miami for the ABA. His teams were always well prepared and they responded to his disciplined style of coaching.

As general manager for the Hornets, Bass was considered the right arm to former owner George Shinn (the team is currently owned by the NBA). Bass, like me, was small in stature, which made us try harder. He was a coach very familiar with the "x's and o's" of the game as well and always prepared his team well. As general manager of the Denver team, he put together the roster. His first selections were Byron Beck of Denver and Wayne

Hightower of Kansas. Both were legitimate players who helped Denver make the playoffs. We both believe in a credo that reflects our sports background: "Win and always look forward to the next challenge. Do not be complacent."

Prior to the merger of the ABA and NBA, Bass served as director of officials for the ABA. His great organizational skills in this capacity were a credit to the ABA. Bass also coached the San Antonio Spurs in both leagues.

Joel Arthur Barker wrote: "Vision without action is merely a dream. Action without vision just passes time. Vision with action can change the world." These sentiments reflect Bob Bass and his philosophy of "doing." He makes things happen. The Oklahoma native surely did himself proud.

The Best Sports Transaction

The St. Louis Spirits were an ABA team owned by Ozzie and Dan Silna, who probably made the best sports deal ever. The team featured 6′8″-foot center Marvin Barnes and a great voice in the field of sports announcing, the one and only Bob Costas. When the merger took place between the ABA and NBA, the understanding was that the ABA teams would "sign off" collectively and all the teams would be satisfied with the deal. Some of the teams wanted out, others wanted some revenue, some wanted to join the NBA, and Ozzie Silna and his St. Louis lawyers and partners agreed to take a piece of the television revenue of the four joining teams for perpetuity. The clubs that agreed to this transaction were the San Antonio Spurs, the New York Nets (currently the New Jersey Nets), the Indiana Pacers and the Denver Nuggets. At that time, television was in its infancy and it was no big deal to those four teams. Today, however, television is huge, and the revenues very substantial. I've said on many occasions that I want Ozzie Silna and his lawyers doing my negotiations on any deals in my future. They did a remarkable job and had good insight about the future of television.

Slam Dunk

Many aren't aware that the first slam-dunk contest was an ABA creation – which Sports Illustrated coined as the "best halftime invention since the restroom." The spirited contest went straight to the heart of the ABA and was important to the league as it became a full-blown show during the team's warm ups. Many ABA fans arrived at arenas early just to watch the likes of Artis Gilmore, Willie Taylor, George Gervin, David Thompson, and of course, the great "Doctor J," Julius Erving, perform their acrobatic aerial shows.

The five contestants at the first contest were Julius Erving, Larry Kenon, Artis Gilmore, David Thompson and George Gervin. Since all of the players competing in the dunk contest were black, Julius Erving took it upon himself to ask head coach Kevin Loughery if they could include a white player in the competition. After some thought they were unable to come up with a white player with dunking talents equal to that of the original five players. During that time in basketball history, white players concentrated their skills on three-point shooting skills. Dan Issel, an ABA center and current general manager of the Denver Nuggets, said at the time that the slam-dunk contest went right to the essence of the ABA.

As popular as the slam dunk contest is in today's NBA gala festivities, the contest was even more popular during its early days with the ABA. Many felt that the awesome dunks were a statement of a player's manhood. The slam dunk became so important during the ABA days that the pregame warm ups became a show in itself. Issel remembers the Nets' Ollie Taylor's pregame rituals each game. He would show off an array of windmill dunks, cradle dunks, reverse dunks, flying dunks and everything else imaginable. The fans would get excited and pumped up before the games even began. It was pure show business – and the ABA believed in show business.

During their days in the ABA, Julius Erving and Doug Moe had great times having fun with and kidding one another. On the day that the first dunk contest was to take place, Moe bet Erving that he couldn't make a dunk in which he took off from the free-throw line – 15 feet away. The bet became the highlight of the game – everyone at the game was aware of it, and more importantly, excited about the wager. George Irvine, Carl Scheer and Vince Cazzetta were the judges for the highly anticipated contest. Scheer remembers the action.

"Julius went to the foul line, turned and began pacing off in the opposite direction from the basket. He cradled the ball in his hand as if it were a baseball – it looked so small. As he paced off, the crowd started screaming. When he got to about three-quarters of the court away, he turned and faced the basket. Then there was total silence from the audience – the crowd knew that it was going to see something special. Julius stared at the basket for a moment. Then he took off with his long and majestic strides. The arena was quiet – you could hear his every step as his shoes touched the floor."

Sheer still remembers Erving's long, galloping stride – as if he were an antelope.

"Julius was off in the air – he brought the ball back from behind himself somewhere – as if he were a helicopter. He rammed it through the rim. Only when the ball hit the floor did the crowd go 'bananas.' They literally went crazy. Doug Moe watched the foul line and to this day claims that Julius' foot was on the line."

The bet has never been resolved, although no one besides Moe seems to care anymore. This was the beginning of the illustrious slam dunk. It will always be a large part of the enjoyment of watching basketball.

The Great "Dr. J"

Many buffs of the great game of basketball regard Julius Erving as one of the premier forwards of the game. He could do anything and everything. He was a precision shooter, a magnificent rebounder and is considered one of the ultimate "slam dunk" artists of all time.

For a time, Dr. J waved his magic wand as an executive vice president for the Orlando Magic of the NBA. I really believe that Dr. J, with his immense talent, helped forge the merger with the NBA. He brought the ABA credibility – he *was* the ABA. Roy Boe of the New York Nets later bought Erving's rights from Earl Foreman, the owner of the Virginia Squires. This allowed the ABA to have a marquee name in the Big Apple. The move increased the interest of the New York press corps. Most people recognized that the New York media outlet helped develop interest in the sporting field and we were right on the button in regard to the great Dr. J, the man from Massachusetts. Not only was Julius Erving a fine basketball player, he was also a dedicated and special individual.

Julius Erving left the University of Massachusetts as a junior and signed as a free agent with the Virginia Squires of the ABA. The Milwaukee Bucks drafted Julius as number 12 in the 1972 NBA draft, but a court order ruled that he should stay with the Squires. He played in the ABA for five years, two with the Squires and three with the New York Nets before signing with the Philadelphia 76ers in 1976, following the merger of the ABA and the NBA. Erving was named both to the All-ABA Team and the All-Rookie Team during his first season in the ABA.

The 76ers got Erving for $6 million; $3 million to the Doctor himself, and $3 million to his former team. He played 11 years in Philly, winning a world championship in 1983. In his first year in Philadelphia, Dr. J's team fell in the NBA finals to the young Portland Trailblazers, who were led by Bill Walton (Erving's sometime broadcasting partner and colleague).

When he was with the New York Nets, he won two ABA titles ('74 and '76) and was named the playoff MVP those two years as well. Dr. J. was the MVP of the ABA in 1974 and 1976, and co-MVP in 1975. He also holds the record for the highest ABA career scoring average: 28.7 points per game. He had a college scoring average of 26.3 to go with his 22.0 NBA scoring average. With the NBA's Sixers, Erving was named the MVP in 1981. He was a perennial All-Star, being selected as the league's MVP twice ('77 and '83). Erving was also a five-time NBA First Team selection (1978, 1980-'83). Before winning the NBA championship, Erving's 76ers made a run for it in 1983, beating the Celtics to advance to the NBA finals, where they lost to Magic Johnson's Lakers. Erving retired after the 1986-'87 season, having piled up 30,026 points in the ABA and NBA combined. With 18,364 points, Erving finished third on the Sixers' all-time scoring list behind Hal Greer (21,586) and Dolph Schayes (19,249). Dr. J. was elected to the NBA Hall of Fame in 1993.

Hubie Brown

Hubie Brown, the great coach and TV analyst, goes around the country giving coaching clinics. One of the most frequently asked questions he hears is: "What was the best team that you ever coached?"

Hubie replies that it's the 1975 ABA All-Star Team, and at least half of his audience looks at him as if he were talking about something in outer space. Hubie then says, "Seriously, that team had a front line of Dan Issel, Artis Gilmore and Wilbert Jones. Issel and Gilmore had monster years after joining the ABA. In the back court, we had one of Kentucky's all-time-greatest shooters in Lou Dampier."

Brown went on to explain that the team had great players, including a great defensive player in "Teddy "Hound Dog" McClain. Brown went on to say that the ABA had some of the greatest forwards to ever play the game: Julius Erving, George McGinnis, David Thompson, Bobby Jones, George Gervin, Larry Kenon, Rick Barry, Caldwell Jones, Maurice Lucas, Marvin Barnes, Danny Roundfield, Billy Cunningham, Bill Knight and Moses Malone. Doug Moe, Connie Hawkins and Roger Brown would later be added to the prestigious list. Talent? You bet. The ABA did have talent.

In Brown's opinion, the ABA had such great talent that they would eventually play in the NBA after the leagues merged. Until that time, they were still a very well-kept secret. Brown maintains that everything that the ABA did is now done in the NBA – with only one exception. They didn't take along the red, white and blue ball. He believes this to be a mistake.

Lee Meade

I first met Lee Meade when we were forming the ABA. We were attempting to put a team in Denver. He was then a young sports editor of the Denver Post, Colorado's leading newspaper. A very people-oriented person, Meade has a charming and informative way, and he never minced words on his positions. He told me up front that Denver was a wonderful city, but that the people were generally "laid back" when it came to new projects. They would be cautious as to their support initially, but once involved, you could not find a better supporting city. He was right on target with his viewpoints.

Lee Meade became one of my very best friends. I found him always sincere, honest and frank about subjects and people. From this first "meet," Lee Meade became one of the five organizers of our new league. He was a key part of the success of our leagues, and over the years, he was a big part of our team. He planned the press conferences, wrote the press releases and dealt with the media representatives of each city on a personal basis. He was very good in his business dealings.

Gary Davidson was the administrator and the leader of our group. I was the organizer, Don Regan did the legal work, Steve Arnold took care of recruiting, and Lee Meade was the director of media relations. Our potent and hard-working team generally got the job done. Later in life, Meade was the sports editor of a suburban paper in Sacramento. He is now retired in Horseshoe

Bay, Texas. He was and is a man of dedication, perseverance and decency.

George Mikan, the "Big Man" and Commissioner

The history books will reflect that George Mikan was the most dominant basketball player of the first half of the 20th century. As a player he was a man who took charge of the boards and one who let everyone know that he was the caretaker of the middle. Players knew that this was his territory. The NBA Minneapolis Lakers stood tall as a team during an era which featured George Mikan as the "big man" for the team, as well as the league. Mikan stood 6'10". He was known as a giant among his peers. He was mean and tough, and he gave no quarter as a player. I was privileged to know him. We were known as the "odd couple" of the league, as I was 5'6" and wide, while he was a tall, thin, giant of a man. We were the "Mutt and Jeff" of the red, white and blue basketball league.

My next-door neighbor, Fred Goff, introduced us. He told me that he had a friend who could perhaps help put it together. Wow, was he right. That friend of Goff's was none other than George Mikan.

Mikan has a strong personality. He is opinionated and firm in his beliefs. He commanded respect and was a take-charge person. Mikan was commissioner of the ABA for two years and during that tenure, everyone knew that when he spoke, they listened. I had a great relationship with George. We did a lot of "zigging and zagging" together, maneuvering and manipulating votes within the ownership ranks. Both of us are politicians – he a Republican and me a Democrat. He ran for Congress in his native state of Minnesota. Although he lost the race, it was close despite it being a predominantly Democratic district. Had he run for office today as an Independent, he most probably would have won using Jesse Ventura's formula of independence.

George Mikan was the key figure in making the ABA happen. He was our credibility, lending us substance and media attention. And to think, his involvement with us came close to not happening. With just 10 minutes remaining before our national press conference in New York, Mikan had yet not signed the agreement. We were still involved in negotiations with his lawyer, Bill Erickson, who maintained that some of his client's demands were not yet met by the organizers and owners. The league was faced with the stark realization that Mikan could have said "no," and who knows what the media would have done if that had become a reality. Needless to say, things were ironed out, and the press conference went well. Mikan did sign and he became our key figure at the time of the announcement, as well as for the years to come.

Bob Cousy

One of the true superstars of professional basketball is the legendary Bob Cousy of Worcester, Massachusetts. The Boston Celtics star point guard is generally listed on most all-time all-star basketball teams. Cousy was highly regarded, and still is, as the "wizard" of the passing game with his dazzling assists to his fast-breaking teammates. Cousy was the commissioner of the IBA 6′4″ and Under League. He was as great a commissioner as he was a basketball player. Everything about Cousy as a former player was a perfect fit for the agenda of the 6′4″ and Under League. Hollywood producer, Rocky Kalish, selected Cousy to help organize the league. The IBA is still playing in Canada. The vitality of Bob Cousy helped to make the league a tremendous success. Bob Cousy still does some commentary work on the Celtics televised games.

The Indiana Connection

The best organization in the ABA's eight-year existence was the Indiana Pacers. Sure, we had other great teams in the league, but year in and out, you could always count on the fact that the men from Indianapolis had to be beaten. They were the New York Yankees of baseball, the Green Bay Packers of football, the Boston Celtics of basketball and the Montreal Canadiens of hockey. The quality of the team started at the top. They had good ownership, top management led by Mike Storen, a dedicated lawyer in Dick Tinkham, and a coach, Slick Leonard, who got the best out of his players. They also had players like Mel Daniels, Roger Brown, Bob Netolicky, George McGinnis and a host of other players on their roster.

Mike Storen came from the Cincinnati Royals of the NBA. He was their business manager and definitely a "Carny" when it came to making trades. An example is when he acquired Mel Daniels from me when we were in financial desperation. We traded Mel from Minneapolis to the Pacers. Mike often claimed that I was a "pirate" in my business dealings, but he was the ultimate thief of the universe. He was able to get Mel Daniels for practically nothing when we moved the Minneapolis franchise to Miami because Larry Shields wanted all the bills paid before we left the city. Larry, who earned a lot of money as a developer in Los Angeles, was a man of high principle. He believed in paying his bills all of the time – so when we moved the team, it was a priority to pay off all the bills before relocating. The Miami owners, whom I got together, were led by Tom Carney. He agreed with Shield's policy of paying his bills, although he knew that in the transfer, losing Daniels would weaken the Floridians.

Mike Storen is a Notre Dame graduate and over the years has taken a lot of my cash when the Irish would beat my beloved Trojans. His daughter, the famous Hannah Storm, grew up in the "Irish atmosphere." She gained a lot of her sports knowledge from her dad. I think she must have learned his superior negotiating skills, as she is the premier woman's sports announcer in North America and doing very well financially. Those "Domers" always seem to have "Touchdown Jesus" in their corner.

Mike Storen and Dick Tinkham were in the league from the beginning to the merger with the NBA. They were the "Rocks of

Gibraltar" of the ABA. They were essential in keeping the league together during good and bad times. I have always considered them friends, as well as complete business executives. Mike Storen has a charming personality and he knew what he was doing. Dick Tinkham kept the league on a straight course and kept us out of a lot of trouble because of his wisdom.

"Former Boston Celtics center Bill Russell studied all of his opponents closely, so that he could actually play the moves in his mind." – Dennis Murphy Jr.

Wilt the Stilt

Basketball purists often argue about who was the greatest center ever to play the game of basketball, and you can fire up a donnybrook just bringing up the subject. Many people claim that Bill Russell was the greatest center of all time because of his defensive play.

To me, there have been great centers in our game, and George Mikan, Moses Malone, Bill Walton, Kareem Abdul Jabbar and Nate Thurmond will all get votes. In the final analysis, however, I think it comes down to three outstanding players: Wilt "The Stilt" Chamberlain, Shaquille O'Neal, and the defensive star of the Boston Celtics, Bill Russell.

Most purists will tell you that Wilt was the all-time best. The modern experts will tell you Shaquille O'Neal should be highly considered. Then there are the Bill Russell fans, who will tell you their man was by far the best. I will not touch this one, but I will say, they were unbelievable athletes and they all made their mark on the game.

Dr. Lenny Bloom of San Diego owned a large portion of land in the Chula Vista area of San Diego County. He envisioned a new sports stadium on his land and he then went to work to attempt to make it happen. He felt that by buying an ABA and WHA team he would then secure 80 dates in the arena. He went to the city of Chula Vista and got their approval to put the matter up to the voters of the city. He signed Wilt Chamberlain to be player-coach for his basketball team and by so doing, felt his chances of securing a favorable vote would be enhanced.

He then bought the L.A. Sharks of the WHA and planned to move them to his facility. It was a well-conceived plan and one that would have worked, but unfortunately for Dr. Bloom, his father got sick and was put in the hospital the weekend prior to the vote. Lenny was extremely close to his father, and this was a major problem for him. He then made the decision that family was more important than vision and thus spent the last weekend of the referendum vote with his pop rather than with steering his ship. Doing the "right thing" left the ship rudderless and in uncharted waters. He lost the referendum by just 13 votes and his dream was derailed.

His ABA team, the San Diego Conquistadors, then played in the San Diego State University's Peterson Gym, and even though it was small in size, the team drew well with Wilt Chamberlain leading the way. If the new arena had been built, the crowds, I am sure, would have been large and very enthusiastic. I respect Lenny Bloom for putting family over ambition, and he should be always complimented for that. People told Dr. Bloom he had no chance to lure Chamberlain from the NBA, but he is a very persistent individual, and he did the best signing job available. Wilt coached the Conquistadors in his last professional year in basketball and gave the ABA another shot in the arm.

Reuben "Ruby" Richman – A Canadian Basketball Man

Toronto's Ruby Richman is a class act in every way. In 1969, Richman, an attorney, came to Florida to negotiate for our Miami Floridians basketball team. He was far ahead of the curve when he felt Toronto would support an ABA team. Was he ever right! The Raptors of the NBA now have the support and excitement of professional basketball. After three days of intense negotiations, our owners felt that they would keep the Floridians in Miami. This was discouraging to Ruby, but as always, he was gracious and classy when we told him of the decision. He said that the ABA would be well-served if we went to Toronto, but he understood.

Over the years Ruby and I have maintained a strong relationship. He was selected to the Canadian Basketball Hall of Fame, and I made one of his endorsement speeches. I did so with honor and pleasure. Ruby, at one time, was a point guard who could shoot the eyes out of the ball from any part of the court. Twenty years later, Ruby joined us in the 6'4" and Under Basketball League. This was especially important to him since he felt that the three-point shot would change basketball. He reasoned that the "little guys" would be able to shine equally as well as "the giants." Philadelphia's Allen Iverson has proven that Ruby was correct in his assessment of the long-range shot.

I have come to respect Ruby's judgment. As a basketball man he has very few equals. Ruby was the general manager of the Chicago entry in ABA 2000 – he paid the price and is a success in life.

My Stay in Denver

After the ABA had been organized, my two bosses, Ken Carlson and Jim Trindle, asked me to go to Denver and get some additional owners for their franchise in Denver. Trindle and Carlson are two of the finest people on this earth, and as my bosses at Voorheis, Trindle and Nelson Engineering in Westminster, California, they treated me with respect and dignity as their director of marketing. They took the Denver franchise ownership in the league knowing full well that their engineering firm would not allow them full time for basketball. Thus, they both felt that they would stay with the franchise, but it would only be on a financial basis.

They wanted me to find some "Denver people" who would do the everyday work as owners of the team. Jack Ashton, who was on the Denver Sports Committee, helped me find a gentleman who owned the Ringsby Truck Lines. Bill Ringsby and his son Don became the majority owners of the Denver Rockets, now the Denver Nuggets. Ken Carlson and Jim Trindle became minority owners of the club. Bill and Don Ringsby were a great father-and-son team. They bought a majority interest and involved themselves in the team. They assembled a good, exciting team, and they hired Texas Tech's Bob Bass as the coach. They brought in Dick Eicher, a Denver banker and former AAU basketball player into the fold as their GM. I was then asked to be the marketing director, which I accepted.

I told my wife about the job offer and that it required moving from California to Denver. She was not keen on the idea, but, because she was a trooper, she went along with it. My wife and I packed our belongings, the kids and the dogs, and away we went. We rented a house in Littleton, Colorado, and became involved in that suburban community. It was a great year in Denver. The people of the city were wonderful and our kids loved it there. The only problem we experienced was the cold weather. That was my downfall, and has been throughout my life. After the first snowstorm and a near accident driving home from a ball game, it was evident and clear that Denver was not for me.

Our family then returned to California. I was not popular with my kids, as they loved the snowball fights and the style of living in Colorado. My kids had made many friends in the city, and our trip back to the West Coast was strained. I'll never forget that on the trip home, we stopped by train tracks to take a break, and a Southern Pacific Superliner bore down on us. It was a job getting the dogs herded back into the car, and for several moments, we thought that one of the three dogs would be a crushed animal. Luckily for all of us, we *did* get them back into the car and in one piece. That's the price of traveling.

The Denver Rockets

The Denver Rockets hold a special place in my heart. I was the first general manager of the team until Bill Ringsby, majority owner of the team, wanted his own man in the position. I was then asked to fulfill the marketing responsibilities, and I did. Since Dick Eicher was the person he wanted as general manager and I immediately agreed; I had heard that he was a real quality guy and would do a terrific job. His reputation proved to be true, and he did a great job. As the team's marketing director I was very involved and loved it. Eicher was a real gentleman and a joy to work for. I enjoyed my stay in Denver and will always be grateful to my Orange County bosses Ken Carlson and Jim Trindle for the opportunity to work there. It was in Denver where I met an outstanding journalist and editor of the Denver Post, Lee Meade. Lee and I became good friends and I learned a lot from him during my sports career.

The Miami Floridians

The Miami Floridians were originally owned by a group of local investors headed by Dr. Tom Carney. The group included Sandy Rywell, Steve Falk, Dr. Dave Schwartz and Larry Shields. Shields was the original owner of the Minnesota Muskies, but retained an interest in the club after the move to Miami. This collection of people operated the team for three years. Jim Pollard, a Stanford graduate and Laker great, was the Miami coach. I was the general manager, and ironically, Rudy Martske, now of USA Today, served as the team's public relations director.

Our Florida basketball ownership group was led by our team president, Dr. Tom Carney, who was also a banker. Under Carney, our team met its bills and responsibilities. As astute a businessman Carney was, he was also a prince of a person. I will always have a special place in my heart for my friend Tom and his family. Carney and his partners were weary of losing money. They felt it was time to concentrate on their own successful professions – the chores of running banks, taking care of patients and making money in the stock market.

In 1970, they decided to sell the team to Ned Doyle, a 75-year-old business tycoon. Doyle was a giant in the advertising business. He made up the "Doyle" partnership of the New York firm, Doyle, Dane and Bernback. Ned and his wife had a condo in south Miami, where they spent most of their winters. Doyle loved sports, and more so, loved being an owner. After making millions of dollars as one of the cleverest advertising executives with his creative Volkswagen ads, Doyle was ready to "settle down" and become a sports owner. He bought the team, while stipulating only one request: that I stay on one year with the team while he learned the business.

Since it was our son's senior year at Norland High School in Miami, that suited me just fine. Ned Doyle was a kind and decent human being – he had a flair about him that was "Irish" all the time. We had gone from a Carney to a Doyle, both of whom shared my own family roots in southern Ireland. Doyle illustrated his advertising genius with his initial breakout ads, which stated: "We fired the team and kept the coach."

This referred to the Miami Floridians barely making the playoffs in 1969, which happened only after we had hired Hal Blitman as our new coach midway through the season. Blitman came south to Miami from the college ranks, more specifically Cheney State, in Philadelphia, – when we were in total disarray and in last place. He was known for taking teams with weak talent and making them contenders – mainly by instilling a team spirit that achieved success. He did the same after arriving in Miami. We were only eliminated from the playoffs after a five-game playoff series against the Indiana Pacers.

My dear friends Slick Leonard and Mike Storen of the Pacers were incensed with me after I placed their club in the Playboy Hotel in Miami Beach while they were awaiting the third game of the playoffs. The Pacers had totally destroyed us in the first two games of the series in Indiana. They had yet to make reservations in Miami before the third game. They had previously thought that Pittsburgh would be their first-round opponent instead of Miami. Lo and behold, we pulled out a win which changed the direction of the playoffs. The Pacers won in five games, but Slick and Mike would never again let me make their hotel reservations - their players didn't sleep much in Miami...

Doyle asked Hal Blitman to coach and asked Jay Deming to be his general manager after I left. I went back to California with great memories of my days in Florida. Like Larry Shields, I loved the warm climate and the nice people and friends that that we made.

Coach Hal Blitman

I have had the pleasure of having a great group of coaches in my professional career. They included Jim Pollard of Stanford University; Bob Bass, the current vice president of the NBA Charlotte Hornets; Terry Slater, coach of the Los Angeles Sharks; and Wayne Rivers of the San Francisco Shamrocks. They all are winners and men who devoted their total attention to the details of running a professional team's operation. I am always amazed at the total dedication these men have devoted to their sport. One of the most intense men I have ever had as an associate is the former Miami Floridians coach, Hal Blitman. Blitman "lived and died" with his team. His players loved him.

So did the fans. He was known in the structure of management as a tower of strength.

I truly loved working with Hal. Over the years we have developed a special friendship. Hal was very intense and he would fight you over a game of Tiddlywinks – he was that much of a competitor. I remember one day when he and his wife were having coffee with my wife, Elaine. Hal literally walked through a clean patio glass window, thinking it was open. Hal is now a high-school principal in Florida who enjoys his wife and family, and playing golf and tennis.

The Dallas Chaparrals

The Dallas Chaparrals were an exciting, hard-hitting and superior shooting team. Bob Folsom, who subsequently became the mayor of his beloved Dallas, owned the team. Colorful Max Williams was the club's GM, former NBA great Cliff Hagen was the coach, and Terry Stembridge, Sr., was the team's announcer. Hagen played in addition to coaching, and players who also led the charge included John Beasley and Cincy Powell. Initially, the Chaparrals were to be owned by Gary Davidson, Don Regan and Mike O'Hara. When the announcement in Dallas was made, Bob Folsom immediately contacted Gary Davidson and offered to buy the team. The offer was terrific and thus the sale was made. Folsom and Joe Geary and their crew did a terrific job with the Chaparrals.

Jerry Saperstein

In this book you will often see the name Jerry Saperstein. He has played a major part in my career. His late father, Abe Saperstein, owned and founded the Harlem Globetrotters. Jerry continued the tradition for four years after his father's death and then sold the team to the Padmer family of Chicago. Jerry has become one of my best friends, as well as being a great consultant through the years. He has been with me in the trenches. Jerry could have retired at a young age and lived the good life; however, like his father, he believed in working and achieving. He has been involved in tennis, hockey and, of course, basketball, on a professional level. In the sports world, the name "Saperstein" equates to perfection.

A credo written by Theodore Roosevelt goes to the soul of the Saperstein family, and a portion of that credo is as follows: *"The credit belongs to the man who is actually in the arena, who's face is marred by dust and sweat and blood... his place in life shall never be with those cold and timid souls who neither know victory or defeat."*

Jerry also tells a story that his father, Abe, passed on to him when he was a youngster. It goes like this: "Son, I hope that you always win, but if you do happen to lose, do so like a champion, because it is not the winning that counts, but that you tried and gave it your all."

Jerry now lives in Florida and commutes to New York. He is now working hard to develop his own summer basketball league, along with devoting much attention to his securities business.

"Build me a son, O Lord, who will be strong enough to know when he is weak, and brave enough to face himself when he is afraid; one who will be proud and unbending in honest defeat, and humble and gentle in victory." – General Douglas McArthur

Earl Foreman, Owner of the Virginia Squires

Earl Foreman, an intelligent and crafty businessman, bought the Oakland Oaks from Pat Boone and moved the team to Virginia, where they became the Virginia Squires. The Squires were coached by Al Bianchi. Foreman built a formidable team by signing Julius Erving, budding star Charlie Scott and shooting guard George Gervin. Foreman's Squires played their home games in Richmond, Norfolk and Hampton Roads. This turned his team into a regional franchise representing the state of Virginia.

The great Dr. J was signed when Foreman had attorney Steve Arnold contact the star while he was a member of the University of Massachusetts basketball team. The rest is history. Foreman, best remembered as being a "hands-on" owner, was the cousin of Dr. Leonard Bloom, who owned the San Diego ABA entry. The pair of cousins had two of the greatest players in basketball history in Julius Erving and Wilt Chamberlain. What a duo!

Larry Brown, ABA Player, NBA Coach

Larry Brown was a winner as a player for the New Orleans Buccaneers and he is a winner today, as the former coach of two ABA teams (the Carolina Cougars and Denver Nuggets) and *nine* different NBA teams. Brown was an intense player, leading the Bucs in their drive for the ABA Western Division Championship in 1968. Brown did the same good work as the head coach of the NBA's 76ers, and he was named NBA Coach of the Year in 2001. He had a natural and terrific guard in Allen Iverson. I was the operations manager of the Miami Floridians back in 1967 and Larry Brown, Doug Moe and Red Robbins loved to break my heart with their magnificent execution of the plays Bucs Coach Babe McCarthy put into play. Over the years, I have always wanted both Doug Moe and Larry Brown to do well. In most cases, they did not let me down.

The only time I wanted Larry Brown to lose was when he coached those men from Westwood, California; the Bruins of UCLA. He got smart and later moved on in his career, and then I again became his greatest booster. I have never seen a more dedicated and involved person than Larry Brown. That's the way he performed as a player, and today, that's the way he coaches. I hope he returns as an NBA coach soon and wins another championship. He is a class person and a winner, all the way.

Coach Doug Moe

Doug Moe played in the ABA and, like Larry Brown, he also coached in the NBA. Moe coached in Denver and had his players hustling at all times. He sometimes seemed like he was not occupied, but Coach Moe coached the game to the maximum of his players' ability. He was well respected and had his players ready to play. Today, Doug keeps busy in the business world. He lives in Colorado and loves the cold weather. He always believed that "Togetherness and teamwork can conquer all adversity."

Bill Sharman, Coach of the L.A. Stars and Utah Stars

Bill Sharman was more than a typical coach – he was a pioneer and an innovator. The shoot-around on game days was his idea. Film preparation and in-depth scouting reports on their opponents were also his ideas. Today, that is standard procedure. Sharman knew more about his opponents than opposing coaches knew about their own teams. He was thoroughly prepared and thus had the edge. So were his players.

Sharman believed that the "little things" made a difference, as exemplified by him having his players keep notes on their opponents. In professional basketball much of the game is about matchups – playing one against one. Bill was a master of putting the right person against a given opponent. He also believed in a special diet. He always had his honey, candy bars and tea in his dressing room. He believed that candy and honey gave players extra energy and that tea fulfilled their liquid needs.

The shoot-around met a lot of moans and groans from players when Sharman first introduced it. His thought was that by getting players up early in the morning, he would get them thinking basketball rather than being lazy and staying in bed. He also used it as a punishment. I remember one night in Florida when I received a phone call at 2 a.m. It was Bill on the line.

"Murph, my club stunk up the joint last night," said Sharman. "I wonder if you would call your trainer and have him open up the gym right now for a practice session."

I said, "Bill, it's 2 a.m."

"It will teach our players a lesson," he responded. "As a favor to me, personally, please do this for me."

I got up and made the call. Bill was on his way. One had a hard time saying no to someone like Bill Sharman. As the years passed I learned that Bill did this frequently with his players. It wasn't unusual for him to take his players right from the airport to the gym, at any time of the day or night. He was a fanatic when it came down to practice.

The Utah Stars were an instant success in Salt Lake. They went into the ABA finals in 1970, losing to the Indiana Pacers. They won it all the following year, beating the Kentucky Colonels in seven games. The toughest series was their battle against Indiana in 1971. It went seven games and was literally a war. The crowds were huge and the excitement intense. The two coaches were a total contrast to one another. Sharman's manner was soft and quiet; Slick Leonard the opposite – loud and volatile. Both were winners, and when the teams met, it was a game that the fans loved. Both clubs gave it their all and played with great pride. In order to beat the Pacers, opponents had to go the proverbial extra mile. Sharman and crew did just that. Sharman was the only coach to win ABA and NBA championships. He was the consummate coach and his impeccable record proved it.

The New Orleans Buccaneers

Each time that we visited the beautiful city of New Orleans, we thought of our original ABA Buccaneers' owners. What a crew. We're talking about the late Morton Downey, Jr., politicians Charlie Smithers and Maurice Stern, and the sweetest horn player in the world, Al Hirt, who was famous for his "southern smoothness."

It was a joy to visit with one of the great musicians of our time, Al Hirt, at his restaurant. We had some lovely evenings talking about basketball and listening to his beautiful horn. Smithers and Stern took care of the business end of the franchise. Downey, Jr. and Babe McCarthy handled matters on the players' end. They had an excellent basketball team, led by one of the most colorful coaches in the business in Mississippi's Babe McCarthy. In the trenches, they had two players who later made it big in coaching – Larry Brown and Doug Moe. Yes, the New Orleans Buccaneers will always have a special place in my heart. They were owned by a group of characters who played well together under a great coach, who also played with devotion and heart.

The New York Nets

Roy Boe, owner of the New York Nets, was the youngest owner in the ABA. He was a flamboyant restaurant owner and a terrific individual. His Nets had uniforms that dazzled the New York fans – two piece, red and white uniforms. Boe traded for Dr. J and was an owner who wasn't afraid to spend his money to build a winning team. He was great for the league and a fabulous owner for New York. Ray Boe is back in the restaurant business today. His contribution to the ABA was absolutely sensational.

Coach Lou Carnesecca

Lou Carnesecca, of St. John's fame, was the first coach of the Nets. Lou is a college hall of famer, a man of high principles and someone who had the respect of his players. He was a giant in the game of college basketball. He was later a giant in the ABA. Coach Carnesseca had a great sense of humor and got along with everyone. He was selected to the Basketball Hall of Fame for his St. John's days. Lou knew a lot about talent as well as being a strong bench coach. He coached the New York Nets for three years and gave the league a lot of credibility.

Charley Finley, Owner, Memphis Tams

Charley Finley was the owner of the ABA's Memphis Tams. His place in the sports world will always be cherished. He was a baseball man who dabbled in basketball. He was the owner of some of the most proficient baseball teams that ever performed. He owned the Oakland Athletics and had on his roster the fabulous Reggie Jackson and star pitcher Catfish Hunter. He also was a business partner of Lenny Bloom and brought excitement and flair to his basketball team in Memphis. His coach and general manager was Bob Bass, the same man who had worked with me in Denver.

Charley Finley was always innovative. He felt that with his experience in professional baseball, he could piggyback it in professional basketball, but as is the case in professional sports, it's difficult to excel in both. What works in baseball does not ensure success in another sport and vice versa. That is why I do not believe in dual-sport ownership. It was a pleasure having Charley "O" in our league, and he did give us all his wisdom and excitement. Charley Finley was a credit to the ABA and we miss him.

A Signing Nightmare

A lot of basketball junkies preferred the quickness of our game, while basketball purists preferred the NBA style of play. The signing of Mel Daniels by the Minnesota Muskies was another big coup for the ABA. He was a 6-foot-9 player out of

New Mexico who was a hard worker and a very emotional player. Daniels was a good rebounder and proficient shot blocker. He was a first-round pick in the NBA, but Commissioner George Mikan and Minnesota owner Larry Shields were determined to persuade him to play in the ABA.

A big squabble ensued between the leagues, but the ABA came out the winner as Daniels decided to play for the new league. Daniels was one of the first of many players who chose the ABA over the longtime established NBA. The first game in Indiana was held at the Indianapolis Fairgrounds. It featured the natural rivalry of Indiana Pacers against the Kentucky Colonels. Because of this rivalry, the game was a complete sellout. Fans were being turned away at the door.

The Pacers got off to a fast start that season, but it immediately it became apparent that Bob Netolicky was not a true center, instead more suited for the power forward position. Mike Storen, who never seemed to stand still, quickly began looking for a center. He settled on Reggie Harding, who had played in the NBA, but had the reputation of being "seven feet of trouble."

After discussing the situation with Tinkham and Stoverman, Storen decided to go after Harding despite his terrible reputation. The negotiations began at 5 a.m. at the airport and were a classic. Storen, in his usual "Irish," tried to charm the giant of a man. Tinkham used his usual to-the-point manner. But despited doing their very best with their blarney, they realized that the negotiations weren't going anywhere, and the issue turned to money.

Tinkham told Reggie to take his pen and write down a figure that would coax Harding to sign with the team. Harding responded. Tinkham came back with the figure of $15,000. Tinkham tied it to a plan. Harding said in his first remarks that with him playing with the Pacers a championship would be ensured. Dick turned that remark around and worked out a formula of wins which would get Reggie to the monetary number he sought. Harding felt so confident of his abilities that he took the offer.

The signing became a nightmare for Storen, Larry Stoverman and the Pacers. Harding was a nonconformist and didn't fare well with authority of any type. He quickly turned into a loose cannon. He refused to wear a coat and tie, which was a rule on road trips. He took off when he wanted to and even missed some games. He once used the excuse that he had to attend the funeral of his daughter, but later it was disclosed he had no daughter. He was truly trouble for the team, and Stoverman couldn't handle him.

Mike knew that Harding couldn't be a Pacer and turned his sights toward a future big-man acquisition. The big man who made the difference turned out to be Mel Daniels.

Spencer Haywood and His Hardship Case

Spencer Haywood was the man who made the hardship case possible for professional athletes. He and his capable lawyer, Al Ross, tested the case in court and won. The ABA invented the hardship rule by which college players (other than seniors) who were in need could sign with professional teams. There really was no reason why a kid not interested in attending college would not bypass college and play in the pro ranks.

Judge Warren Ferguson heard the case and ruled in favor of Haywood and Ross. The same Warren Ferguson was once the city attorney of Buena Park, the city where I was mayor back in the 1950s. What a small world. It was reasoned that a player, if good enough, should be able to play and not use up the most financial and productive years of his life doing something else or just sitting at home. The best part of his life was becoming a basketball player rather than a teacher, scientist or scholar.

Haywood signed with Denver of the ABA, and after being named ABA Rookie of the Year and MVP for the 1969-70 season, was courted by Sam Shulman of the NBA's Seattle Supersonics – all in one season. The hardship rule was now in full bloom. Shulman defied his fellow NBA owners and signed Haywood, thus breaking the barrier. Today hardship cases are a fact of life and are now in the mainstream of NBA vocabulary.

Haywood's agent Al Ross is a scrappy L.A. lawyer who takes pride in representing his basketball and sports clients. He resents being called an agent – instead preferring to be called "the best sports attorney and business manager around."

"I do a heck of a job for my clients and I am proud to represent them in their battles with owners," said Ross. "Some nights I don't sleep, because I *do* care about my clients."

He also said that the Gary Davidsons and Dennis Murphys of the world are the greatest things that could have happened to sports, as they provided new opportunities for the players and fans alike.

"I am not a fast-buck artist," said Ross. "I put in a lot of hours and sweat into my work. I pay the price of success."

Al Ross now lives a good life in Newport Beach, California. He has a beautiful home, ambitious children, and a wife who keeps him working hard and tending the lawn.

Arthur Kim

Arthur Kim was the owner of the ABA Anaheim Amigos. Prior to the Amigos, Kim owned the Washington Generals, the entertaining opponents of the Harlem Globetrotters. Kim had a vast knowledge of the game of basketball, which quickly became an asset to Gary Davidson and me. Art knew the game backwards and forwards – and along with his lawyer, Jim Ackerman, he did a great job managing the Amigos. The Amigos played their home games in the cozy confines of the Anaheim Convention Center – a venue that seated around 7,000 fans. The Amigos drew an average of about 3,000 fans per game – this without the aid of "giveaways," something that Kim didn't believe in.

Kim was a feisty owner, who ran a tight ship. He sold his Amigos to Jim Kirst, a Los Angeles construction owner, after the team's first season in Anaheim. Kirst moved the team to Tinsel Town, where they became the Los Angeles Stars and played their home games at the Los Angeles Sports Arena. Jim Hardy was the team's general manager, and they were coached by the legendary Bill Sharman. The Stars won the Western Division championship in their first year in L.A. (1968).

The team subsequently moved to Salt Lake when they were bought by cable icon Bill Daniels. With the move, the team named Vince Boryla as the general manager. Sharman remained as the team's coach. The Salt Lake team featured ABA greats Zelmo Beatty, Willie Wise and Mack Calvin. The team presently plays in Utah in the NBA as the Jazz, continuing its impressive basketball heritage.

The Referees

At the ABA's beginning, the referees were very inexperienced, and this created problems. Getting experienced referees was an obvious solution, so we offered NBA referees a $25,000 signing bonus and doubled their salaries. Dick Tinkham negotiated the deal and made it happen, giving our fledgling league a great boost. We were very proud of our corps of ABA referees and thank Norm Drucker and Thurlo McGrady for assembling such a fine group of officials. Special thanks go out to Earl Strom for giving us a much-needed shot in the arm when we needed the referees' help.

In 1969, the ABA's coup not only surprised the NBA; it stunned the entire basketball world. We were able to get four of the NBA's top officials in Norm Drucker, Earl Strom, John Vanek and Joe Gushue. Those four men were considered the "cream" of the NBA referee crop. Referees and umpires are often just "accepted" and not given the true credit that they deserve. Their importance is reflected in the results of many strikes by the officials. They usually win their points because they do make a major difference to the players, coaches and fans. We often take for granted how much work it requires to be a proficient official. They learn their craft much in the same manner as the players do. It is a science to know where to be and call the game with consistency and knowledge. Games can be won or lost with the referee corps. They truly make a difference.

In 1969, when George Mikan resigned as commissioner, Jim Gardner, the former governor of North Carolina, was chosen to lead the ABA. One of the first things he did was to lure four of the top NBA officials away from the established league. Ralph Dolgoff, a renowned financial planner who was the inventor of the Dolgoff Financial Plan, was working closely with the ABA in developing a pension plan for the league. He was a neighbor of Norm Drucker, who subsequently became our chief referee. The referees in the early 1960s didn't make any money and had very little clout. Their NBA union seemed very weak, making it apparent that it would be a good idea to raid the NBA ranks.

The Three-Point Shot

The exciting and innovative three-point shot was first utilized by the old American Basketball League, which was organized in 1964 by Abe Saperstein. Unfortunately, the league played just a half season before disbanding on Christmas weekend. We felt that in order for our fledgling league to be successful, we would have to bring back hot-shooting forwards and guards. We believed that acceptance of the three-point shot would enhance excitement and revolutionize the game.

The NBA possessed a strong contingent of centers which dominated the game prior to the acceptance of the three-point shot. Things changed after we got the three-point shooting guards. The fight with our board of governors over the establishment of the three-point shot was a terrific battle. Commissioner George Mikan, Gary Davidson and I favored the play, while the basketball purists, namely Mike Storen and Dick Tinkham, fought against it.

After two days of rugged debate, Mike Storen, representing the Indianapolis Pacers, switched his vote, making it 7-5 in favor of the three-point shot. The NBA called us the "Mickey Mouse league," and continued to try to humiliate us. We stood our ground, and today the three-point shot is well respected and is a standard in high schools, colleges and with the pros. It's been rewarding to see the Reggie Millers, Kobe Bryants and Vince Carters hit those threes, making the game even more exciting. The three-point shot was a test that indeed proved to be a winner.

The Troubled Stars

The first superstar to play in the inaugural year of the ABA was Connie Hawkins of the Pittsburgh Pipers. Hawkins, along with Charlie Williams, Roger Brown, Tony Jackson and Doug Moe, was banned from the NBA for various reasons. George Mikan investigated the banning and felt their punishment was much too severe. He offered them a second opportunity to play the sport that they loved. Hawkins was playing in an industrial league in Pittsburgh when Gabe Rubin signed him. Hawkins, who had a wife and two children, at the time, was living very poorly. He had just about hit bottom, but his basketball skills hadn't deserted him when the ABA became a reality. It gave him the chance to shine again.

Hawkins had very large hands and was able to control the ball effortlessly. He was a legend on the playground. People would come just to watch him perform his dunks as he glided over his opponents. Even fellow professional basketball stars would watch in awe when he performed. Steve Jones said: "The Hawk gave the ABA instant credibility and brought a lot of fans out to see him perform throughout the league."

Hawkins was the main ingredient in Pittsburgh winning the inaugural ABA championship in a seven-game series against New Orleans. Pittsburgh's winning lineup consisted of Hawkins and Charlie Williams, two players denied an opportunity to play in the NBA. They also featured NBA castoffs Tom Washington, Art Heyman and Chico Vaughn. Many experts felt that Pittsburgh, especially with Hawkins, could hold its own against any NBA team. The 1967 ABA championship landed each winning player a ring, $2,200 and a team trophy. These NBA "rejects" were especially thankful for the opportunity to play basketball on a professional level again.

In its first season the ABA drew 1,200,000 fans, which averaged out to 2,800 fans per game. Considering that this was a new league, the attendance figures were very respectable.

The ABA All-Stars

The league's first All-Star team consisted of forwards Hawkins and Moe, pivot man Mel Daniels, and guards Larry Jones and Charlie Williams. This group would have been serious contenders in the NBA. The NBA, which originally banned Hawkins, suddenly became interested in him as his fame blossomed in the ABA. His lawyer, who for years had been denied, all of a sudden had his phone calls returned.

Herbert Francis de Bower wrote: "Some men succeed because they cheerfully pay the price of success, and others, though they may claim ambition and a desire to succeed, are unwilling to pay that price." The individuals named above were willing to pay the price, and by sticking it out, deserved their success. Connie Hawkins received an annuity which was to pay him $30,000 per year starting at age 45. It was a terrific change in his life, and those who knew him were happy indeed.

The loss of a superstar like Hawkins was a major blow to the ABA. The fault of his jumping to the NBA was solely that of the ABA. Gabe Rubin decided to move his Pittsburgh Pipers to Minnesota, and it turned into a disaster. Imagine, selling out the arena on his final championship, with his team catching on in Pittsburgh, and he decides to move to Minnesota. Rubin felt that with his championship team, and specifically with his star, Connie Hawkins, he could capture the Minnesota market. This was a huge mistake on his part and ended up hurting the league. The people of Pittsburgh weren't happy with the team's move, which some ABA officials believed took place because George Mikan wanted a team in Minnesota. This, however, has always been conjecture. We all make mistakes, but this was a colossal one for Gabe Rubin and the ABA.

Vince Cazzetta, the Pittsburgh Pipers' coach, was a healer and a person the players respected and trusted. When Rubin decided to move to Minneapolis, Cazzetta was reluctant to move. He had six children and was happy living in Pittsburgh. In order for him to move he wanted a long-term contract, which Rubin refused to give him. When Cazzetta refused to move, Rubin hired a very strong disciplinarian to be his new Minnesota coach. His name was Jim Harding.

Harding was a college coach from Loyola of New Orleans. As it turned out, he unfortunately didn't adjust to the professional coaching style. Coaches who have made the jump from college to professional ranks learn that on the professional level players are highly skilled and do not take to the "go get 'em style" prevalent in the college ranks. This was a factor in Harding's tough adjustment to the handling of his players. The chemistry between the players and Harding was not there and the record of the team showed.

In Pittsburgh, the team won the championship; in Minneapolis, the club struggled and was eliminated in the first round of the playoffs. Connie Hawkins had been injured in Minneapolis and played in only 47 games. Some insiders felt that one of the many reasons for Hawkins' injuries was because he felt that Harding didn't like him. The NBA Phoenix Suns were looking for a player who could help their team become an instant contender in their league. Connie Hawkins was just that player. After playing two years in the ABA, Hawkins was given the opportunity to play in the NBA. He signed a five-year contract for $410,000, with a bonus of $250,000,

Great Pride

I take great pride in knowing that the ABA signed players Julius Erving, Doug Moe, Larry Brown, Rick Barry, Moses Malone, George Gervin and Dan Issel – and broadcaster Bob

Costas – and gave many more their start in their professional careers. Over most of our history in the ABA, we were ridiculed by some fans, media and especially our competition at the time – the NBA and its owners.

We had a lot of "funny" times in the "New League," as it was referred to back then. Many strange and wacky things happened to us as we tried to make it through those wonderful years. We did delight those fans who didn't have major league professional sports teams at the time – and in some cases wouldn't have professional teams today had it not been for the ABA.

The years have passed – and now that I'm in the twilight of my life – I can see affection and appreciation for some of the things that we were able to bring to the fans. Because of the ABA, we see some of the artistic gains of the game now in place in the NBA – namely the adoption of the three-point shot and the flashy moves and flying dunks which have helped make the NBA the exciting game that it is today.

Good luck always and God bless you, Dad.

Love, Dawn and David Mee

The Murphy grandkids love you, Grandpa.

Melissa and Chris Duralde
Mindy and Ben Sexton
Dina and Matt Grubb
Debbie and Michael Williams
Denise and Casey Carasco
Danielle Mee, Sean Murphy and Michelle Haarlammert

SECTION III: THE WHA

The World Hockey Association (1972-1979)
Written by: Dennis Murphy, Sr., aided by Jack Armstrong,
Walt Marlow and Larry Robbins

"No matter how often you drop, you are not down, until you refuse to get up." – Dennis Murphy

A Piece of Cake

Unlike the ABA and our other leagues, the World Hockey Association was a piece of cake to organize once we got the Canadian contingent aboard. Gary Davidson, Don Regan and I had gone through all of the growing pains of the ABA; therefore, we did not make the same mistakes with the WHA. Regan kept the documents from the ABA, which made our legal position sound. We already knew that the NHL management and ownership would fight us, but we also knew what our parameters were.

The WHA put together a strong team to run the league office in Newport Beach. Gary Davidson and I brought in the famed Ed Fitkin, who for years had been a member of "Hockey Night in Canada" broadcast crew. Walt Marlow suggested that Ed Fitkin knew all the players in the media world and the hockey establishment. Fitkin's addition would give the WHA a needed hockey presence. Davidson then picked the late Jim Browitt to replace me as the administrator of the league when I took over the Los Angeles Sharks.

Browitt was a top-notch troubleshooter who proved to be invaluable to the WHA. Lee Meade of Minneapolis became the public relations director. Max Muhleman, who subsequently became one of the top marketing geniuses of the sports world, assumed the marketing chores. Don Regan was the league's counsel and stayed in that capacity. Vern Buffey became the director of officials, while Steve Arnold and his partner, Marty Blackman, handled the player personnel activities. It was a strong, good team, which shook the rafters – especially the old-time NHL hierarchy.

Many of the Canadian media dubbed the World Hockey Association, the "Wishful Hockey Association." President Clarence Campbell of the NHL boastfully stated that the WHA would have no chance of getting off the ground. He felt his league was ready to go to the mat with the hockey upstarts. The WHA, unimpressed with the paper threat of the NHL, moved forward with our plans. In November of 1971, a major WHA press conference was held in New York City.

Learning from our mistakes of the past, Don Regan and I hired public relations director Joey Goldstein of New York to take charge of the conference. Goldstein put on a first-class affair at the American Hotel. All of the shakers and breakers of the national media were present. (Pat Brown, the former governor of California, a part owner of the Los Angeles entry, would drop the first puck.) We announced that Chicago, Calgary, Edmonton, Los Angeles, Miami, New York, San Francisco, Winnipeg, St. Paul and Dayton, Ohio, had qualified for franchises. The league would add two additional teams prior to the opening of our first season, which was scheduled for October, 1972.

The WHA made six changes prior to its first season of play. Miami moved to Philadelphia, Dayton to Houston, and San Francisco relocated to Quebec City. The WHA added Ottawa and Boston to the league and moved Calgary to Cleveland when Calgary owner Bob Brownridge was stricken with cancer. For the most part, these moves were positive. The league gained strong ownership in Howard Baldwin of Boston, Nick Mileti in Cleveland, Paul Racine in Quebec City, and Bernie Brown and Jim Cooper in Philadelphia. Paul Deneau, after losing his lease in Dayton because of political upheaval in his city, moved to Houston. Doug Michel, an Ottawa businessman, took the team in the Canadian capital. The league was now composed of four Canadian teams and eight from the United States.

Breaking the NHL's Reserve Clause

With our expertise relating to the reserve clause, we needed to be very careful in our dealings with the players. The NHL had two-way contracts with its players that allowed ownership and management to ship the players to the minors at their beck and call. This could be done at salaries they could adjust, based on whether the players played in the majors or in the minors. Don

Regan felt that this clause would not stand up in court, and he was right. From the beginning, we acquired many NHL players, whereas in the ABA, the major-league players had to sit out for a year. This was a major reason for our success with the WHA.

The WHA did away with the reserve clause which had bound players to a team for life. The new league's presence opened the pocketbooks of all the owners in both leagues, allowing the players to make a decent wage for their efforts. The grandest coup of the WHA was the signing of the legendary and great Bobby Hull. Hull was to the WHA what Julius Erving was to the ABA. The legacy of Winnipeg's Ben Hatskin will always be his signing of the all-time, slap-shot great. Along with Hatskin, Abe Simkin, Blackie Simkin and Sol Simkin also must be given credit for Hull's signing. They all came to the forefront to guarantee Hull's fabulous contract.

The NHL was convinced that its reserve clause would stand up in court. Don Regan was convinced it would not, and he was right. The NHL owners stood firm and agreed collectively that they would not capitulate to their players' demands. As a result, many NHL players jumped to our new league. Money was flowing like wine and the WHA made major inroads on the establishment. Bobby Hull, The Golden Jet, started it all. At the WHA draft in Anaheim, California, he was selected by the Winnipeg Jets as their first pick. No one in the NHL took the pick seriously. They reasoned that no new league could possibly match this superstar's salary.

Ben Hatskin and his partners, the Simkins, were tough businessmen who knew the value of a superstar. They were also dead serious in acquiring Hull. They began serious negotiations with Hull's lawyers and accountants. Quietly, they offered him $1 million to sign a contract, with the entire contract worth $2.7 million over 10 years. Bobby Hull was the first athlete in the world ever to receive such a salary and bonus. He was worth every cent of it, and should always be credited as being the first person in any sport to escalate players' salaries.

Ben Hatskin felt that our league had to stand up to the bullies of the old-time NHL. He felt that the NHL only understood strength, and that we had to be the aggressor in our fight with them. He was the one who convinced our league to institute litigation procedures against the established NHL. Hatskin, together with Bill Hunter, had fought the NHL in their junior hockey days, and he understood that the NHL controlled hockey completely through a series of agreements with the various amateur groups and with the minor hockey leagues. Hatskin insisted that we press our legal positions and urged Don Regan to take up the challenge.

With the assistance of Hatskin and Hunter, the WHA filed a $48 million antitrust suit that charged the NHL of illegal restrictive practices that enabled them to control all of hockey. Don Regan then used the following arguments in the suit against the establishment:

1. The NHL used the reserve clause to make it difficult for a competing league to do business. 2. The NHL used its power to control the entire hockey world through their control of the minor leagues and youth hockey programs.

The first step for Regan was to get the two-way contract set down; the second was to take on the reserve clause. On November 8, 1972, Judge A. Leon Higginbotham rendered a major decision. It read: "It is hereby ordered that the National Hockey League, its member clubs and teams, along with those acting in their behalf, are enjoined from further prosecuting, commencing, or threatening to commence, any legal proceeding pursuant to and/or enforce the so-called reserve clause of the National Hockey League's standard players contract."

The hockey establishment, along with the entire sports world, was given a wake-up call. That ruling eventually changed the sports community.

In February, 1974, the case was settled out of court, with the NHL making a cash payment to the WHA and agreeing to a mutual recognition of contracts. This helped to eliminate the so-called reserve clause and to allow intra-league competition. Thus, it allowed the WHA a joint working agreement with the minor and junior hockey leagues. This was a major victory for the WHA and gave pro hockey players, for the first time in their careers, a chance to play for someone other than an NHL-controlled team. This action opened the doors for players in all professional leagues, and so the WHA upstarts helped give players partial freedom from that time on.

The WHA was fortunate that the NHL didn't take the new league seriously. Over a period of six decades, the NHL had consisted of six teams: the Montreal Canadiens, Toronto Maple Leafs, Chicago Blackhawks, Boston Bruins, New York Rangers and Detroit Red Wings. In 1967 the NHL added six more expansion teams. They sold new franchise for the unbelievable amount of $2 million each, adding Los Angeles, Oakland, Philadelphia, Pittsburgh, St. Louis and Minneapolis. This changed the complexion of the league from regional to national status. They were fortunate that television was just coming on the scene, which coupled with the new expansion, enabled new fans to watch NHL hockey.

The big problem that occurred, however, was with the massive expansion was that parity in the league was unfair. Greed got in the way and the new teams were being clobbered. Howard Baldwin always felt that in the early years of the WHA's existence, the owners of the league, after the Hull signing, were dedicated to going after NHL players. He also believed that after seven years of struggle, owners in both leagues became weary of laying out big money for marginal players – they believed the only thing to do was to merge with the NHL.

Baldwin felt that by paring the league to seven teams in the 1978 season, it would allow the league to work more closely together for the purpose of making a merger work. Signing players like Gretzky, Vaive, Goulet and Messier would put the WHA into a better position to end the battle. In 1978, the WHA, in the difficult position of survival, also achieved parity among the six playing teams. Indianapolis collapsed early in the 1978 season leaving Winnipeg, New England, Edmonton, Quebec City, Cincinnati and Birmingham. The talent within those remaining teams was highly skilled, as exemplified by the WHA All Stars defeating the Moscow Dynamo in all three games of a three-game series played in Canada. The Dynamo were considered by most as the best team in Russia – everyone respected their talent and ability.

The Winnipeg Jets were sold in 1978 to a group headed by Michael Gobuty. They signed John Ferguson as the general manager. By signing Ferguson, the ownership group thought it would enhance their chance of being included in the merger with the NHL. Ferguson was a highly skilled general manager who had a fabulous reputation in the NHL. He was highly respected. Ferguson desperately attempted to get Wayne Gretzky to come to Winnipeg when the Racers collapsed, but Peter Pocklington of Edmonton moved quickly to get "The Great One" to join the Edmonton Oilers for $800,000 in cash and future considerations. Pocklington made his biggest "coup" and the heist of his life when he got his superstar, because Nelson Skalbania had money problems and was forced to sell his half of the team. Pocklington will always be remembered for his acquisition of the NHL's all-time leading scorer, Wayne Gretzky, who is considered the greatest player of all time.

John Bassett was a visionary and tough competitor. He felt that the NHL only understood strength and power. He felt that it would be a big mistake to deal with them with kid gloves. He had his battles with Harold Ballard in Toronto. Bassett, together with the Eaton family, owned the Toronto Toros. They rented the Maple Leaf Gardens at a very high price. This was accomplished because Bassett had visions of building his own arena in Toronto. Ballard would not stand still for this.

Feeling the threat of a new rival, the NHL added two new teams to their roster; one in Atlanta and the other in Uniondale, New York. The NHL was selling their teams for $2 million each. We had upped our fees to $250,000 from $25,000 before we dropped the first puck. Competition does have its benefits, and in the professional hockey world, the players reaped huge perks, with most salaries jumping to respectable levels. The NHL owners had things going their way for so many years that the players, as a whole, were treated very poorly. The WHA helped to escalate the salaries and benefits for most players in both the new league and the NHL.

The NHL attempted to put our league down, but the Philadelphia legal ruling in 1972 that prevented the NHL from enforcing its reserve clause allowed intra-league play, and we won the majority of games (33-27) in head-to-head competition. Gary Davidson, Don Regan and I felt we would do well, but others did not, particularly the NHL. The first of these games was played by the NHL's St. Louis Blues and the WHA's Houston Aeros in September, 1974, and the Aeros were victorious, 5-3. The good showing by the WHA proved to all that the league had a good nucleus of talent. Most hockey experts said that the WHA was the strongest expansion league of all time. We knew that we had outstanding talent and, once again, we were proven correct. The great WHA was truly major league.

The WHA has to thank the NHL for its arrogance, which made it possible for Hull to jump leagues. The NHL thought that their legal position would keep Hull in check. Don Regan and his WHA lawyers proved them wrong.

The WHA's Many Characters

We also organized our group of owners differently. I personally called the shots on bringing in the group of owners. Gary never interfered and Don was too busy doing the legal work. I had lists of potential buyers, which I had kept from the ABA days. Other than Nick Mileti of Cleveland, we did not allow dual ownership with any other sports leagues. This, of course, was a major advantage, as we received full attention from the potential ownership groups without distractions. They all had one goal in mind, and that was to make our league successful. We had many "characters," and we did make many mistakes.

The New York crew was a case in point. Our lead owner there was Richard Woods, a New York attorney. He had assembled a group of successful area businessmen who knew nothing about sports. We hooked them up with Marvin Milkes, a baseball executive who knew every aspect of the sports business. I can remember clearly the day Marvin called me from his Madison Square Garden office and said, "Murph, these owners want to have their own wives cook the meal for the New York Raiders initial press conference."

They felt that their wives could organize and cook a wonderful and tasty home-cooked meal at a minimum cost. They did not know the media. I had to explain to them that they would be laughed at, even though their intentions were good. They relented and we had a great press conference. Marvin Milkes thanked me over the years many times for restoring that professionalism.

On the whole, our WHA had a group of outstanding owners and professional general managers. The league had exceptional coaches and topnotch people in the front offices. Our teams were competitive and our loyal fans enjoyed our style of play.

Larry Pleau and the New England Whalers

The general manager of the St. Louis Blues for 13 years and now the team's VP and senior advisor, Larry Pleau was the first player to be signed by the first-year Avco Cup champion New England Whalers. A native of Lynn, Massachusetts, Pleau liked the idea of playing professional hockey near his hometown. Pleau was an outstanding player in the Montreal Canadiens system, but like many players, was stymied in his progress because the Canadiens were so loaded with talent that it was tough to make the big club. The Whalers' first GM and coach, Jack Kelley, saw an opportunity to latch on to this outstanding talent, and he made a major run to sign him.

"After checking out the WHA structure, and specifically the Whalers, with my advisors, I signed a contract with the new team in Boston for $180,000 over a three-year period," Pleau said later.

Pleau's signing was typical of many by players looking for an opportunity to play in the pros. The money offered by the new WHA gave incentive to other players to jump from the NHL's "slave wage" to the WHA, where the money was definitely major league. Pleau was a credit to the league.

Visionary Thinking

Hall of Famer Bobby Hull helped launch the WHA in 1972-73 when he jumped from the NHL's Chicago Blackhawks to the Winnipeg Jets.

"One thing the WHA will always be remembered for is how it helped hockey grow into an international sport," Hull said. "Business is global today, and the Winnipeg Jets were thinking that way 20 years before anyone else. It's true that Börje Salming was the first Swede to come over and play with the Toronto Maple Leagues, but the arrival of Anders Hedberg, Ulf Nilsson and Lars-Erik Sjoberg brought the second wave of players... the Willy Lindstroms and the Danny Labraatens. It was the World

Hockey Association's visionary thinking that made the game of hockey the big winner."

Bobby Hull, "Mr. WHA"

He was the "slap shot," and he was the first million-dollar professional athlete. Bobby Hull was also one of the best public relations men who ever played any game. He would sign autographs until the last kid had disappeared. Apparently, when Bobby was a kid, he had waited hours for a star player to acquire an autograph and the player left before reaching him. Bobby was deeply hurt. He vowed that if he ever made "the big time," he would never disappoint a kid. He was that type of person. The public loved him. He was a terrific interview, and he always took time out to talk to people, especially the little ones. He felt that all of us put our pants on the same way, and that he was blessed to be a star hockey player. He remembered his roots.

Don Regan, the WHA lawyer, could not believe that the Chicago Blackhawks let Bobby get away to us. It was a colossal blunder that cost the NHL dearly. Ben Hatskin, the owner of the Winnipeg Jets, and Bobby Hull liked each other from the very beginning of their relationship. Ben told Bobby, in no uncertain terms, "We want you to play for the Winnipeg Jets and the WHA, and we won't take no for an answer."

"If we can come to terms, I would be proud to play for you and the WHA, and you won't be sorry, Ben," Bobby said.

Bobby Hull was not only the franchise, he was the league. He brought with him more than 60 players from the NHL and he brought credibility to the WHA. He helped the league develop, and he did everything in his power to build up the image of the WHA. In every city that the Jets played in during the first year, the home club would have a local press conference just for Bobby, and he responded; oh, how he responded. The media recognized him as a true superstar. He also got along with the owners of the league. He reasoned that if he helped the owners, they in turn would help his counterparts, his peers. His attitude carried over to the other NHL players who had jumped leagues and, willingly, the players helped the local clubs in their publicity and public relations in each of our cities. This attitude helped the league and the franchises, and it was wonderful to watch, especially in contrast to today's society, where there is so much animosity and jealousy.

Bobby Hull was an enigma to most of the competitive WHA teams. He especially loved to beat the Los Angeles Sharks. His first wife was from California and Bobby loved the beautiful weather in L.A., especially in the wintertime. He would always bring his golf clubs on the trips. He would play golf in the morning and then take extra delight in beating us that evening. I always thought that he was taking out his golf frustrations that he had experienced in the morning on us that night. I suspected that our goalie, George Gardner, who was a proficient golfer on his own, had possibly suckered Bobby into playing golf that morning and now Bobby was getting even. The fact that Bobby played golf came out after the Jets had beaten the Sharks nine times in a row. Terry Slater and I, in our frustration, felt that we had to win just once that season, and we kept hoping. In the fifth meeting of the series in L.A., we held a 4-3 lead with 20 seconds left on the clock. The faceoff was in our end and Winnipeg's owner Ben Hatskin came over to me and said, "Murph, you finally did it."

I looked over at him and said, "Benny, don't count on it," and sure enough, they won the faceoff and Bobby got the puck and put it in the corner of the net with his famous slap shot. This tied the game in regulation play, and then in overtime, they naturally beat us. Can you imagine losing 10 straight games to one team during the inaugural season?

I went down to see Bobby Hull after the game, and he said, "Murphy, that damn goalie Gardner cost you."

I asked why, and he said that Gardner had taken him for $200 that morning in golf. Bobby added that he told Gardner he'd get it back that night. He did. I then looked for Gardner after the discussion, but he was nowhere to be found. I wanted to fine him $200 in return for his indiscretion.

When Bobby Hull signed his Winnipeg Jets contract, the city came to a halt. More than 20,000 people attended the noon signing downtown. His signing brought more Winnipeg more press than ever before. He was the man of honor to those in Winnipeg, but he was the "man of the year" to the WHA. In all of my years in sports, I never saw such an impact on a community or on a league as Bobby Hull had by signing his contract with our league. As president of the WHA, Gary Davidson stated many times after the Hull signing, "He did not come easy, but he was well worth every dime."

Gordie Howe, "Mr. Hockey"

Gordie Howe is considered not only the greatest hockey player to have played the game, but also one of the greatest athletes of all time and in all sports. To think that most professional hockey players play an average of five years in the big time, and then to consider that Gordie played as a professional in five different decades (1940s-1980s), it's unbelievable. I would also like to warn all of you golfers to be very careful with your wallet when you play the old fox. He has been known to pick some pockets on the fairways. Player after player will tell you that it was a great honor to play with or against Gordie Howe. André Lacroix, a great player in his own right, related it best when he said, "Gordie Howe and Bobby Hull had such admiration for each other. When they both made commitments to the WHA by signing up with the new league, they both fulfilled those commitments. Bobby got the league off the ground, and Gordie and his sons got the engine to roar."

Gordie has often said that had Bobby Hull not joined the WHA, he would never have had the opportunity to play with his own kids. If you ask former players, they will tell you that just to be on a line with Gordie for one shift was an honor they will always cherish. Joe Noris of the San Diego Mariners played on the

Howe line in the WHA All-Star Game in Hartford in 1977 and was awed by the smoothness and finesse the old fox had even at the age of 52. Jacques Caron said that Howe was the most complete player he had ever seen. He could shoot the puck from any part of the ice in stride, and he never telegraphed his shot. Even modern players like Mark Messier (Edmonton Oilers, Vancouver Canucks, and New York Rangers) will tell you that Howe was an amazing athletc and that it was an honor to play against him, especially at the beginning of their own professional hockey careers.

Howe was "Mr. Elbows." Everyone has stories about those elbows, and a great many players – including John Cunniff, Rick Dudley and Rob Ramage of the WHA – experienced the punishment they caused. They will tell you that for them, it was a badge of honor to get Howe's famous elbow during a WHA game. I'm sure that NHL players will tell you likewise, as the "elbow king" played 26 years in the NHL in addition to his six years in the WHA, and he used those same elbows on those players as well.

In 1972, the Houston Aeros became one of the charter teams in the WHA. Owner Paul DeNeau originally purchased the team to play in Dayton, Ohio, with the understanding that the city would build a new arena for his team. When that didn't happen due to a city election that turned out of office the councilmen who advocated for the arena, DeNeau moved his club to Houston. The team became a tenant in the Sam Houston Coliseum, and

DeNeau hired Houston attorney Jim Smith as the team's first president and GM.

Bill Dineen was the Aeros first coach. He had spent years in the game and was a man of immense integrity and experience. He played six years in the NHL and had many stops in the minor leagues. In 1970, he became a player-coach for the Denver Spurs of the Western Hockey League. After the WHA developed, he was a great choice for the Aeros, as he had already developed a strong relationship with the hockey community. Dineen was considered one of the "nice guys" in the sports industry. He said that he had a major advantage over some of the other WHA coaches, as he came out of the player ranks. He had a sense of timing, and his tentacles were established, especially in the high-minor leagues, where most of the WHA players would come from.

"When Bobby Hull signed with the Winnipeg Jets, I knew the league would get off the ground, and I knew that we would get players to come over, "Dineen said after signing with Houston.

The Aeros drafted 120 players at the original WHA draft, and Dineen and Smith arranged the pecking order of those players before signing them. Dineen sought a team that had experience, muscle and speed. The first year, a lot of Western Hockey League players were on his draft list. Together with Smith, he was able to sign André Hinse, Larry Lund and Wayne Rutledge as a trio from Denver. He then added NHL players Murray Hall,

Ted Taylor, John Schella and Paul Popiel to form a strong nucleus for the Aeros.

In their first season in Houston, the Aeros finished second in the Western Division. Much of the credit for the team's strong showing was given to NHL Hall of Famer Doug Harvey, who served as assistant coach to Dineen. During the WHA's first season's playoffs, Dineen and Harvey were convinced that the Aeros needed a proficient scorer to become the league champions. Their goal was to get one during the off season. Needless to say, they got one in the legendary Gordie Howe. As a bonus, they got Marty and Mark Howe as well. What a coup the Aeros garnered!

Dineen was fondly called "Foxy," in the industry. He was and is a shrewd negotiator, and people often said, "When dealing with Dineen, don't get fooled by the softness of his voice and his quiet disposition, as he is skilled and he knows what he is doing at all times."

Foxy and Jim Smith made a strong negotiating team for the Aeros. In 1973, Dineen and Doug Harvey were scouting the Canadian Junior Hockey Championship. They specifically watched Mark Howe put on an awesome display of his abilities when the Toronto Marlboroughs (Marlies) beat Medicine Hat to win the Memorial Cup. Medicine Hat had on its roster junior players of their own, such as Tom Lysiak, Lanny McDonald and Tiger Williams.

The more that Harvey and Dineen watched the 16-year-old Mark Howe perform, the more determined they were that, one way or another, they were going to sign him and his brother Marty. As fate would have it, the two spotted Colleen Howe immediately after the game, and Dineen asked, "Are Mark and Marty going back next year to play for the Marlies?"

Colleen told him that she felt that the Canadian Junior Hockey system was wrong, and that the kids should be able to play for more than $35 a week, which was what the junior players were being paid at the time. She implied that the two boys would look into playing for a WHA team.

Colleen Howe was not only a dedicated mother and a great partner to her husband, but she was also a very astute business-woman. The family works close together. Dineen called his friend Gordie and said that he and Harvey had watched Mark at the Memorial Cup and wanted him to play for the Aeros. Dineen reasoned that Mark was an American kid playing in Canada, and now was not eligible to play in the Olympics because he was considered a professional by playing in the Canadian juniors' programs. Thus, why not make some real money playing for Houston?

Gordie then asked what Dineen wanted to hear the most: "Foxy, could you also use another Howe as well?"

Dineen blurted out, "Gordie, that is what I had in mind all the time!"

"Foxy" Dineen had accomplished his mission and his goal, getting Gordie *and* both of his sons to play for the Aeros.

Gordie and his family will always have a special place in my heart, as they are class all the way.

Colleen Howe knew that Gordie had a dream of playing alongside his two boys, and realized how much it meant to Gordie. She had even contacted Gary Davidson with a plan, so that when Bill Dineen made his pitch, she agreed it was worth the try. Negotiations started in earnest and Bill Dineen and Jim Smith brought the WHA, then in just its second year of operation, another major coup – the signing of the Howe threesome of Gordie, Mark and Marty.

As this signing took place during my watch as president and commissioner, I was elated. To think that in just two years our league had signed "The Golden Jet" Bobby Hull and Gordie "Mr. Hockey" Howe! I then asked the question: which was the real major league, the WHA or the NHL? This debate ran on for years. We always felt that our talent was equal, but the media was reluctant to acknowledge it. Even after our Edmonton Oilers won four Stanley Cups in their first six years in the NHL, like Rodney Dangerfield, "we got no respect." Second leagues always have that problem.

Gordie felt that he was in good shape, having retired just two years prior, and he worked out constantly. He especially had the extra desire after Clarence Campbell, the commissioner of the NHL, announced that Gordie should not play again because he could suffer the fate of some other aging stars by playing too long. Campbell said, "It would make me sick, if instead of applause, Gordie Howe was greeted by boos by the fans." Though Campbell's concern was understandable, Gordie Howe had a dream that he wanted to play out, and he was determined to do so.

In a last-ditch effort to keep the Howes from going to the WHA, the NHL offered Gordie a $500,000 contract to act as the league's public-relations ambassador. Gordie refused the generous offer and played the next six years with his sons in the WHA. He was the main reason that the Houston Aeros became a dominant force in the WHA. Gordie was a physical marvel and played until he reached the grand young age of 52.

Gordie Howe is not only one of the greatest hockey players who ever laced up his skates; he's also one of the nicest people I've ever known. We had a lot of fun talking about some of the tricks he pulled on his old commissioner. He would do things such as flicking ice shavings on me during warm ups when I was giving an important speech. I will always remember a special time in Quebec City when I really got the Howe treatment, and with a smile.

It was right after the final game of the Houston Aeros had defeated the Quebec Nordiques in four straight games to win the 1975 Avco Cup championship series. The game was being televised back in Houston and the director of the broadcast came to me and said, "We have a very limited time for this presentation. You must keep your remarks to a minimum as we want the people back in Houston to see the cup presented to Gordie."

The Quebec fans were naturally very disappointed over the four-game sweep. The custom in Quebec is to always, through an interpreter, make comments in French first, and then follow it up in English. Prior to the game, I had a beautiful three-minute speech prepared, that I read, in French, to the audience. I had our league's finance director, Linda Zenk, prepare it, as she had a French background and spoke French fluently. The speech went over great with the audience, and I was pleased. Immediately after the game, I took the microphone from the Houston directors and had just started to congratulate Gordie and the Aeros in English. The fans started booing. I knew we had to get off the air quickly, so I asked Gordie why they were booing.

"Murphy, you have got to speak French first," he said.

"Gordie, I don't speak French," I said.

"Then say 'parley-vous français,' " Gordie said.

I parley-voused, and then I *really* got booed. Gordie grabbed the mike from me and, in flawless French, thanked the fans and me. His speech received a huge ovation.

Gordie then gave me his famous wink and said, "I saved your butt again, Murph."

After the WHA merged with the NHL, Gordie played another NHL season with the Hartford Whalers before hanging up his skates. One of Gordie's replies to questions relating to his age was, "There may be a little snow on the roof, but there's still a fire in the furnace." He truly was and is a legend of our times.

The Birth of the Los Angeles Sharks

I left the league office and became the president and general manager of the Los Angeles Sharks for the 1972-1973 season. Our team was going to be an aggressive and bruising club. Our coach, Terry Slater, told me, "When those other clubs come into our building, they will know that they're in a war. We will be after them from the first whistle." He instilled the word "intimidation" as our battle cry.

Slater was one of a kind. He asked me when we hired him, "Do we have a lot of money, or is it going to be tight?" When I asked him why, he said, "If we have a lot of dollars, I'd go for a finesse and skating team. If we're tight on cash, I'll put a bruising team on the ice."

I told him that we would meet our bills, but that it was going to be a tight ship. He said, "Fine, let's go for the tough guys."

Slater was an owner's dream. He looked out for the team's needs, but he was frugal with the dollars. Terry was a college graduate and a very intense man. He lived and died for hockey. He was in the game 16 hours a day. Terry had charts, was on the telephone with his scouts, and was constantly in touch with his players. We became close friends and our lines of communication were open at all times.

I was always in love with the game of hockey, but did not grow up in it. I loved the action and felt that I knew the game as a fan. I did not know the technical side of the game. In the very beginning of our relationship, Terrance, as he was affectionately known, knew that I would handle the business side, and that he would make the decisions relative to the operation of the team. Terry ate, slept and dreamed about hockey. We always maintained that understanding. Terry made all the personnel moves and was a joy to work with. He was intense to a fault. He was also a student of the game and a master psychologist. He got the best out of his players and they loved him as a person. He kicked butt when it was necessary, but he also patted them on the back when they did things right.

Celebrity City

In the first year, our club finished third in the Western Conference and we made the playoffs. We finished over .500 and surprised the experts, especially my friend Bill Hunter of the Edmonton Oilers. The hockey fans of Los Angeles loved our style of hockey and came to the Sports Arena knowing that they were going to be entertained. Being in Tinsel Town, our staff went all out.

We maintained a hospitality room under the watchful eye of Assistant General Manager John Kanel. Kanel made our VIP room the talk of the sports world, as he always kept it filled with celebrities, great food and booze. People fought to get into the room, as they never knew who would be present for any specific game. We had movie stars galore at the games – Telly Savalas, Kevin Dobson (Savalas' sidekick on Kojak), June Lockhart, Donald O'Connor and Angie Dickinson. The room was a "sign of our times," and soon became a hot topic of discussion with the media. The television anchors from

Channel 4, Kelly Lange and Stu Nahan, were constant guests. They loved our food and the action and excitement at our games. Every game night, the room boasted famous personalities from the world of sports, motion pictures, television and politics. One of our owners was the former governor of California, Pat Brown.

There was a crowd meter at the Sports Arena, which from our command post we were able to keep informed as to how many fans were in attendance. I was always an impatient general manager when 7 p.m. rolled around. I regularly would lambaste my assistant general manager John Kanel as to the whereabouts of the fans and why they weren't there. My longtime friend, Charlie Marchese, who stood no more than 5 feet tall, would come to the defense of John whenever I went into one of my tirades, by saying, "Murph, the fans will come. Don't get on John's case."

Los Angeles is, and always has been, known as a "late crowd" town. Typically at 7 p.m. there were no fans in the seats. When 7:30 p.m. rolled around, we had our normal 6,000 fans. One night I thought I would play a joke on Charlie Marchese by telling Dan Parma not to allow Charlie, who was a frequent visitor, to the "Bullpen Room" as it was called. Dan proceeded to carry out my request – he did just that – he didn't let Charlie into the room. Needless to say, he was irate. Typical of his style, Charlie in a fierce manner, confronted John Kanel, and asked why he didn't know anything about what had just transpired. I loved every minute of their "discussion." With this stunt we were able to get even with his numerous previous defenses of Kanel regarding the fan count. It was fun times like this that I will always cherish – we did have a lot of good laughs while we were with our Los Angeles Sharks.

We had fun doing our jobs, and we did them well. We had a boiler-room operation, headed up by a carny named Dick Gerdsen. He was a master at getting people into the building. He always told the "white lie" and he always surprised John Kanel and our marketing director Carl DiPietro with the presence of our crowds. He and his crew never told us what to expect, and he surprised us all with his substantial numbers. For example, he insisted that we have a game on a Sunday morning, and we all thought he had gone off the deep end. We reluctantly consented to do it – and he pulled 13,000 fans into the building on a promotion of coffee and crumpets at 10 a.m. The game was televised in Quebec City and no one could believe it. We found out later that he had worked out a promotion with the Catholic diocese with a special $3 ticket. The churches would receive $1 from each ticket for every person at the game who attended early mass in Los Angeles.

The Catholic Church bulletin read, "God, Church, Family and Breakfast with the Los Angeles Sharks." It was a huge success and people talked about it for years to come.

I tell a story about Coach Terry Slater that describes his intense attitude toward hockey. We had a game in Los Angeles on New Year's Eve. The game started at 6 p.m., and both teams headed for the airport to catch a plane to Philadelphia where we would play the Philadelphia Blazers the next evening on New Year's Day. Jacques Plante was the Philadelphia goalie, and as everyone in the hockey world knows, he was the very best in his profession. Plante was an especially hot goaltender at the time, and in the first game at the Sports Arena in L.A., he stopped 40 shots on goal while the Blazers only had nine shots on our goalie. Naturally, they scored on one of their nine shots and we got shut out. This infuriated Terry Slater, and he was a bear on the plane to Philadelphia.

The next evening, Plante went back in goal, and we shot 43 times and did not score. Philadelphia shot 13 times and scored once. We had lost two games in a row after outshooting the Blazers, 83-22. Immediately after the game, Terry and I walked to cool off. As we were walking and talking, Terry saw a garbage can and proceeded to kick it in frustration. For his trouble, he broke his foot. On New Year's Day, he was in the hospital with his foot elevated in a splint. It is comical today, but at the time, it was a major crisis. Imagine losing two games to Plante and then having our coach in a Philadelphia hospital with a broken foot.

What a way to start a new year. This was life in the WHA. Terry and his wife Aggie were our personal friends as well as business associates. We had some great times together, and in three years of association, never once had nasty thoughts or words between us. After that first season, I suggested that Terry and Aggie, Elaine and I, and Jeannie and John Kanel go to Hawaii and have a chance to reflect on the completed season and have some rest and relaxation. We got our travel agent to get us special rates and away we went.

We stayed at the Mauna Kea Resort Hotel, which is one of the very best hotels in the world. The site is breathtaking and we had rooms on the beach side of the hotel. About 3 a.m. one night, I became restless and decided to go out on the patio and watch the ocean in its majestic glory. It was restful, and as I reflected, I looked over to the next patio to my right and lo and behold, Terry was doing the same thing. We shot the breeze for a while and I asked him if all was well.

He said, "No. Me and Aggie had an 'Irish debate' and I needed to cool down."

Two months later, Terry stormed into my office. "Remember that night we had our talk on the patio?" Terry said.

"Sure I remember," I said.

"Well, Murphy, I cooled off and went back to bed," he said. "Now I've been told that Aggie and I are going to have a new addition to our family. You and your psychology. Now I have another mouth to feed."

Our times together always did bring up the unexpected. Today I know that Terry would have been especially proud of his son, Grant Slater, who organized a junior hockey league in California and had teams in Los Angeles, San Diego, San Francisco and Bakersfield.

California Governor Pat Brown

In my political days, I rubbed elbows with some of the top politicians. Jesse Unruh, my classmate at USC, turned out to be one of the movers and shakers in the California State Legislature.

"Big Daddy," as he was endearingly known to his friends, became the speaker of the California Assembly. He introduced me to the late California governor Pat Brown. Pat and I struck up a wonderful friendship and I served as one of his co-chairmen when he ran for reelection. After his election to a second term as governor, I convinced Pat to work with me on the creation of the WHA. He subsequently became an owner of the Los Angeles Sharks and helped the league tremendously.

We drew a lot of political figures at Sharks' games. As it turned out, our playing arena, the Los Angeles Sports Arena, was where John F. Kennedy had been selected as the Democratic candidate in 1959. Talk about history and nostalgia. I was Kennedy's campaign coordinator in Orange County when he was running for president.

The Sharks roster was comprised of some big hitters, "thumpers," as I like to refer to them. The group included Ted McCaskill, Steve Sutherland, Tom Gilmore, Jim Niekamp, Earl Heiskala and J.P. Leblanc – our "Little Tiger Sharks." The Sharks' goaltenders were Russ Gillow and George Gardner of Vancouver. The team was a winner.

The Los Angeles Sharks included several former NHL players, including Jim Watson, Gerry Odrowsky, Ralph MacSweyn, Russ Gillow, Jim Niekamp, George Gardner and Mike Byers. The other team members came from the high minors. Team captain Ted McCaskill gave the club great leadership and followed his playing career by being a coach. Ted lives in Phoenix, Arizona, and runs his own apparel business. His son Kirk was a winning pitcher for the California Angels of Major League Baseball.

Dr. Leonard Bloom

I have hung out with lot of great and decent owners, as well as some downright nasty ones in my day. One of the nicest guys of the group was Leonard Bloom, who owned the WHA's Los Angeles Sharks. This is not to say that we didn't have our battles when I was the Sharks general manager. Lenny, as he was most commonly referred to, had some very innovative ideas and was very creative at times. He was a person of high integrity, who had a heart as big as his wallet.

While owner of the team, he signed many top-notch hockey players, including Marc Tardif, Ted McCaskill and Gordie Roberts. Lenny was also owner of the San Diego Conquistadors, an ABA team. His noted general manger at the time was Alex Groza, and Alex and I had monthly duels. We would scramble scramble to see who could position himself in the best spot for payday. The first one to see Lenny received the team's first pay check. Unfortunately for me, Alex was bigger and smarter, so my guys always got paid second. One thing we always knew for sure, however, was that Lenny always paid us. That was not always the case with some of the other teams.

While serving as Lenny's general manager, I was asked to be the second commissioner of the WHA in the league's second season. I have always kidded Lenny that he helped me upstairs so that he could get rid of me. He never denied or accepted this point of view, which has always piqued my curiosity. Lenny was, and still is, a very successful real estate developer. Over the years, Lenny and I have been involved in the development of many leagues. Some of his teams have made money, some have not, but Lenny always ran a "good ship" and treated his employees well. When Lenny bought the Los Angeles Sharks, he became an integral part of the league's development.

Over the years, he has mellowed some, and today he owns Paramount Entertainment, Inc. He is also working on developing a new spring/summer football league. His dedication, drive and decency stands well in making a league a success if he decides to proceed.

One Friday afternoon the phone rang in the Sharks office. Our secretary, Sandra Lee, came running in and said that Lenny was on the phone. I quickly dropped everything and picked up the phone. He told me that he wanted me to get John Kanel working on getting him a landing pad for his helicopter at the Sports Arena complex. I told him that I would get right on it. Kanel, in his usual way, began to research the details. He found out that no one had ever received permission from the Sports Commission to do so, including President John F. Kennedy, Governor Pat Brown and other major dignitaries. John reported back and told me he thought it was going to be tough to do, but he'd try. In his usual efficient manner, he got the job done. Commissioner John Ferraro of the Sports Commission went to bat for us. Together with Councilman Gil Lindsay of Los Angeles, they steered the request through. Lenny Bloom got his helicopter pad, and once again, John Kanel came through. We have kidded Lenny on this over the years, and he has responded by saying, "We were their largest tenant and we deserved it."

As always, Lenny traveled in style and was first class in his demeanor. John and I have always remained his friends. While I was recovering from my stroke, Lenny was working on his football league, but in his decent manner, he helped me in my time of need. I thank him for that.

If you're lucky, wrote Sarah Ockler, "In your entire life, you can probably count your true friends on one hand." I have been lucky indeed, and Dr. Lenny Bloom is one of those "fingers" on my hands. Thank you, Lenny, for being my friend.

Wild Bill Hunter

The owner of the Edmonton Oilers, "Wild Bill" Hunter was the most dynamic salesman I have ever known. He was also one of the best speakers in the world. He was "Mr. Hockey" of Edmonton and one of the premier promoters around. He loved Canada and hockey. To Bill, hockey belonged to Canada like basketball belonged to the United States. I had a lot of fun with Bill on this subject and we both enjoyed many laughs over his outbreaks at World Hockey Association meetings. At most WHA meetings, Bill would give the Americans his wisdom, and when he disagreed with us Americans on hockey items, Bill would bellow, "Sit down, you Americans. You don't know anything about hockey, especially you, Murphy."

After the first full season of the WHA, together with our mutual friend Ben Hatskin of the Winnipeg Jets, I decided I was going to get even with the "White Fox." I served as the president and general manager of the Los Angeles Sharks, and Bill held a similar job in Edmonton. That season, the Sharks had finished third in the Western Division, and Edmonton had finished fourth. At our annual meeting in La Costa, California, we got into our usual debates, and Bill, in his usual fashion, got up to give me another lecture. I figured he would, and I was prepared.

At the right moment during the meeting, and with Ben Hatskin's approval, I requested a five-minute break. I had a huge banner made up with the final standings of the season clearly defined on it. It showed, in bold type, that the Sharks were third and Bill Hunter's Oilers were fourth. I had our L.A. coach, Terry Slater, dress up in red, white and blue and our radio announcer, Gary Morrell, ready with a huge bass drum. At a given signal, they walked into the meeting and paraded around the room, keeping in step with the beating of the drum. I then stood up, looked at Bill Hunter, and said in my best Melvin Belli manner, "I rest my case." Bill didn't speak to me for more than two whole weeks.

Not long after the meeting, Bill mellowed on this matter of "Americans versus Canadians" in hockey. Bill Hunter, Ben Hatskin and Scotty Munro were pivotal in the establishment of the WHA. These three Canadians turned the corner for all of us, and gave those of us in management instant credibility in our drive toward making the WHA a success.

Walter and Jordan Kaiser

The Kaiser brothers, Jordan and Walter, were the sole owners of the Chicago Cougars hockey club. The team played its regular season games at the world-famous International Amphitheater. The Kaiser brothers were and are major real-estate developers in the Chicago area. The Cougars' first coach was Marcel Pronovost, and the team featured talented players like Reggie Fleming, Rosaire Paiement, Pat Stapleton, Dave Dryden and Darryl Maggs, all former NHL players. After the first year's operation, Pat Stapleton became player-coach. Jacques Demers was his assistant and the director of player personnel.

The Kaiser brothers started the Lakeshore Athletic Club in 1972, the world's first full-service indoor fitness center. Since that time, they developed fitness centers throughout North America. In the fall of 2002, they opened a club in London, England, in partnership with Reebok International. The Reebok Sports Club, Canary Wharf, is now the premier health club in London and on the continent. In addition to their health-club business, they have major real-estate developments throughout the country, primarily in the Midwest.

New England Whalers' Owner, Howard Baldwin

During the early days of the WHA, I received a telephone call from Howard Baldwin, who was then from Boston. I had always had a special place in my heart for New England, because that is where the Murphy clan originated. My dad was from Beverly, Massachusetts, and he loved his roots. Every chance I had to travel to Boston, I made that particular trip. My Aunt Irene lived there, and I loved visiting with her and listening to her stories about my dad growing up. New England people are special. They ooze charm and grace, and are warm and kind people.

They also are great hosts, and in my aunt's case, great cooks. My Aunt Irene made the best corned beef and cabbage in the world. When Howard Baldwin asked me to visit with him and his partner, John Colburn, in Boston, I jumped at the opportunity.

When I arrived by plane at Logan Field, I found two young men in their 20s waiting for me. Howard Baldwin carried the conversation, with John Colburn listening carefully. Baldwin told me that he and his associates felt that Boston should be included in our WHA development plans. He said that he was working with the Philadelphia Flyers and felt that he knew enough about the business to make it work. He thought that he could get into the Boston Garden and gain fan support in New England because the game's popularity could sustain two teams. He would not divulge their moneyman, but he made it clear that they would be financially sound.

Truthfully, I thought that both he and John had rich relatives and that they would be sound investors. I did not know at the time that they had approached millionaire Bob Schmertz, who owned Leisure Technology of New Jersey, and who had subsequently bought the Boston Celtics, to support their team. Howard Baldwin not only turned out to be a friend of mine, but he was one of the backbones of the WHA. He attended our very first WHA meeting and was the president of the league at the time of the merger with the NHL.

The Whalers, as the New England entry in the WHA, were one of our original 12 charter members. Very few people gave us a chance for survival, and certainly not past the first season. Every team in our league had its own auspicious start. Baldwin has often chuckled about a specific headline that appeared in the Boston Herald American after the announcement was made that Boston had received a WHA franchise: "Two local kids got the franchise. Their chances for success are slim and none." As fate would have it, the Whalers not only finished the season, but also won the first Avco Cup Championship. Not bad for a couple of kids from New England.

Howard Baldwin put together a strong franchise. He had strong ownership in Bob Schmertz, a great coach in Jack Kelley and a workaholic marketer in Bill Barnes. Although he made an impact in Boston and developed a cadre of fans, the Bruins were so entrenched that a move to Hartford only made sense.

I was extremely proud of Howard Baldwin. I remember back to our first-ever meeting at Boston's Logan Airport where he said to me that by allowing John Colburn and his associates to join the league, we would all be proud. He was a man of his word. I also enjoyed a special friendship with Coach Kelley. To-gether with league attorney, Don Regan, we formed the "Irish Mafia" of the league. At many meetings the three of us would gather and sing Irish songs. Kelley had a great voice; Regan and I sounded more like leaf blowers, but we had fun as we drove others at the meeting up the wall with our rendition of "Irish Eyes Are Smiling."

As I look back at the early days of the WHA I remember that we had a great camaraderie among the owners, general managers, coaches, and especially, the players. We all realized that we were in a fight with the established NHL. And, because of their threats, we stood together. It was a great time in my life – and certainly a busy one.

Great men have dreams, hopes and aspirations, average men do not. It is the strength, the will, and the determination that leads men to fulfill dreams that seem impossible. Howard Baldwin had dreams and pursued them with backbone and soul, and his internal fire was strengthened after each battle.

First-Year Playoffs

After some setbacks in the first season, the WHA's first championship series featured the New England Whalers and the Winnipeg Jets. The Whalers won the series in five games. According to Bill Barnes, one of the Whalers' founders, championship night was made even more special when majority owner Bob Schmertz, making his first visit to a celebrating team's locker room, had four bottles of champagne poured on him by the players.

Hours after the yelling and screaming was over, Howard Baldwin issued a challenge to the NHL. Baldwin dared the NHL's Stanley Cup champion Montreal Canadiens to play the Whalers at a neutral site in a one-game affair. The NHL chuckled over this one and laughed at the brash and bold WHA owner.

Many cities at the time were aggressively building new arenas, and the Whalers, even though satisfied with their first-year championship performance in Boston, felt that they had to move on. They moved the team and its operations to Hartford, Connecticut.

Ben Hatskin

In every man's lifetime, there is usually a group of people who have helped him on the way, financially or with their guidance. I was fortunate to work with people in that mold, and the leader of the clan was "Gentle Ben" Hatskin. Hatskin was the first owner of the Winnipeg Jets, a member of the Winnipeg Hall of Fame, and co-founder of the International Basketball Association along with his business partners, Murray and Sol Simkin. Ben also played center for the Winnipeg Blue Bombers of the Canadian Football League. Hatskin was a great humanitarian and leader. Just prior to his death, he was elected to Winnipeg's Hall of Fame. In my opinion, he was and will always be, "Mr. Winnipeg." I truly believe that had Ben stayed around, the Jets never would have left Winnipeg. He was that type of a leader and visionary.

It was because of Ben Hatskin's persistence that the great Bobby Hull made his historic jump to the WHA. Hatskin made up his mind that "The Golden Jet" would play for the Jets, and he made it happen. He is also credited with putting together the hockey line of Hedberg, Nilsson and Hull. This line has been proclaimed by many hockey experts as being the best ever to play the game. The line was so good that the NHL insisted it be disbanded at the time of the merger. (One of the concessions for the four WHA teams merging into the NHL was that each team could only keep two players.) The NHL knew that the Jets would have made their presence felt, and probably would have won the Stanley Cup in the NHL's first year after the merger if they came in as a unit. There was no way that the NHL was going to allow that to happen. (Gary Davidson and I have often said that if the NHL had come at us at full speed they could have broken our backs. They seemed to be overconfident. They believed that their control of the hockey world at the time would stand up to the test. Some of their owners were monopolistic and arrogant. In my opinion, that is why we got out of the box.)

Ben Hatskin stood by me through the development of the WHA and was always my personal confidante and leader after I became president of the league. The chemistry between us was sincere and trustworthy. I always knew where he stood. Ben always rolled with the punches, and I always wanted his support when the chips were down. Hatskin was born in 1917 and earned his first dollar making wooden boxes. Later, he was involved in the corrugated box business. From there, he became involved in the lumber, real estate and nightclub business. He also owned racehorses. He teamed up with the Simkin family of Winnipeg to buy the Winnipeg Jets after spending time as the owner of the Winnipeg Jets junior hockey team in the Western Canada Hockey League. He had a growl that sounded mean, but Gentle Ben was truly a pussycat and a man who stood by his word. He knew when to get tough, but he also knew when to pat you on the back. Ben was the one who engineered my interim presidency in the WHA, and he was the one who brought stability to the Jets and kept the WHA running.

Make no mistake – the success of the WHA can be attributed to Ben Hatskin's leadership. He was a tough linesman for the Winnipeg Blue Bombers of the Canadian Football League, and his motto was to "win at all times." He and his wife, C.C., had residences in both Winnipeg and Palm Springs, California. It was in Palm Springs that Ben suffered a stroke. Even though he was impaired physically, his mind and manner remained as sharp as when he was in his prime. I visited him often after he had his stroke. He was a pearl in the rough, and to me, he will always be the man who was responsible for making the WHA whole and a reality.

The late Ben Hatskin left his imprint on the world of hockey, and it will always bear his signature. Let me describe him in the following way: Ecclesiastes 6:16 says that "A faithful friend is the medicine of life." His love for you is tops when you are at the bottom. He helps you to look up when the rest of the world looks down on you. He shows you the meaning of friendship, not the meanness of it. He stands behind you when you are taking bows and beside you when you are taking boos. That was my man Ben Hatskin. God bless him always.

The European Connection

The European style of play in the 1970s emphasized stick handling, skating and crisp passing. The NHL and WHA styles were
toughness and going for the body. The fans of North America
liked the checks, fights and rough stuff. For the European stars,
it was a difficult transition. Anders Hedberg will tell anyone up
front that if it had not been for Bobby Hull on his line, he would
have returned to Sweden. He abhorred the Philadelphia Flyers'
style of hockey and loved the Winnipeg Jets' style of moving the
puck and skating with intensity and at a level that no other team
in North America had. Hedberg said that the WHA opened up the
involvement of European players in the NHL and that the
Winnipeg Jets' play was the forerunner of the style that the game
has evolved into today.

The European players' impact on the WHA was another major
reason for the league's success in acquiring a bevy of stars. The
line of Bobby Hull, Anders Hedberg and Ulf Nilsson has been
considered by many as the greatest line to play the game. The
two Swedes and Hull wowed the fans with their finesse, grace
and fine skating abilities and formed one of the most exciting
lines ever. The trio played well together, further helping to establish the European style, which featured finesse skating, puck
handling and quickness in North America. This style of play was
a stark contrast to the North American's style of dumping the
puck and digging in the corner. In 1974, the WHA drew more
than four million fans to our games. It's no surprise that it was

the same year that the Winnipeg Jets signed both Nilsson and Hedberg.

The Swedes were the forerunners of the explosion of European players into North America. The New England Whalers signed brothers Christer and Thommy Abrahamsson. The Toronto Toros signed Czech stars Vaclav Nedomansky and Richard Farda. The WHA European explosion of hockey was also a contrast to some of the brutish style of play that was the norm for the North American teams. There was a constant debate among the owners and administrators within the league as to what style of hockey the fans preferred.

Ben Hatskin, with his visionary foresight, felt that the WHA should go after the European stars. He had made many trips to Europe in his business capacities, and felt that after seeing many European games, North America was missing a great opportunity when they neglected going after European players. After the Jets signed Ulf Nilsson and Anders Hedberg, they added Willy Lindström, Dan Labraaten, and Lars-Erik Sjoberg to their roster in the mid-1970s. The Swedish connection captured the hearts of the Winnipeg fans with their style of play. Today the NHL has players from all over Europe.

As Anders Hedberg once said, "The WHA opened the eyes of North American fans by introducing European players and featuring their exciting style of play."

Hatskin reasoned that if a player had talent, it didn't matter where he was born. Today's European players come from countries like Sweden, Germany, Finland, Czechoslovakia, Norway, Russia and more. Their talent speaks for itself, and the NHL now has an international flavor.

When Glen Sather took over as general manager of the Edmonton Oilers, he put together a style of play similar to Winnipeg's. He brought in a style of finesse and skating that made Edmonton the "team of the 80s." The combination of Gretzky, Messier and Kurri was a great one for the Oilers. They made the Oilers the most dominant team in the NHL. They won four Stanley Cups in the first six years of the team's play in the NHL.

In the 21st century, the hockey explosion will carry into many more European countries and into Asia, where the game is starting to jell. Bobby Hull credits the WHA and its visionary leaders for the transition of professional hockey into a global sport. Hull reminds people that hockey is a global business today, and that the WHA was the forerunner in bringing in the Hedbergs, Nilssons, Sjobergs, Lindstroms and Labraatens to North America. Like the Russians, these players could flat out play.

Today, international hockey is flourishing. The teams in Europe are very competitive and countries like Germany, Italy, the United Kingdom and Spain have joined the hockey explosion. New facilities are being built throughout Europe and the fans are coming in droves.

I was surprised that the European countries had a lack of facilities in the 1970s. Most countries had huge outdoor soccer stadiums that held over 70,000 seats, but very few arenas that had between 10,000 and 20,000 seats. This situation is changing quickly. For example, in the 1990s, the United Kingdom built beautiful new buildings in Manchester, Sheffield, Newcastle, London, and Birmingham, with a lot more on the drawing board. The same explosion can be seen throughout Europe, with 100 new facilities opening up during the early 21st century on the continent alone. Professional sports will be going global in the next century and my view is that pro sports, now only in its infancy, will bear fruit. I just wish I was a college senior graduating in business administration today so that I would feel pretty secure about my future.

The Greatest Hockey Line

There will always be major arguments and friendly confrontations when discussing the "greatest" of anything. People have their favorites on any topic. Gretzky, Messier and Kurri composed a powerful line that was very productive for the Edmonton Oilers. However, most students of the game will tell you that the Winnipeg Jets' line of Bobby Hull, Anders Hedberg and Ulf Nilsson was poetry in motion. They could skate, they could score, and they had finesse on the ice like no other group of hockey players. It was a line that worked together and could come at you from any direction. Bobby Hull, who had one of the hardest slap shots ever, made the line tick. Ulf Nilsson was the "quarterback," and Anders Hedberg was the all-purpose player.

It was a line made in heaven, and the fans of Winnipeg were happily astonished by their performance.

I have been asked many times what made the WHA different. "Our players were special," is how I respond.

They cared about the game, their community and their fellow man. They were always working to sell the greatest game of all, and it showed. Throughout this book, we have talked about Bobby Hull. It is now time to talk about the fabulous Swedes. They were the forerunners of the great European explosion that has taken place in hockey today.

In 1975, the Jets' trio of Hull, Nilsson and Hedberg scored a total of 362 points. "If I passed the puck to Hull, I would hear it from Anders, and if I took a shot myself, I would get an earful from both of them," Nilsson said. "However, it was a joy to play with both of them as we kept the scoreboard moving upwards." The Swedes brought excitement to the WHA and to their fans throughout the league.

Ulf Nilsson

"It's hard to understand the drafting system in American sports," said Swedish superstar Ulf Nilsson. "The draft goes completely against the principle of freedom of choice that Americans so proudly proclaim. When I first came to North America, I did not have the freedom of choice in the NHL, thus I signed with the WHA and played with Anders Hedberg, Erik Sjoberg and Bobby Hull of the Winnipeg Jets. What more could a hockey player ask for? I then played on a line with those famous stars, Hull and Hedberg."

It certainly worked out for Nilsson.

Many hockey experts have suggested that the line of Hull, Hedberg and Nilsson was the greatest ever. Nilsson has said that from the first time the three stepped on the ice, it was magic in the making. He added that he had the toughest job on the line, as both Hull and Hedberg wanted the puck, and when he took a shot himself, he got grief from both of them.

The line was a great draw in WHA cities. The smoothness of the skating by all three was artistic and aggressive, and the fans loved it. This great line wanted to score goals and worked to make them happen. Nilsson joined the New York Rangers after they made him an unbelievable offer. He was a star quality player, and in his personal life, he was a star as well. Bobby Hull always said that, "Ulf Nilsson was one of the best skaters in either league."

We were proud that he was one of the international stars that started the trend.

Nick Mileti

It was a beautiful Ohio night and Nick Mileti was at the height of his career. He was inaugurating the new and spacious Coliseum at Richfield, and he had planned a special weekend of events to celebrate the opening of his magnificent building in 1974. The first night was Frank Sinatra, and "Old Blue Eyes" performed as only he could. The arena was packed to capacity and those of us in the ownership and administrative levels of the WHA were Nick's special guests. We were seated in the center row of the orchestra level and it was a magnificent night – Frank wowed everyone. The audience was in awe of one of the greatest enter-tainers of our time as he sang his heart out. If Tony Bennett left his heart in San Francisco, Frank Sinatra left his heart in Cleve-land that night.

The second night was supposed to be WHA night, and the Cleveland Crusaders were scheduled to play the first profession-al hockey game in the building. The facility was packed and the fans were excited. Unfortunately for Nick and the rest of us in the WHA, the ice did not freeze properly that evening. After two 30-minute delays, Nick came to me and said, "Murph, we are not going to be able to play the game. Would you please tell the fans that they will all get a rain check and two free tickets to a future game?"

During my life, I've had many tough tasks to perform, but this one was one of the toughest. Everything worked out fine, how-ever, as the people in Ohio are some of the most understanding in the world. Over the years, I was privileged to become Nick Mileti's friend, and I learned why the people of Ohio appreciated him. He was also a real team player in the WHA and one of our noted leaders.

Nick was one of the WHA representatives who worked with the NHL on a potential merger. Those negotiations took place at the very beginning of my being appointed league president. The merger did not work out at the time, but Nick did all that he could. He tried to convince everyone in both leagues that by not merging, it was going to cost both leagues millions of dollars in losses. To his eternal credit and foresight, he was right. He was ahead of time and could have saved everyone a lot of money early on. The merger actually took place five years later.

The 1974 WHA Season

When I became president of the WHA in 1974, taking over for Gary Davidson, we drew more than 4 million fans, continuing our growth pattern. Bobby Hull scored 77 goals in 78 games, and his impressive goal-scoring spree matched Maurice Richard's NHL record feat of 50 goals in 50 games. New stars like André Lacroix, Danny Lawson and Ron Ward were rapidly coming into their own after having outstanding seasons the previous year.

The 1974 Summit Series

The WHA was honored to have its players take part in the series between the world's two hockey powers at the time, Canada and the Soviet Union. The Canadians in the WHA took charge of the event, and as an American, I felt that it was appropriately their show. Ben Hatskin was the chairman of Team Canada, Bill Hunter was the GM, and Bill Harris took the reins as coach. Team Canada was strong and featured such big names as Bobby Hull, André Lacroix, Frank Mahovlich, Gordie Howe and his sons, Ralph Backstrom and Whitey Stapleton. Since I was the president of the WHA, my wife Elaine and I went on the trip to the Soviet Union as a representative of the league.

We had a wonderful time in Russia and I was fortunate to meet many of the Russian politicians and sports leaders. In addition, we were able to visit the Moscow Circus and the world-famous Moscow Ballet. The series was very exciting, and although Team Canada lost, the players performed with grace and style, and represented their country well. Ralph Backstrom was honored as the series' MVP, and all of the players had a ball. Despite Team Canada losing several of the games, the entire event went very well. Fans at the games and watching at home on television greatly enjoyed themselves. The WHA received a ton of goodwill and publicity. Larry Gordon and Bill Hunter were the chief marketers of the event and they did a wonderful job. We were all pleased that the league's talent was showcased to a wider audience. Fans in the Canadian cities where the games were played loved the hockey and were impressed by the league's credibility, which now seemed to be broadcast throughout the universe. The WHA had indeed made it to the big time.

John Bassett

Majority owner John Bassett bought the original Ottawa Nationals from Nick Trbovich and Doug Michel. Together with the Eatons of the Canadian department store fame, they developed and operated the Toronto Toros. After years of squabbling with the owner of Maple Leaf Gardens, Basset moved the Toros to

Birmingham, Alabama, in 1977. He then renamed the team the Birmingham Bulls. John and his partners always ran a first-class operation in Toronto and Birmingham. While with Birmingham, Bassett signed Canadian Junior League underage players to WHA contracts.

The signing of the juniors was another coup for the WHA – it was the only way the league would survive. With this, the Bassett's foresight again came to the forefront. After the Toronto Toros moved to Alabama and became the Birmingham Bulls, Bassett assembled the "Baby Bulls," potential first-round draft choices of the NHL that included goaltender Pat Riggins, defenseman Rob Ramage and forward Michael Goulet. They were situated in the south and fit in very well with the southern fans. After Bassett took the lead, other WHA teams followed suit. Other players signed: Danny Geoffrion to Quebec; Mike Gartner to Cincinnati; Jordy Douglas to Hartford; Dave Hunter and Wes George to Edmonton. (Bassett later owned the Tampa Bay Bandits of the United States Football League. Bassett's legacy will always depict him as a man of creative vision and dedication. He had Steve Spurrier as his football coach.)

The biggest signing, however, was made by the Indianapolis Racers, when they signed "The Great One," Wayne Gretzky, who at the time was earning a mere $75 per week. They also signed future star Mark Messier. Gretzky went from earning a pittance to signing a million-dollar contract. Messier received a $250,000 contract. This, too, a far cry from the $75 a week he was making as a junior.

Howard Baldwin believed that by signing the young junior hockey talent to the WHA, the league would have all the stars in future years. He felt that would make the NHL become serious in merger discussions. He was correct.

In 1978 the WHA became a six-team league. A charter member of the league, the Houston Aeros, decided not to play that year. It was a sad day for general manager and coach, Bill Dineen. Dineen was with the club from its inception. He had built a strong franchise and honestly felt that with the club he had assembled, they would be a very competitive team in the NHL. He had talented players like André Lacroix (the WHA's all-time leading scorer), Morris Lukowich, Jack Stanfield, Rick Preston, and, of course, the Howes. The essence of his feelings was that the WHA teams were competitive and could hold their own with anyone.

A Good Stepping Stone

Mark Messier, who won a Stanley Cup with the New York Rangers in 1994 to break the team's 54-year championship drought, played in the WHA with the Indianapolis Racers and Cincinnati Stingers in 1978-79, his first year in pro hockey.

"The WHA was a good stepping stone for me and a number of other young guys," Messier said. "I had one year under my belt, and the next year, when I went to training camp in Edmonton, I felt more comfortable and prepared. The WHA helped me realize what I had to do to make the Oilers. I have no regrets about playing in the WHA. I recall playing on a line with Robbie

Ftorek and Mike Gartner in Cincinnati. I was 17 years old and Mike was 18. Robbie was among the league leaders that year, which is quite remarkable, considering I only scored one goal."

Ice Capades

Hall of Famer Harry Howell, who also captained the New York Rangers, completed his pro career with the WHA's New York Golden Blades, Jersey Knights and San Diego Mariners. "I'm trying so hard to forget that I wore white skates," Howell said. "They ran something like $350 a pair. It was just ridiculous. On opening night, the Blades introduced us with a big spotlight. The fans, instead of cheering, were whistling. It was like we were in the Ice Capades. When I became player-coach, the first thing I did was have the players paint the boots of the skates black. We didn't play great hockey, but at least we looked like a hockey team. I got an opportunity to play three years longer than I should have, but the money was good and I am forever grateful. I was 43 years old when I stopped playing. That's pretty ancient for a hockey player. Personally, it was nice to see young talents like Anders Hedberg and Ulf Nilsson come in from Europe. Those two lads were as good as anyone I've ever seen play hockey."

Fighting Alphabetically

Former NHL referee Paul Stewart played in the WHA with Edmonton and Cincinnati and was better known for his fists than his wrist shots.

"When I signed with the Stingers, I knew I was going to be tested immediately," Stewart said. "We had something like three of the first 10 games against Birmingham. I scanned the roster and took on the Bulls alphabetically, fighting Frank Beaton, Gilles 'Bad News' Bilodeau, and then Steve Durbano."

Quick Change

Derek Sanderson jumped from the Boston Bruins for $2.6 million to sign with the Philadelphia Blazers. He only played eight games before injuring his back, and wound up back in the NHL before the 1972-73 season was finished. "The WHA was like owning a motorhome," Sanderson said. "There are only two great days – the day you buy it and the day you sell it. The WHA brought hockey along, salary wise."

Big Thrill

John Tonelli got his start in the WHA with the Houston Aeros before shifting to the NHL to play for the New York Islanders. He played on four Stanley Cup championships teams in his 14-year NHL career. "One of my biggest thrills was opening night at the Summit in Houston," Tonelli said. "I centered a line with

Gordie Howe on right wing and Mark Howe on left wing. Gordie was 48 years old or so at the time. I remember going to training camp. I was just trying to make an impression and Gordie skated past me, saying, 'Hurry up, kid. Let's get it going.' Gordie was a fabulous skater and an amazing athlete and person."

True Pressure

Mark Howe, the son of Gordie Howe, played six years in the WHA and 16 more in the NHL before retiring after the 1994-95 season. "For Dad, it was a thrill, a dream to come back and play hockey," Howe recalled. "Marty and I felt pressure to a point because we were only playing because we were Gordie's kids. We both felt we had a job to do, a career to start, and names to make for ourselves. We both wanted to be contributing members of the hockey team. The first three days of practice in Houston, I had to miss some of the workouts because of severe migraine headaches just from thinking about playing well. I had put so much pressure on myself because I felt I had to prove to people I could play hockey because of my abilities, not because I was Gordie Howe's son."

WHA General Managers and Coaches

The WHA was blessed with formidable managers and coaches. I always talked with pride about our professionals who chose the players in the WHA. People like Jack Kelley, Bill Hunter, Terry

Slater, John Hanna, Rudy Pilous, Bill Dineen and others put together their teams by using their extensive hockey knowledge and their contacts throughout North America. For example, Jack Kelley, a former college coach, was selected by owner Howard Baldwin to take charge of the New England Whalers. Kelley was a total gamble, as he had no experience as a professional coach, and many old timers in the NHL questioned Baldwin's choice. However, that evaluation was very short-lived, as Kelley and his staff put together a winning team and Kelley won the Avco Cup in his very first year as a professional coach.

The WHA players were a joy to work with. They appreciated the fact that they were finally getting paid a decent salary for playing professional hockey. It was a normal routine to encourage our players to become part of the local community and be a part of its activities. Our players went to hospitals, girls and boys clubs and community centers, and they worked especially hard with youth groups in their particular cities.

Hockey players are a special group of young men. They are tough between the lines, but off the ice they are warm and compassionated individuals. They have special rules and guidelines to follow. The fighting that takes place on the ice stops there. They often wait until the next game before retaliating. Ted McCaskill and Earl Heiskala, two of the Los Angeles Sharks' enforcers on the ice, were community leaders off the frozen surface. Both men were highly intelligent and are now doing very well in civilian life. McCaskill never backed down to anyone, and he loved to mix it up on the ice. Younger players on other clubs were always looking to test him, and, for the most part, it proved to be a big mistake.

I will never forget a classic fight between McCaskill and Paul Shmyr of the Cleveland Crusaders – the two men were butting heads and blood was everywhere. As the gladiators were escorted off the ice, McCaskill yelled at Ron Ego, the referee, "Why, oh why didn't you let it go? We were having a ball and the fans were loving it," he yelled.

Terry Slater

Terry Slater, who coached the WHA's Los Angeles Sharks, was one of the nicest men I have ever met. He was one of a kind – a decent human being with a heart of gold. Terry was a total team player – he always looked out for his players, but still worked closely with management.

Slater came to Los Angeles after an exceptionally colorful career as a player and coach. As captain of the St. Lawrence University hockey squad, Slater set an all-time scoring record and made All-American two consecutive years before joining the Montreal Canadiens of the National Hockey League. Slater's outstanding coaching career began with the University of Toledo, where his teams won two Mid-American Championships before taking over the coaching duties of the last-place Toledo Blades. Slater then proceeded to lead the Blades to an International Hockey League championship in his first year.

In 1969, Slater moved to the Des Moines Oak Leafs of the International Hockey League, where he took the team to the second round of the playoffs. His ability to produce instant winners was well known and respected in the hockey world. Slater was a compulsive winner, and he brought that winning record to the Los Angeles Sharks.

Following his stint as coach of the Sharks, Slater became the coach of Colgate University, a college powerhouse. Today, Terry resides in Heaven with our God. Terry's lovely widow, Aggie, lives in beautiful Tampa Bay, Florida. Todd and Grant Slater, Terry's sons, are active in the business world. Todd is assisting Howard Baldwin in making movies. Grant put together a West Coast junior hockey league. The Slater brothers are surely go-getters, much like their father.

John Kanel, Los Angeles Sharks

The detail man and GM, John Kanel was my associate for more than three decades – 38 years to be exact. I have often compared him to a saint for his ability to cope with my mercurial personality for that many years. His loyalty and strength deserve a Congressional Medal of Honor for all the wars we went through together. John Kanel had the temperament to break a tense situation with a timely joke that he brought from his early theatrical background. He studied theater arts in college at the University of Missouri. His loyalty was his legacy to my career. John always reminded me that he was elected six times as a councilman and mayor of his beloved city of Cypress, California. In contrast, the people of Buena Park, California, where I served as mayor, elected me only once (though I only ran once). I have always conceded that he was a better politician than me.

I was proud to have his support, especially in regards to the WHA. He was the assistant general manager of the Los Angeles Sharks when I served as its first general manager. I often reminded him that when I was the GM, the team finished second in the Western Division, and when he took over from me, the team finished last. His response was always that I accepted the presidency of the WHA when I knew that I had a weak team, and that I bailed out at the right time.

As life has moved on, I realize more than ever that John Kanel was responsible for the multitude of details that helped keep me out of trouble. For that, I will always be indebted to him. He was not only my associate, he was also my friend. John Kanel worked his fingers to the bone to give a friend a hand. His friendship and loyalty were the kind you couldn't lose – even when you deserved to. He was a faithful associate. I have equated John's association not with material success, but with a person whose reward was always doing a job well, helping a friend in need, and achieving by being a man of decency. He was the mayor of Cypress for 20 years and they named a street in his honor. John was a dedicated soldier for the WHA.

Coach Jacques Demers

Jacques Demers coached in both the WHA and NHL. He is a colorful figure and someone who usually gets the most out of his players. His last stint as a coach was with the NHL's Tampa Bay Lightning in 1989, and like Frank Mahovlich, is now a senator in Canada. In WHA All-Star competitions, Demers coached a line made up of Wayne Gretzky and Gordie and Mark Howe. He said it was an honor to have two of the greatest players that ever played on the same line. Demers was a winner all the way.

Coach Jack Kelley

Jack Kelley coached in college and then made a successful transition to the professional ranks. He was the coach of the first Avco Cup champions. Kelley always had his players ready for action, and he built his teams with that in mind. His teams featured players like Larry Lund, Rich Ley, Teddy Green and Larry Pleau. Kelley was a member of the "Irish Mafia Singers" along with Don Regan and yours truly. We kept the Irish background in the foreground. Howard Baldwin hired Kelley to coach the Hartford Whalers, and together they put together a strong team that played in the WHA and then in the NHL after the merger.

At one point, they acquired Gordie, Mark and Marty Howe. That was a successful move, and the Whalers were very competitive. Jack Kelley now lives the retired life in Florida. He was, and is, classy in everything he does.

Coach Whitey Stapleton

Whitey Stapleton was the player-coach of the Chicago Cougars. He was a part owner of the team after Jordan and Walter Kaiser decided to sell the team. Whitey was an All-Star defenseman and he played many years in the NHL before joining the WHA.

Coach Glen Sonmor

The St. Paul Fighting Saints of the WHA fit the name to a T. Glen Sonmor was their coach and GM, and his players followed his lead. One of my main jobs as commissioner and president of the league was to levy fines to both the players and coaches when necessary. I venture to say that Sonmor received more fines than the norm. He was a feisty and controversial coach who backed down from no one. I will always remember the night in San Diego when he charged the fans. There happened to be fans from the U.S. Navy in the stands, and Sonmor thought someone in the stands had thrown something at his players. The battle proved to be fierce as elbows flew and teeth were lost. I would have fined Sonmor for his actions, but he stood his ground and argued that security in the arena should have been fined instead of him. He had a point, but I fined both him and the owner of the San Diego Mariners. This got everyone upset with me, but that's life as a commissioner. Sonmor was a successful and terrific coach.

Coach Bill Dineen

Bill Dineen was the successful coach of the Houston Aeros. He led this team to the Avco Cup twice. Dineen had a plan and he knew that getting that plan to work would be by using his wit. He lived by his integrity, and the plan began to work. He got his wish with the signing of Howe and his sons, and the rest is history. After the merger of the WHA and the NHL, Bill Dineen coached the New England Whalers. His formula for winning also worked for the Whalers. He is, and always will be, a winner.

Glen Sather

Glen Sather, the current president and GM of the New York Rangers, played a pivotal part in the success of the Edmonton Oilers successful dynasty. He was the GM for both the WHA and NHL Oilers franchises, as well as a former NHL player. Sather always was a man of distinction, whether it was competing on the ice or behind his desk as the team's general manager. When the two leagues merged, Sather led the Edmonton Oilers to four championships in a six-year period. This is a perfect example of his leadership skills. Sather always led a team that was plentiful in grace and finesse. It also didn't hurt having Wayne Gretzky on his roster.

Jack Stanfield

Jack Stanfield was a player and coach in the WHA in the early 1970s. He has been active in the development of regional sports networks and helped establish the Prime Sports network. Stanfield played with the WHA's Houston Aeros and was the team's GM upon retirement, replacing Jim Smith. Until recently, Jack was the executive VP of Fox International Sports Division, headquartered in Houston, Texas, where he lives with his family and is involved in community activities. Jack and I have had a lot of fun and laughs about his playing days. It just so happened that he scored a playoff goal with 30 seconds left in regulation against my Los Angeles Sharks, and I've never lived it down. He is a beautiful person who knows how to get his viewpoints over. He played alongside "Mr. Hockey," Gordie Howe, and often says what a great honor it was. It seemed that the Houston Aeros had a lot of great players, good chemistry and men of conviction who made their lives a pattern of success. Jack Stanfield fits that mold very well.

Rejean Houle, General Manager, Montreal Canadiens

The former general manager of the famed Montreal Canadiens played in the WHA for the Quebec Nordiques as a premier star. He was an exciting player, a strong skater and a scorer. His hard-work ethic stood him well as a player and as a GM. Houle has strong connections to his native Quebec and he is well-respected in the sport he loves. Houle was on the Team Canada roster in the second Summit Series against the Soviet Union. Houle has always been a winner and is one today.

The WHA Teams

1. Alberta Oilers: Now the Edmonton Oilers. Dr. Charles Allard, Zayne Feldman and "Wild Bill" Hunter owned the team. Hunter, who had owned and operated the Edmonton Oil Kings junior club, was the founding father of the Alberta Oilers. Despite concerns that Edmonton could never support a big-league club, Hunter bulled forward with his tunnel vision of bringing major-league hockey to the city. In the first year, the Oilers proved to be consistent performers, finishing the season with a winning record. In the years to follow, the Edmonton Oilers won the Stanley Cup four times in the franchise's first six years after the merger with the NHL. In its initial years, the team played in the Edmonton Gardens before moving into the 17,000-seat Edmonton Arena. Ray Kinasewich was selected as the team's first coach. "The Great One," Wayne Gretzky, was the mainstay of the Oilers and is considered one of the best players of all time. He teamed up with Mark Messier to form the dynamic duo that kept pace with the world of hockey. Early on, the Oilers signed NHL players such as Jim Harrison, Al Hamilton and Val Fonteyne. Wild Bill Hunter also signed top junior players from Western Canada. It was a strong team and was among the leaders in its first season. In the years to come, it was the most recognizable WHA team and is now a member of the NHL.

2. Chicago Cougars: The Cougars chose Chicago in hopes of capturing the attention of an already enthusiastic hockey crowd.

One of the team's first strategic moves was to sign longtime bruising Blackhawk Reggie Fleming and longtime NHL star Marcel Pronovost, who became the team's player-coach. However, despite these choices, the Cougars struggled to score goals during that first season. That would not last for long, as by the WHA's second season, the Cougars improved their standings by 27 points. This was due to the addition of players like Ralph Backstrom, Pat Stapleton, Larry Cahan, Jim McLeod and Rosaire Paiement. Backstrom won the Stanley Cup six times while playing with the Montreal Canadiens for many years. Brothers Jordan and Walter Kaiser, two Chicago developers, owned the club. The team played its games at the Chicago National Amphitheater, which seated 9,000 fans. The team was very colorful and very competitive. Ralph Backstrom is now the president and owner of the Colorado Eagles of the ECHL.

3. Cleveland Crusaders: Nick Mileti, a lawyer and sports mogul, also owned the Cleveland Indians of Major League Baseball, brought the Crusaders into the WHA after he had been bypassed by the NHL in their expansion program. Fortunately for Cleveland, he succeeded in joining the WHA, and Mileti's skaters proved to be one of the strongest teams in the new major-league hockey league. Mileti signed Gerry Cheevers, the outstanding former goalie of the Boston Bruins, as his premier player. Cheevers was an All-Star goalie three times in the WHA's first three seasons. Other notable Crusader players included Roy Buchanan, Paul Shmyr and Jerry Pender.

The Crusaders played their initial season at the Cleveland Coliseum and then moved into the 17,000-seat Richfield Arena.

4. Houston Aeros: The Aeros played their games at the Sam Houston Coliseum. Jim Smith, the team's president, hired Bill Dineen as his first coach, and signed Murray Hall, John Schella, Ed Hoekstra and goalie Wayne Rutledge away from the NHL. A year later, Smith signed the Gordie Howe family to play for the Aeros. This move was a major highlight in the success of the WHA. It featured all-time great Gordie Howe and his two sons, Marty and Mark Howe. The signing was a fabulous idea and helped make the WHA credible in every way. The Aeros proved to be more than simply a team with some marketing savvy; they were also one of the most successful WHA franchises, winning back-to-back championships in 1974 and 1975 after finishing second to the Winnipeg Jets in the league's first season. Jack Stanfield, who later became an operations and general manager for Fox TV, became the Aeros' GM after Jim Smith resigned. Irving Kaplan was the team owner.

5. Los Angeles Sharks: Art Rhodes, a business executive from Kansas City; Pat Brown, the late governor of California; Don Dyer, a Long Beach lawyer; and Dennis Murphy, a co-founder of the WHA, owned the Los Angeles Sharks. The team played at the Los Angeles Sports Arena. In their inaugural 1972/1973 season, the Sharks opened up in grand style, attracting more than 13,000 fans for their very first game. This beginning caused quite a stir with their crosstown rivals, the NHL's Los Angeles Kings. The Sharks were led by their very animated coach Terry Slater, who built a team of bruisers and headlined the team with goalie George Gardner of the Vancouver Canucks. The Sharks also featured Alton White, a black hockey player from New York. White was the first major-league black player since the renowned Willie O'Ree. The team acquired Ted McCaskill, Earl Heiskala, Steve Sutherland, Tom Gilmore and Jim Watson, all of whom where respected for their pugilistic abilities. Some of the finesse players included Gary Veneruzzo, Bart Crashley and J.P. LeBlanc. The team captured the fans of L.A. with their aggressive style of hockey. In the first season, the Sharks finished above .500 and won more games on the road than they did on their home ice.

6. New England Whalers: The team was owned by Howard Baldwin, John Colburn and Bob Schmertz. Baldwin later became the managing partner of the NHL Pittsburgh Penguins. Baldwin hired Jack Kelly as his GM and coach. Kelly was a highly respected college coach from Boston University who had won the NCAA hockey championship for two consecutive years. The team played most of its games at the Boston Gardens. Kelley, with his reputation, was able to get some of the big names from the NHL. He signed Ted Green, the popular Boston Bruin; Tom Webster, a 30-goal scorer; and Brad Selwood, Jim Dorey, Rick Ley, Larry Pleau and goalie Al Smith. The Whalers were the first Avco Cup champions, ultimately beating the Winnipeg

Jets in the first WHA playoff championship.

7. Minnesota Fighting Saints: The Saints represented Minnesota and were one of the original 12 teams in the WHA's inaugural season. Lou Kaplan, a St. Paul businessman, was the team's president. He and his partner, businessman Len Vanelli, hired former New York Ranger Glen Sonmor as their coach. Sonmor, a former NHL coach, believed in having a tough team, and he signed up the infamous Carlson brothers (featured as "the Hanson brothers" in the movie Slap Shot starring Paul Newman), along with Wayne Connelly, Jack McCartan, Mike Curran, Ted Hampson and John Arbour. Other noted players included Dave Keon, Mike Antonovich, Rick Smith and Bill Goldthorpe. Len Vanelli was a leader of the Fighting Saints in marketing and sales. He would later become president of the team. Attorney Wayne Belisle of St. Paul took charge of the team during the 1973 season. Harry Neale, the noted broadcaster, served as coach after Sonmor. They played their games in the new St. Paul Civic Center and drew decent crowds. During their five-year existence, the Saints drew more than 1 million fans and qualified for the playoffs three times. St. Louis loved the Saints and the club responded with a hustling and talented team.

8. New York Raiders: Gary Davidson, Don Regan, Bill Hunter and I felt we had to have a New York entry in the WHA. We had an inquiry from a young New York attorney by the name of Richard Wood. Needless to say, we moved quickly on this inquiry. Wood and his partner Sy Siegel paid their league fee and hired a baseball executive named Marvin Milkes of the California Angels to be the team's general manager. Milkes signed Camille Henry, a popular former New York Ranger player, as the coach, and then signed several outstanding and exciting players, including Bobby Sheehan, Ron Ward, Norm Ferguson and Garry Peters. Wood worked out a lease with Madison Square Gardens and played all the Raiders games at the Gardens. Some NHL owners were upset that the Gardens leased out the arena to those "upstarts" from the WHA. As one longtime NHL owner stated, "It's like inviting a thief into your house for dinner." The Garden was under the threat of a lawsuit engineered by WHA attorney Don Regan and was not about to fight the allegations of an anti-trust violation. Although the Big Apple was well represented, the crowds were small. The attendance was so small that the team had to move to Cherry Hills, New Jersey, and became the New York Golden Blades before being renamed again as the New Jersey Knights. They were subsequently sold and moved to San Diego, California.

9. Ottawa Nationals: Doug Michel, a young Ottawa businessman, owned the team. Ottawa, the capital of Canada, had no chance of getting an NHL team at the time, so the WHA decided that the city could be a potential winner. Michel selected Bill Harris as the coach and Bud Houle as the general manager. The games were played in the Ottawa Civic Center. The team featured Guy Trottier, Gavin Kirk and Les Binkley as their marquee players. Although the Nationals only played one season, they set a positive tone in the community and demonstrated that major-league hockey would be accepted in the Canadian capital. The city now has an NHL team.

10. Philadelphia Blazers: The Blazers were owned by attorney James Cooper and millionaire trucking executive Bernie Brown. The team played at the Philadelphia Civic Center. Phil Watson, a fiery former NHL star who eventually moved on to Buffalo, coached the team. Bernie Parent, one of the all-time great goal-tenders, was the club's marquee player. Cooper also signed Boston Bruins stars Derek Sanderson and John "Pie Face" McKenzie. The remainder of the club included numerous minor-league prospects. The club played one season in Philadelphia before moving to Vancouver, British Columbia, where Canadian businessman Jim Pattison became its owner.

11. Quebec Nordiques: Shopping-center magnate Paul Racine owned the club, which played its games at the 13,000-seat Quebec City Coliseum. Racine loved Quebec City, the Chateau Frontenac Hotel, his Quebec Nordiques hockey team and the WHA. He was a gracious and benevolent host – a leader who owned a major shopping mall in the city of Quebec. He showed the kind of business acumen that let us in the WHA entrust him with the responsibility of the WHA treasury. Racine was also a competitor who loved to beat the Toronto Toros, a team owned by his good friend John Bassett. He said that when he did beat the Toros, he would open up his best wine and savor every sip of it. And the wine, you can be sure, did not come from a screw-top bottle. I can truly say that Racine was one of our best owners. May his soul rest in peace with our Lord in Heaven. Racine owned a boat that he truly loved. At the drop of a hat, he would take guests on it. He loved taking Bobby Hull out on it, as he got The Golden Jet's viewpoints about Racine's beloved Nordiques. Maurice Filion coached the team and Marcus Fortier was the general manager. Fans took quickly to the team and it was one of the WHA's strongest franchises. NHL Hall of Famer J.C. Tremblay was the star of the team, and he was named a WHA All-Star defenseman. Marc Tardif joined the club in 1974 and was voted the most valuable player in the WHA twice. The club also featured Boom Boom Geoffrion and goalie Serge Aubry.

12. Winnipeg Jets: The Jets were the flagship team of the WHA. Legendary Ben Hatskin and Winnipeg's Simkin family owned the team. The Jets may have done more for the league than any of the other teams when they were able to sign the great Bobby Hull. That signing gave the WHA a stamp of approval and had an impact on all of hockey. Bobby Hull was the franchise and the league's marquee star. Hatskin hired Annis Stukus as his GM and Nick Mickoski as the bench coach. In addition to Hull, the team signed the Swedish sensations Ulf Nilsson and Anders Hedberg. The Hull-Hedberg-Nilsson line became one of the greatest in hockey history. The team played at the Winnipeg Arena, which at the time held 11,000 seats, but the Jets built additional seats to serve the growing crowds. The Jets won the Western Division championship in 1972-'73 against the Houston Aeros in an exciting and memorable series that established the quality of WHA hockey. The Jets lost to the New England Whalers in the Avco Cup championship finals.

13. Vancouver Blazers: Beginning in the 1973 season, the Philadelphia Blazers relocated to Vancouver, British Columbia. They remained there for two seasons before the club elected to suspend operations. During the Blazers' two years in Vancouver, they posted 64 wins, 89 losses and three ties. Key players included Ron Ward, Larry Lund, Danny Lawson and Bryan Campbell. Joe Crozier, a longtime NHL favorite was the team's coach. The Blazers became the Calgary Cowboys in the 1975-'76 season.

14. Phoenix Roadrunners: The Roadrunners entered the WHA in its third season and qualified for post-season play on two of three occasions. In their inaugural season, the team finished with 39 wins, 31 losses and eight ties in the very tough Western Division. Key players included swift-skating Dennis Sobchuk, Robbie Ftorek and the steady Jim Niekamp. The Roadrunners played in the Veterans Memorial Arena in downtown Phoenix, and were led by owner Karl Eller, an advertising genius, and Bert Getz, a banker. The hockey team was built around Ftorek, who later became the coach of the NHL's New Jersey Devils and

Los Angeles Kings. Bill McFarland was the club's GM and president. He was a former NHL player who was well established and connected, and he hired longtime minor-leaguer Sandy Hucul as his coach. The team managed to draw good crowds. A proficient golfer, Robbie Ftorek won the golf tournament at the WHA Reunion.

15. Calgary Cowboys: The Cowboys began operations in the WHA in the league's fourth season. During their two seasons in the WHA, the Cowboys averaged close to 5,000 fans per game and qualified for the playoffs in their first season. The team's most notable players included Danny Lawson, Ron Chipperfield and Don McLeod.

16. Cincinnati Stingers: The Stingers competed in the WHA's final three seasons. The Stingers' most productive season came during the 1976 campaign, when they finished in second place in the Eastern Division behind the eventual Avco Cup champions, the Quebec Nordiques. Terry Slater coached the team, and Rich LeDuc, Blaine Stoughton and Rick Dudley were a few of the key players. All three went on with their hockey careers and became owners or officials in the front office of various clubs.

17. Michigan Stags/Baltimore Blades: The Michigan Stags entered the WHA and eventually moved their operations to Baltimore. The move did not change the club's luck at the box office and the Stags/Blades could not grow roots in the WHA.

Their three key players included Gary Veneruzzo, J.P. LeBlanc and Tom Serviss. The club moved from Los Angeles (Sharks) and played in the Baltimore Civic Center. Young businessmen Pete Shagena and Charles Nolton owned the team. Johnny Wilson served as the coach.

18. San Diego Mariners: The Mariners participated in the WHA from 1974-1977. During their three seasons in the league, they qualified for the playoffs each year and averaged more than 6,000 fans per night. The Mariners' roster featured such stars as Kevin Morrison, Joe Noris and André Lacroix. They were coached first by Harry Howell and then by Ron Ingram. In three seasons, the Mariners posted 119 wins, 106 losses and 14 ties. Despite the long history of the sport in San Diego (the Pacific Coast Hockey League), the Mariners were the only major-league ice hockey club to ever play in the city. They played at the San Diego Sports Arena, which was owned by the Hahn family. Joe Schwartz was the first owner of the team, Skip Feldman was the GM, and my brother John Murphy was the marketing director.

19. Toronto Toros: In 1973, the Toros presented another major-league hockey club to the city of Toronto. The Toros' roster included big-name players like Paul Henderson, Frank Mahovlich and Vaclav Nedomansky, who created quite a stir in this legendary hockey town. In the Toros' three seasons, the Toros qualified for the playoffs twice and averaged more than 8,000 fans per game. Their most productive season was in 1973 when they posted a 41-33-4 record and finished in second place in the Eastern Division.

20. Denver Spurs: Although the Spurs only lasted for one season in the WHA, they entertained the citizens of Denver with some of the outstanding names in hockey. They featured four-time Stanley Cup champion Ralph Backstrom, J. P. LeBlanc, and the renowned Peter "the Rat" Mara.

21. Indianapolis Racers: The Racers may best be remembered as the team that introduced Wayne Gretzky to professional hockey. "The Great One" was 17 when Racers' owner Nelson Skalbania signed him to a personal-service contract. Although Gretzky's stay in Indianapolis was brief, the event will go down in history. The Racers had other notable characters involved in their organization, including Pat Stapleton, David Keon and Coach Jacques Demers. The Racers' most successful season came in 1975-76 when they won the tough Eastern Division championship.

Gordie Howe and His Best Seller

Gordie Howe and his wife Colleen wrote their own book, which has become the all-time best-selling hockey hardcover autobiography of all time. Written together with Tom DeLisle, the book can be purchased online. It is about "Mr. Hockey," and is interesting reading. I recommend it highly. Power Play International, Inc., (248) 960-7500, www.mrhockey.com.

Wayne Gretzky, Number 99, Mr. Everything

In the annals of hockey history, Wayne "The Great One" Gretzky will always be one who stands out. Number 99 will always be the symbol of excellence, integrity and class. The number 99 is and always will be, to the hockey purist, his, and only his, immortal number. Number 99 started his professional career as a skinny 17-year-old with the Indianapolis Racers of the World Hockey Association. His owner, Nelson Skalbania, offered him an initial contract which he could not turn down. His greatness is now history, and what a run it has been. He is also considered the all-time playmaker.

As an Edmonton Oiler, both in the WHA and the NHL, he did it all. He was the spark that led to all of those NHL Stanley Cups that the Oilers won. He was a joy to watch skate and perform. He knew where his passes were headed, and he knew how to put the puck into the net. Wayne Gretzky was really and truly is "The Great One."

His trade to the Los Angeles Kings from the Oilers in 1988 helped develop hockey interest in Southern California. He was always there for the Kings' fans and was a super high-profile star. His signing by then-Los Angeles owner Bruce McNall was one of the biggest sports stories in the 20th century. After the merger between the WHA and the NHL took place, Gretzky led the Edmonton Oilers to four Stanley Cup championships. As a team, they were awesome, and number 99 was the main ingredient in the Oilers' success. The wins in Edmonton proved to the hockey establishment that the WHA was truly a talented league and very underrated.

Thank you, Wayne, for helping to make professional hockey the sport it is today, both in the United States and in your native Canada. The Vince Lombardi credo exemplifies Wayne Gretzky in every way. It goes like this: "Leaders are made, they are not born." They make all things happen because they are willing to pay the price. We all, therefore, should pay the price to achieve our goals. It is becoming difficult to be patient with a society that is tolerant of the misfits, the maladjusted and the losers. Have sympathy for them, help them, but let us not condone them. We need to stand up and cheer for the doer, the achiever and the winner. Wayne Gretzky always was, is now, and always will be a winner.

Ralph Backstrom, Mr. Class Act

Ralph Backstrom is known by his peers as a great skater, a true gentleman, a tough but clean player, and a team player. Ralph Backstrom is "Mr. Integrity" and "Mr. Respect" to his peers. Ralph exemplifies the good of the NHL, the WHA and professional sports in general. A native of Kirkland Lake, Ontario, Canada, Backstrom was the captain of the 1958 Memorial Cup champions from Canada. He was considered one of the best junior hockey players ever to play the game. He originally signed with the Montreal Canadiens and has had his name inscribed on the Stanley Cup six times. There are only nine players in the history of the NHL who have won more than six Stanley Cups in their careers. Backstrom's many credits include being selected as the most valuable player for Team Canada in the Summit Series against the Soviet Union in 1974. Backstrom was a finesse player. Though he never looked for trouble, he did not back down from anyone, either.

Many believe that Ralph Backstrom will be selected to the Hockey Hall of Fame because of his record. He deserves it. He played 15 years in the NHL and four seasons in the WHA. Ralph went into coaching, where he spent years with the Los Angeles Kings, Phoenix Roadrunners and with the University of Denver. Now Ralph and his wife, Janet, live in Denver, Colorado. He has three children, Martin, Diana and Andrew. Together with his many friends in the world of professional hockey, Backstrom gave instant credibility to the new sport of roller hockey by helping in the development of Roller Hockey International. He served as RHI's commissioner and today he is the president and owner of the Colorado Eagles of the ECHL. As a member of the Los Angeles Kings, Backstrom met a California businessman, Maury Silver, in 1972. Together they have been credited with pushing forward the development of the modern inline skate. Backstrom has always said that anything in life is possible for those who believe.

Frank Mahovlich, "Mr. Senator"

In 1974, with John Bassett as the team's principal owner, the Toronto Toros signed Frank Mahovlich. Frank was a longtime Toronto Maple Leaf and former Montreal Canadiens superstar. He was third former NHL player with more than 500 career goals to join the WHA. (Bobby Hull and Gordie Howe were the other two.) It was indeed another shot in the arm for the WHA.

It was especially gratifying for me that both Gordie Howe and Frank Mahovlich came into the league on my watch as WHA president and commissioner. Frank had a distinguished career in the NHL and he was the premier player for the Toros. He later made the Hockey Hall of Fame, which he fully deserved. Frank is now a senator, representing his country in the Canadian government. He is a politician who makes friends easily. He and his family now reside in the Toronto area. At Mahovlich's signing, Toros owner John Bassett said, "We are indeed proud to have Frank Mahovlich in our league. He is a superstar who has strong ties with the community and his very presence will add immensely to our league's credibility."

Mahovlich played on the Team Canada squad in 1974 that played against the Russian All-Stars. He was a well-respected member of that team and was immensely involved in the superb performance of Team Canada.

André Lacroix

André Lacroix was a center who had the uncanny ability of always knowing where his wingers were on the ice. He was a terrific skater and was known for his passing wizardry. André was also a good public-relations man for the San Diego Mariners and the Quebec Nordiques of the WHA. As president of the league, I frequently managed to visit San Diego to watch the Mariners play their home games at the San Diego Sports Arena, a venue that seated 13,600 fans. I was always in awe of the finesse with which Lacroix handled the puck. He was a class act who was as classy off the ice as he was on. Lacroix was rhythm in motion and a credit to the WHA. Lacroix was the captain and leader of the Joe Schwartz- and Skip Feldman-owned Mariners. Harry Howell and Ron Ingram coached Lacroix. Lacroix was a great friend to my brother John, and all three of us loved to swap stories with each other.

Peter Graham owned the Sports Arena when we first played there, but the Hahn family subsequently bought the arena and did a great job of upgrading and improving it. They were very positive people. Ron Hahn was a Stanford man who made things happen.

Scotty Bowman, a Tough Adversary

In my opinion, Scotty Bowman is *the* hockey coach of the 20th century. Not because of his championship rings, his knowledge of the x's and o's of hockey, and not because of his competitive spirit, but because Scotty is a "people person." He takes pride in what his players accomplish and he is the teacher who commands their attention and respect. Scotty never joined our WHA. He was always protecting his players on the Montreal Canadiens, especially his great goaltender, Ken Dryden.

In the early years of the WHA's war with the NHL, Los Angeles Sharks coach Terry Slater and I thought that we would try and pick off one of the best goaltenders in the NHL for our Sharks. I arranged a meeting with Ken Dryden at the Marriott Hotel in Los

Angeles. To this day, I don't know how Scotty found out about our proposed secret meeting, but I found out very early on that he was not going to let his superstar goalie get away.

As I arrived at the hotel, I found a hostile Scotty Bowman in the lobby. He approached me, and in a firm voice, said, "Murphy, get out of here or they will be picking up your bones in the parking lot. Ken Dryden is staying with the Canadiens."

Slater and I turned around and left the hotel without talking to the goaltending legend.

I learned early on that Scotty Bowman respected his players and would go to the mat for them anytime. His successful record and his place in hockey history are well established. One of my early losses in putting together the WHA will always be a badge of honor for me. I wish we would have had Scotty's services and dedication with our great WHA, but he was a National Hockey Leaguer. Albert Einstein once said, *"Try not to become a man of success but rather try to become a man of value."* Bowman put his faith in love, sacrifice, dedication and loyalty, and he, the victor of success, has received dividends tenfold.

The Lawyers

The legal profession is often knocked; frequently, deservedly so. However, this was not the case in the World Hockey Association. The WHA was blessed with outstanding lawyers. Our three main lawyers were Don Regan, his associate Tim Grandi, and Telly Mercury, a Canadian. We were also helped by Gary Davidson, our president, who was also a lawyer, and Robert Capporale from New England, who helped us in the properties division. This group of men was a very strong team. They also related well with the team owners and their personal lawyers. Our team took on and beat the best in the legal profession.

In Philadelphia, Don and his team faced off against Edward Bennett Williams and his phalanx of lawyers. We scored the legal goal. The NHL's reserve clause was broken and the WHA had free access to NHL players. Ben Hatskin, the WHA chairman, supported our legal effort and supplied his own personal attorney, Telly Mercury, to help us on Canadian matters. Telly, Tim and Don were the trio who forged great working relationships and provided the knowledge and stability necessary to help steer us through rough legal waters. With these lawyers, we were able to make our projects successful because of their dedication and their belief in the league. Don Regan, as our chief council, was the man who put together this strong team. His experience and guidance enabled us to succeed in breaking through the NHL's roadblock. Thanks, guys.

Gary Davidson, My Partner and Longtime Friend

I have been associated with a lot of decent people on this earth; however, none have touched my life with the same effect that my friend Gary Davidson has. He is without a doubt, a 180-degree contrast from my style of operating. He is UCLA, I am

USC. He is a stout Republican, I am a conservative Democrat. He is a great dresser, I am a laundry bag. He is a fiscal genius, I am known as a free spender. He is a basketball player, I played baseball. He is a handsome dude, and I, well... you can find your own description. This scenario can go on forever, but I think you get the picture.

We are indeed opposites. He worked his way through college, established his own law firm, and is a consummate administrator and chief executive officer. I first met Gary when I was helping to organize the American Basketball Association. A mutual friend, Roland Speth, brought us together and the rest is history. Gary and I were indeed an odd pair, but we did organize well together. When you consider that we were instrumental in the formation of both the ABA and the WHA, it is truly amazing. We did not team up on the World Football League, which Gary did himself.

The World Football league was a great idea, but the economy at that time was in a bad recession, and the league suffered. Gary helped organize the league, and after the first season, Chris Hemmeter of Hawaii took over as its second president. In the second year of operation, Hemmeter and his associates pulled the plug and a great idea went down the tubes. Gary took the fall hard, but in reality, and in my mind, he was not in control at the time and should not be blamed for the league's misstep. I have said on many occasions that had Gary retained the leadership role in the league, the WFL would be thriving today. Davidson was known for his calm demeanor under fire.

A story I enjoy telling is about the time we lost two proposed WHA teams during our organizational/developmental period, Miami and Calgary. The loss created a terrible setback for our fledgling league, and when the announcement broke in the media, our phone lines went crazy. Reporters wanted a league statement, and when I could not locate Gary, I went into a panic. Before I spoke to the media, I wanted to discuss with Gary what our response should be. I finally found him at the Balboa Bay Club playing tennis, and I let him have some of my choice Irish words.

Gary waited for my tirade to subside and then he calmly said, "It has only been a couple of hours since the announcement broke, and Murph, life will go on. Let's get a hold of Nick Mileti and John Cooper and get Cleveland and Philadelphia to join the league. This way, the statement we make to the press will be a positive one instead of a negative one."

As usual, Davidson was right and we did exactly that. We turned a negative into a positive without missing a beat. It is better to take one step backward and then take two steps forward. Gary Davidson has always been a strong leader, and his guidance was invaluable for our new entity. Gary is now the owner of the Windstone Group of Orange County, California, which provides substance-abuse counseling. Gary is a person who motivates others.

A quote by Franklin D. Roosevelt sets it in proper perspective: *"People acting together as a group can accomplish things which no individual acting alone could ever hope to bring about."*

In conclusion, I am reminded of a quote from General Dwight D. Eisenhower, which exemplifies Gary Davidson so well:

"Motivation is the art of getting people to do what you want them to do because they want to do it."

Donald Regan

Don Regan is UCLA. His wife, Sarah, is also UCLA. One of his sons was Notre Dame, and one a Bruin. Consequently, Regan's allegiance is with UCLA and Notre Dame… anyone but USC. Boy, have we had some debates. I won some money during football season; he won it back during basketball season. Don Regan is a terrific lawyer. He helped to break the reserve clause. Regan was the "quiet giant" behind the scenes, the man who got the job done. Gary Davidson and I got to rely on Don. He was always the one who kept us out of trouble. He was also the one who served as the referee when Gary and I got into a shouting match. When all was said and done, Don Regan is the one who should get a lot of credit for the success of the ABA, the WHA and World Team Tennis.

He and his family were on the road so much that he always took along one of his children when he traveled North America and helped us put our leagues together. Those of us in the trenches should always be grateful for Don's wisdom, intelligence and dedication to the development of the hybrid leagues. Don Regan and his partner, Gary Davidson, have had some major basketball confrontations. The blood flowed and neither man gave any quarter. Who won is still a mystery. Over the years, I have discovered that as a sports attorney, there was none better than Don Regan. Thanks Don, for your great advice and help.

Telly Mercury, General Counsel

Telly Mercury was a young and enterprising lawyer from Winnipeg who was the attorney for both the Winnipeg Jets and WHA chairman Bent Hatskin. Mercury had been a world-class judo expert who competed in national competitions throughout Canada. He helped put together the package for Bobby Hull and worked closely with Don Regan and Gary Davidson. When the league office moved to Canada from Newport Beach, California, Telly became the league counsel and commuted to Toronto from Winnipeg. Ben Hatskin had complete confidence in Telly Mercury and he did a yeoman's job for the association.

Telly is now practicing law and business in his beloved city of Winnipeg and he represents some major companies and individuals. He is a real gentleman who can be tough when necessary. He has always been a "bottom-line" attorney with compassion and integrity. He served as the legal counsel to Team Canada in the series against the Russians. He and his friend John Kanel formed the Greek coalition in the league, and we all had a lot of fun kidding those outstanding Greeks. Mercury played a major role with Ben Hatskin in signing the Golden Jet, Bobby Hull. He was involved with Hull's attorney from the very beginning of the negotiations.

Larry Gordon, WHA Marketing Director

Larry Gordon was a terrific addition to the WHA office. He was the marketing director for the association and he did his job well. Together with Ben Hatskin and Bill Hunter, he played a major role in the WHA's Summit Series with the Soviet Union. Gordon was a workhorse who always got things resolved. Ben Hatskin put a lot of trust in Gordon's abilities, putting him in charge of the negotiations with the Russians as well as the top marketers in North America. Gordon served as president of the International Hockey League, and he owned the IHL's Cleveland Lumberjacks.

Loyalty is a virtue only a few men have, and those men who have it are few and far between, and this could be said of Larry Gordon. Gordon and I were the co-chairmen of the 26th WHA reunion in Windsor, Canada, a few years ago. We had a successful event and he did a great job helping to coordinate the affair. He and his wife have homes in Cleveland, Ohio, and in Mexico.

Max Muhleman

Max Muhleman is a marketing genius. He was the man who helped secure the sponsors and advertisers in the United States and Canada for the WHA. We were lucky to have his services in the U.S., and with Larry Gordon, they made a good team. Muhleman concentrated his efforts on Wall Street, and Gordon excelled in Canada. Today Muhleman has his own offices in Charlotte, North Carolina. He is very involved in sports marketing, with a strong emphasis on car racing and the Charlotte Hornets NBA team.

Walt Marlow

The man who helped make the WHA was our L.A. Herald Examiner writer and friend, Walt Marlow. Walt got the founders together with Canada's Wild Bill Hunter and history was made. Walt was a beat reporter for the Examiner when he got interested in our project. There is no doubt that without meeting with the Canadians, which Walt arranged, we would have had a difficult time making the WHA a success. The Canadian media was tough on us American organizers, and without the "Canadian Connection," things would have been difficult. The league hired Walt in 1973. When the league offices moved to Canada, we asked Walt to move there, and he did. The great work he did in Newport Beach was transferred to Toronto. He stayed with the WHA until he moved back to California. We thank Walt for his contributions. Now retired, Walt lives in Santa Ana, California, with his wife, Blanche.

"No one so thoroughly appreciates the value of constructive criticism as the one who's giving it." – Hal Chadwick

A Major Debate

We had a major debate among the league leadership as to whether or not we wanted to go into the city of Ottawa. It is the capital of Canada, had a lot of government workers, an adequate arena and a population base of 600,000, including the suburbs, yet a few of the leaders in our league felt that we'd be better off in one of the U.S. cities. I liked Ottawa and I cared for Doug Michel, who was my kind of guy. He was a jewel and a man who had determination and love for his city. He had very little money, but some strong contacts, and I felt that, one way or another, Michel would come through. I feel that those who want something badly enough can succeed, and Michel was one who did not take the word "no" gently. He and his family had a powwow and agreed to mortgage their home to put up their franchise fee. This, to Michel's credit, was his ultimate feeling – that Ottawa could and would support a pro hockey team.

Michel found a strong partner from Buffalo, New York, named Nick Trbovich, and away they went. In the first season in Ottawa, they hired Billy Harris as coach and Buck Houle as GM. The team feature Guy Trottier, Wayne Carlton, Kevin Kirk and Les Binkley. They set a positive tone in the community, and today, as Michel predicted, they have an NHL team. It reminds me that if a person honestly does believe, he someway and somehow will make it happen. Doug Michel is that kind of man. After the first season in Ottawa, both Michel and Trbovich decided to sell their team to John Bassett, who moved the team to Toronto and called it the Toronto Toros.

Jim Pattison, Owner of the Vancouver Blazers

When people talk about the city of Vancouver, the name of businessman Jim Pattison always moves to the forefront. He was always a symbol of excellence to many people and a big booster of one of North America's most beautiful cities. He was the CEO and president of the highly successful 1986 World Exposition in Vancouver and the owner of the WHA's Vancouver Blazers. His team featured some of hockey's most colorful characters – Coach Joe Crozier and star player John "Pie Face" McKenzie come to mind. The Blazers played their games at the Pacific Coliseum in Vancouver. As a coach, Crozier installed a hard-hitting team that kept the fans in the game.

Paul Deneau

Owner Paul Deneau of the Houston Aeros was a character. A highly successful businessman from Dayton, Ohio, who owned the city's largest skyscraper, Deneau was a gracious host at all times. He loved Dayton and wanted to bring it a WHA team. My task was to talk him out of putting a team in Dayton; our leadership group felt that we needed the big cities during the league's initial stage of growth. This turned out to be a battle with Deneau, as he felt very strongly that Dayton could be the "Green Bay" of the WHA. During the formative stage of the league, I think we had more meetings and conferences on Dayton than any other subject.

Fortunately for us in the WHA management, the city council was facing a tough election battle and the faction that supported Deneau was defeated. The new council refused to give Deneau a lease in the civic auditorium for the interim period. As a result, he took the franchise to Houston, which wanted a team in our league. Deneau has since passed away, but he will always be a fond memory to those of us in the WHA.

Jim Cooper

After the Miami franchise decided to drop out of the WHA's original 12 teams, the Philadelphia contingent, led by lawyer Jim Cooper and bankrolled by trucker Bernie Brown, took the club. They hired Jim "Pie Face" McKenzie as their player-coach and the Philadelphia Blazers played their games at the Philadelphia Civic Center. Goaltender Bernie Parent led the team in net, and the team was exciting from the very beginning. After receiving an offer from Vancouver's Jim Pattison, Brown and Cooper sold the franchise to Vancouver.

Dr. A.C. Allard

As owner of the Edmonton Oilers, multimillionaire Dr. Allard was a class act. He and his GM Bill Hunter not only put a competitive team on the ice, but they helped build the beautiful Edmonton Coliseum. Dr. Allard always remained quietly in the background, but he loved his Edmonton Oilers and was always there for Bill Hunter, Zayne Feldman and his partners.

Nelson Skalbania

During the WHA, we had some flamboyant owners. The first time I met Nelson Skalbania, the eventual owner of the Indiana Racers, was at the Santa Monica Airport. His private jet landed right on time, and his friendly and contagious personality took over. He exemplified money and electricity. Like all of us, Skalbania had ups and downs in life, but with his business acumen, he always seemed to bounce back. He was always there for me as a friend. He is a master psychologist and planner. His successful business friends like Peter Pocklington, Jim Pattison and Michael Gobuty have only nice things to say about him. He will always have a special place in the great WHA. It was Skalbania who signed the famous number 99, Wayne Gretzky, to a personal-services contract at the tender age of 17. At the time, Gretzky was making just $75 a week. Mark Messier received a $250,000 contract after making the same paltry salary as Gretzky. Skalbania has often said that Gretzky had "that extra something special" that guarantees success. Signing the contract with such a superstar made headline news throughout the world at the time. It helped build the league's credibility immeasurably.

Ray Kroc, Owner of the San Diego Mariners

A giant in the restaurant business whose fortune grew exponentially after he bought out the founders of McDonald's, Ray Kroc stepped up to buy the San Diego Mariners when the initial owner, Joe Schwartz decided to sell the team. Kroc's son-in-law Ballard Smith was placed in charge of the club, and he was a tower of strength to San Diego and to the league. Smith was a hands-on director in the league. Former NHL stars Harry Howell and Ron Ingram were excellent coaches for the Mariners. Skip Feldman served as GM, and my brother John was the team's marketing director. André Lacroix and Kevin Morrison led the team. The club played at the 13,000-seat San Diego Sports Arena and was well received by the fans in town.

The Acquisition of Players

One of the areas of major concern for our new WHA was getting players. The NHL had most of the best hockey players under a two-way contract. This meant that the players could, at the NHL team's insistence, go down to the minors at any time and be paid accordingly. It was then an NHL "owner's market," and they milked it dry. Don Regan felt that the two-way contract could be challenged in court and that we would win. As usual, he was correct.

In the early 1970s, the Western Hockey League was made up of six cities – San Diego, Phoenix, Denver, Seattle, Vancouver and San Francisco. The players were a notch below the NHL players in skills at that time. It was a developmental league for the NHL, but some of the teams were independent and not beholden to the bigger league. We looked at their structure and felt that it was here where we could test the NHL. It was a good strategy, and in our first year of existence, most of our players came from this source. We picked up potential players in colleges in Canada and the United States. In both countries, college hockey is played with enthusiasm.

Raiding the NHL for Players

At my insistence, the WHA decided to follow in the footsteps of Al Davis, the former commissioner of the American Football League. After an initial consultation with our lawyer, Don Regan, we decided to acquire some of our star and marquee players from the NHL establishment. We then started raiding NHL rosters. With the money offered by our owners, the league gained many stars instantly. The war was on... and the players benefited. In addition to the NHL players, the WHA owners and general managers worked hard to pick up the emerging stars of the minor leagues. Lots of time and energy was given to the rosters of the NHL's minor-league teams, and we gained many players from this area.

Gary Davidson, Don Regan and I decided early on that the timing of starting a new league was perfect. The interest in hockey was growing throughout the continent, and the cost of acquiring a new NHL hockey franchise had escalated to staggering numbers. The WHA owners found out early that their costs were considerably less by joining our league than if they had attempted to join the NHL. The greedy leaders of the NHL had established a $2 million entrance fee into their league. The founders of the WHA, on the other hand, offered our teams entry for $25,000.

We held our draft in Anaheim, California, and we made it a total media production. We invited Alan Eagleson, the NHL players' lawyer, to the meeting, and I have always suspected that he was a spy for the NHL owners. Eagleson showed no enthusiasm toward the WHA, even though the WHA was the vehicle that helped his NHL players' salaries escalate. In fact, he said some disparaging things about our league to the press, which we had to dispute and offset.

The Al Davis formula of raiding players from the establishment brought more than 60 players to the WHA in its first year. It created salary demands by the existing NHL players with their NHL owners. The WHA only needed three or four marquee players per team in order to establish credibility. The NHL, on the other hand, had to protect their total rosters or lose credibility. Outrageous demands became the order of the day.

The WHA wanted to create a higher-scoring image. We established the overtime period in order to try to cut down on the constant ties. We did not whistle down icing from the shorthanded team's defensive zones, thus speeding up the game. We attempted to get colored pucks like the ABA's red, white and blue balls, but this move was not successful, and we reverted back to the standard black hockey puck. The league was innovative and willing to try different ideas, even though some did not work. With 12 teams in place to start the season in 1972, the

WHA had proved to all that it was ready to take an active position in the emerging sports community.

The commissioner's office was in Newport Beach, California. Releases, TV interviews and radio announcements were flowing throughout the continent. The teams were in training camp and everyone was enthusiastic about the future. More than 60 NHL veterans who had jumped leagues joined 150 minor leaguers to fill our team rosters. Most of the coaches had proven NHL experience, and the reports filing out of the camps were that the talent, skills and enthusiasm was of high quality. It was quite obvious that the brand of hockey was going to be of a quality vintage.

The Jumpers

There are many reasons why some National Hockey League players and players in the high minors jumped ship, but the paramount reason for most was the money. The average salary in the NHL prior to the establishment of the WHA was in the neighborhood of $25,000 per year. The elite players were in the $40,000 area and top players in the high minors averaged around $12,000. After the WHA made its presence felt, most of the NHL players and top minor-league players increased their salaries immensely. The battle for the elite players became intense, and many of the stars played one league against the other and increased their salaries dramatically. Most players generally did aim high, and they often discovered that when their talents were set free, they could achieve unlimited goals.

Those who jumped from the NHL to join our league were not hesitant to escape the accepted path and, in most cases, it was the right decision. Take, for example, goaltender Gerry Cheevers of Boston and J.C. Tremblay of Montreal. Both of these great players took the plunge knowing that the money they received for their so-called gamble was worth the chance, and they were proved right. Both the Cleveland Crusaders and Quebec Nordiques, respectively, were very satisfied with their new acquisitions, and the players reaped the benefits of our new league.

The WHA did not win most of the battles, but the NHL players did – stars like Brad Park and Vic Hadfield of the New York Rangers stayed with their teams and benefited because the Rangers upped the ante to keep them in the Big Apple. This scenario played out all over the NHL. Competition was terrific for all, especially for the players.

Stars of the WHA Staff

In 1974, I was very supportive of the board of governors' decision to have Bud Poile join us. He was a consummate professional; detailed, stubborn and strong willed. Those virtues stood well with the league leadership because we had many points of view. Poile was a great sounding board on the various committees within the board of governors. Some of our WHA advocates were skeptical of Poile's involvement in the WHA because he was always considered an NHL insider. Many thought that his purpose in joining the WHA was to divide and conquer our league. Some of our American contingent, especially, urged me to watch Poile's every move and not to trust him. However, Poile was loyal, both to me and to the league. His hockey experience, knowledge and counsel kept me out of hot water on many occasions. I came to respect him and have considered him a friend.

Larry Gordon is one of the most efficient men in the world. He was our director of merchandising and he did an outstanding job in developing our products division. Gordon put together the Summit Series with Russia and was instrumental in bringing hundreds of thousands of dollars into our league's coffers. Gordon was active in the International Hockey League as the former owner of the Cleveland Lumberjacks, and they could not have acquired a finer leader.

Frank Polnaszek was the statistician and historian for the league, and what a glorious history it had.

Walt Marlow was our point man. He kept us on the front lines of the sports pages. His work was respected by the media and his help will always be remembered and treasured.

Linda Zenk kept the books on behalf of the league. She kept us on our toes and watched our expense accounts like it was her own money.

Upon leaving the Los Angeles Sharks as GM, John Kanel joined the WHA office and became the league administrator. Kanel, who was my associate and friend for more than 35 years, was one of those special types of men who come around to someone just once in a lifetime. He was a pleasant Greek who was always there in stressful and troublesome times. He had a way about him that allowed him to say just the right thing to break up a stressful situation – usually when talking to a "barracuda" businessman. He'd come up with one of his typical "Kanelism" quotes, causing laughter and easing the tension.

John was detail oriented almost to a fault and managed to save me from chaos and disaster many times. Although I hate details, I realize they have to be completed. John's attention to the fine points in our business deals and developments were integral to many of our company's greatest accomplishments.

As my personal secretary, Elsie Hill was a pillar of strength. She helped with our agendas and made sure that our owners were updated at all times.

Jim Browitt was a leader in the league's transition and was our director of operations for a time.

A member of the original "Hockey Night in Canada," Ed Fitkin was hired by Jack Kent Cooke as the Los Angeles Kings first television/radio color analyst. He then joined the WHA, where his expertise was invaluable.

Our WHA staff believed in the principle that a team effort can make miracles happen. We all pitched in to make our league office run smoothly. Every letter, every phone call and every personal contact we made was a statement about the caliber of service we offered. Being the "second league," we knew we had to set a tone and try harder. We all took the attitude that when we thought we were exhausted and that all the possibilities were used up, we would keep going. We all felt that we had to fight one more round because we never understood the word "quit."

I always told our staff members that minds are like parachutes; they only function when they're open. So much of everything is shaped by our power of perception. I told our people that because we were perceived as the "second league," we had to set goals that did not interfere with reality. I felt that our enemies would compound our mistakes, and as a result, we had to make as few mistakes as possible. Our office staff maintained good communication with our owners and was dedicated to the league. The WHA staff gave the owners and me great service. I could never express enough thanks.

WHA Rule Changes

When changes were contemplated in the rules at any of our WHA meetings, the leadership of the league treaded lightly. It was apparent from the very beginning that our Canadian friends wanted to keep the game intact. For this reason, we called on our chief of officials, Vern Buffey, to create the rules structure. Buffey had been and was highly respected in the profession and he did not want to significantly change the rules. He did, however, feel that there were too many ties in the NHL and thus supported a 10-minute overtime period for games tied after regulation. This rule change was strongly supported by our Canadian friends, and with the urging of Jim Pattison, Bill Hunter, John Bassett and Ben Hatskin, that rule was adopted by the WHA board of governors.

The decision had a major effect on cutting down the number of tie games. It also gave our WHA fans something to hold on to in establishing a different style of play. I credit Buffey for his foresight and good sense in developing our rules, and at the same time, maintaining the integrity of the game. He contributed in developing our own legacy in the hockey world. Buffey put together a strong corps of referees. He prided himself as one who "took charge on the ice," and he stood by his referees. Gary Davidson backed Buffey's dedication and presence. Buffey has now joined the long list of our faithfully departed, and those of us in the trenches will be forever grateful for his development of our new league's rules. The WHA was fortunate in having a core group of referees led by Buffey and, later, by chief official Bob Frampton. They took pride in their work and dedicated themselves to making our league a success. They contributed and were partially responsible for the success of the great WHA.

WHA Officials: Our Refs

The WHA had a dedicated group of officials in the nine years of the league's existence. WHA's officials were largely longtime minor-league officials, and they were guided by our referees in chief, Vern Buffey and Bob Frampton. Buffey and Frampton were veteran referees from the NHL and were men of high integrity who ran their crew with a firm hand. We will always remember the majesty of referee Bill Friday. He was one of a special breed. When he took the ice, everyone in the building knew who was in charge. His demeanor oozed authority and strength. The lead referees, Ron Ego, Bob Sloan, Bob Kolari, Ron Harris and Wayne Mundey took no baloney on the ice, but at the same time, they showed the players great respect. Those of us behind the scenes will always be grateful for the "gentle policemen" who controlled the game on the ice.

Director of Officials: Vern Buffey and Bob Frampton

Referees: Bill Friday, Bob Sloan, Ron Ego, Brent Casselman, Wayne Mundey, Bob Kolari, Ron Harris, Alan Glaspell, Ron Asselstine.

Linesmen: Pierre Belanger, Gene Kusy, Mike Entwistle, Ross Keenan, Eric Manship, Graham Hern, Dennis Dahlmann, Wayne Bonney, Joey Dame, Ron Foyt, Max Hansen, Tom Shamshak, Tom Marek, Glen Sherwood, Ken Pierce, Kevin Weatherby, Michel Chartre, Ron Rishagen, Mike Chee, Gord Kerr, Daryl Havrelock, Ron Renneberg, Paul Corcoran, Dick Haigh.

A Start Toward a Merger

In 1978, the New York Rangers, under John Ferguson, offered the two Swedish stars of the Winnipeg Jets, Ulf Nilsson and Anders Hedberg, huge dollars to join the Rangers. Imagine, in just five years, the Rangers had increased their offer from $10,000 to $600,000 per year. Meanwhile, the Jets had been sold to a group headed by Michael Gobuty. Stunned by the Rangers' offer, the new ownership group decided not to match it. This was a major setback for the WHA and indicated to the league's eight team owners that the NHL was going for the jugular and that their future was in jeopardy. This act alone helped spur the WHA to work harder for a merger.

The war between the two leagues was counterproductive. Fans and the media were talking about the losses that the WHA was sustaining, but in reality, the ownerships of both leagues were biting the bullet. It was then up to WHA President Howard Baldwin and NHL Commissioner John Zeigler to work out the details. It was fortunate that both leagues had leaders who were realistic and able to compromise. Baldwin and Zeigler knew that keeping up the battle was utterly foolish. The only way to bring sensibility out of chaos was to work out a settlement.

Baldwin and I have often been asked if another major league could be established against the existing "Big Four" – the National Football League, Major League Baseball, the National Basketball Association and the National Hockey League. We both respond with a resounding, "No!" I do not believe we will ever see a rival to those established leagues because the money involved is just too enormous. We were lucky, because our timing was right, and because of the arrogance of the Harold

Ballards of the world. I personally think that if leaders like Howard Baldwin and John Zeigler were running the big boys today, they would understand the games and never let another league start.

Beginning the Merger Talks

As the new president of the WHA, one of my first acts was to ask Nick Mileti, our Cleveland Crusaders owner, who had many friends in the NHL, if we could arrive at a consensus. He contacted Sam Pollock, the icon of the Montreal Canadiens and Bruce Jennings of the New Rangers to see if we could start preliminary discussions in forming a structure for a merger. I knew that when and if a merger came to pass, I would lose my job, as I was certain that the NHL would insist on keeping Clarence Campbell as commissioner. This did not deter me in my decision to work on the merger, as I felt confident that there would be something for me. I believed that if we could get both leagues together, it would be good for all of us.

Nick reported back that both Jennings and Pollock thought that a merger was a good idea, and that we should move toward that direction. It was agreed that nothing would be said preliminarily and especially not to the media. When I look back and reflect, I believe that one of the best-kept secrets in professional sports was our negotiation with the NHL. The planning was done in secret and, until both leagues met in New York, a lid was kept tight on the talks. Ben Hatskin and I put together our three-man committee and the NHL did likewise. Nick Mileti, Howard Baldwin and Paul Racine represented the WHA; Pollock, Jennings and Bill Wirtz of the Chicago Blackhawks represented the NHL.

The committee worked tirelessly and made a tremendous amount of headway. One of the stumbling blocks was dual-city representation. The main problem was in Chicago where the NHL's Blackhawks and our WHA Cougars played. The NHL wanted only one team in each city, and that was a major problem – our owners in Chicago were successful developers Jordan and Walter Kaiser. They felt that they could get the financing to build a new arena, and with that, could become the dominant team in Chicago. The Wirtz family, which owned the Chicago Blackhawks, insisted that they *were* Chicago, and under no circumstances would they allow a second team in the Windy City. We had no problems with the owners of WHA teams in Boston, Los Angeles, Philadelphia and St. Paul, all of which had both WHA and NHL franchises. The WHA's Boston franchise moved to Hartford, Los Angeles moved to Baltimore, and Philadelphia and Minnesota were willing to join with other ownerships in our league, and those matters were worked out in committee. Only Chicago didn't work out, as Jordan and Walter Kaiser stood up for their position. As both the NHL's and WHA's ownership groups stated that a merger would only happen with a unanimous vote from all the owners in both leagues, we were at an impasse.

The WHA had the Kaisers balking, and the NHL had to contend with Harold Ballard of the Toronto Maple Leafs. From the WHA's inception, old man Ballard never did and probably never would have given us any credibility. Even when he rented his building, Maple Leaf Gardens, to the WHA's Toronto Toros' ownership of John Basset and the Eaton family, he still felt that we were a bush league with bush owners who were not worthy of joining the NHL. Even with the stubbornness of the Kaisers, the Wirtz family, and Harold Ballard, our merger committee felt that we should have separate owner meetings in two different hotels in New York to see if we could hammer out an agreement. Ben Hatskin thought we were wasting our time and said no, but he was quite willing to hold the meeting in the best interests of both leagues.

Credit should be given to our joint merger committee of owners, as they worked night and day to see if something could be worked out. The NHL owners felt that, one way or another, they would get their hardnosed Harold Ballard in line, and we felt we could get the Kaisers to join with some other club in our league and forge ahead. Unfortunately, after two hard days of bargaining, we did not move the Kaisers, and the NHL could not sway Ballard. The result was downright disappointing and, in my mind and others, foolish. The war went on.

Six years later, after millions of dollars were lost by both leagues, the warring factions finally did merge. Much of this success must be credited to Howard Baldwin, our New England owner, who relentlessly pushed for a merger.

One of the first people I became acquainted with in the NHL establishment was Emile Francis. Francis was running the St. Louis Blues and recognized early on that a war between the two leagues was counterproductive. Emile led the charge for a merger with the NHL; however, three teams, the Montreal Canadiens, Boston Bruins and (naturally) Harold Ballard's Maple Leafs stood firmly against it.

The fans in WHA cities, especially in Canada, were furious with the hardliners of the NHL. The Montreal Canadiens, who were owned by the Molson Brewery, became the target of fans in Winnipeg, Quebec and Edmonton, who began a major boycott of Molson. The company suffered financially – a full 63 percent of the beer sold in Western Canada, where the Oilers played, was Molson.

Fans by the thousands switched beers and the boycott had a major impact on Molson throughout Canada. Morgan McCammon, a spokesman for the Montreal Canadiens, reconsidered his opposition to the merger after gunshots were fired at the Molson office on Furby Street. He not only switched his position against the merger, but took a leading position in its favor.

The NHL board of governors asked Commissioner John Zeigler to hold a special meeting in Chicago, and on March 22,

1979, the governors voted 14-3 to unite major league hockey. Montreal voted with the majority and, in retrospect, carried the day for the pro-merger forces. The fans of North America have mostly had little to say in decisions made by the owners and players of major sports, but the WHA/NHL merger can partially be attributed to the fans' pressure to force the issue by their economic boycott of Molson. I have often felt that some of the ridiculous labor battles we see could – and should – be settled by fed-up fans.

WHA President Howard Baldwin had always promoted the idea of going after NHL players, but after seven years of struggle, he believed that team owners in both leagues were getting tired of laying out big money for marginal players. With just six teams in the WHA in 1978, Baldwin felt that a merger made more sense than continuing to fight the NHL. Signing players like Gretzky and Messier had certainly given the WHA credibility and put the league into a better negotiating position with the NHL, but Baldwin believed that the endless battles over players damaged both leagues.

While fighting for survival against the NHL, the WHA had achieved parity among its remaining six teams – Winnipeg, New England, Edmonton, Quebec City, Cincinnati and Birmingham. The league's highly skilled players had proved that emphatically by winning all three games of a series against Moscow Dynamo in 1979. Dynamo was the best team in Russia, and everyone respected their talent and ability.

WHA President Howard Baldwin

Unfortunately for everyone, the recession in North America of the 1970s ruled against building a new arena in Toronto, so John Bassett moved his team to the Deep South – Birmingham, Alabama. During the 1978 WHA summer meetings, the league received some major body blows. Hedberg and Nilsson decided to jump to the New York Rangers (already mentioned), John Tonelli left Houston to join the New York Islanders, and one of the top coaches in the WHA, Harry Neale, left Cincinnati for the Vancouver Canucks.

In my judgment, Baldwin was the leader of the United States' contingent to the WHA. His team won the first Avco Cup Championship and was always strong and competitive. He was a leader who kept the pieces together in times of stress and trouble. Later in the NHL, he served as the managing partner of the Pittsburgh Penguins. As history will show, Baldwin was the only owner to win the WHA's Avco Cup and the NHL's Stanley Cup. Baldwin helped engineer the merger with the NHL and helped keep the mystique of the WHA alive in the NHL.

Throughout the seven years of the WHA's existence, Howard Baldwin was the most vocal WHA team owner pushing for a merger. After Baldwin assumed the presidency of the WHA in 1978, many of the NHL brass started a personal vendetta against him. It was totally unfair, but it was a fact. He became the whipping boy for the WHA and took a lot of heat from the

NHL-controlled media. Baldwin did not become discouraged. He felt that the WHA had changed the sports world and understood the bitterness that some people in the NHL – particularly Harold Ballard – had for the league.

Within the WHA, John Bassett, the owner of the Birmingham Bulls, was a hawk. He did not like "pussy footing" negotiations and reasoned that the WHA should fight back hard, just like the Ballards of the world. He felt that the NHL only understood strength. In retaliation, he began targeting the Canadian junior leagues and signed Ken Linesman, a great teenager from Canada. Bassett reasoned that for survival, the WHA had to sign the world's top juniors, and he wanted to continue to punish the NHL. It was the only way that the WHA would survive, and Bassett's foresight once again came to the forefront. From the juniors, he put together the "Baby Bulls," all potential NHL first-round draft picks. They included stars like goaltender Pat Riggins, defenseman Rob Ramage and forward Michel Goulet. He situated them in the Deep South with his Birmingham Bulls, and they clicked with the southern fans.

After Bassett took the lead, other WHA teams followed suit. Players from the juniors that signed included Danny Geoffrion (Quebec), Mike Gartner (Cincinnati), Jordy Douglas (Hartford), and Dave Hunter and Wes George (Edmonton). However, the Indianapolis Racers made the most important signing. They signed "The Great One," Wayne Gretzky, and future star Mark Messier. Nelson Skalbania, the owner of the

Racers, should always be given credit for this master stroke.

The Aggressive NHL

In 1978, the NHL was becoming very aggressive in breaking up the upstarts from the WHA. For six years, the new league had made some major inroads and gains on the established league. There was a growing feeling by most NHL owners that they should either merge with the opposition or destroy it. The majority of the owners felt that the best way was to work with the WHA on a compromise. Meanwhile, the WHA was being tested to the hilt. To combat the aggressiveness of the NHL, the WHA turned over the leadership to a young and vigorous Howard Baldwin of Hartford. The eight owners still in the battle reasoned that in order to make a better deal on a merger, they needed to stay alive, and at the same time, negotiate. Baldwin was their man.

The NHL also hired a new commissioner, attorney John Zeigler, who was a young, forward-thinking leader. He replaced Clarence Campbell, who had always aligned himself with the hardliners in the league, especially Montreal, Boston and Toronto, and wanted no part of the new league. Harold Ballard of the Toronto Maple Leafs led the hardliners, and he wanted to destroy the WHA. Ballard was a crusty old man who had served time in prison in Canada after being found guilty of defrauding shareholders of Maple Leaf Gardens. His philosophy was to shoot down those ingrates of the WHA and not give them a bloody inch. He called the new WHA president, Howard Baldwin, "a mackerel fisherman from Providence." The fact and truth was that Baldwin was from Cape Cod, Massachusetts. Ballard, most of the time, did not know what state or country he was in, let alone city, but he was tough and obstinate.

Two major problems hit the WHA in 1978. A storm of a century hit the New England states and caused havoc in the Northeastern belt of the U.S. Many buildings toppled in Hartford, and one of the most damaged was the new Hartford Civic Center. It suffered considerable damage to its roof, and games could not be played the arena. The Hartford community, especially the insurance industry, banded together and helped to pledge funds to support the team while the building was being repaired. The club temporarily moved to the Springfield Arena in Springfield, Massachusetts, to finish the season.

The second major disappointment to hit the WHA was the NHL's aggressive fight to recapture some of the players that it had lost to the WHA in the six prior seasons. The NHL was determined to go after many of the star players they had lost to the WHA, and the older league was successful at doing so many times.

The Last WHA Game

In the final game in Winnipeg in 1979, WHA Chief Executive Officer Ben Hatskin presented the final Avco Cup to his beloved Jets. Hatskin, who had signed Bobby Hull to the unprecedented $1 million dollar contract in 1972, mentioned the four WHA teams that would be merging into the NHL the following year: "Quebec won the championship, New England won the championship, Winnipeg won it three times, and it's too bad that there wasn't a cup for Edmonton; they deserved one as well."

Edmonton, with Wayne Gretzky and Glen Sather, won the Stanley Cup four times in their first six seasons in the NHL. That was indeed their reward, and what a fitting one it was. It also proved to the world that the WHA did have great talent, and in the end, did play a major part in hockey history. The leadership of both leagues felt that it was time to walk away with each other and show the way. Both the WHA and the NHL felt that it would be better counsel to learn the lesson than to continue to self-destruct.

The 26th WHA Reunion

The WHA alumni were very fortunate to have Larry King of CNN as the main speaker at our 26-year reunion in 2002. King made a great speech and enjoyed the atmosphere of Windsor, Canada. More than 400 players, coaches, staff, management and coaches appreciated the reunion. Robbie Ftorek won the golf tournament, Bobby Hull and Gordie Howe joined their many friends, and it was an evening that will be remembered by all. The stories flowed like wine and the exploits became more outrageous as the evening moved on. Harry Neale, the famed announcer and former coach of the Minnesota Fighting Saints, was the master of ceremonies.

The Avco Cup

The Stanley Cup has always been the symbol of hockey excellence. The Avco Cup was to the WHA what the Stanley Cup was to the NHL. How the Avco Cup came to be goes back to my youth. I graduated from University High School in Los Angeles, and one of my classmates and a longtime friend, Wally Merryman, just happened to be the chairman of the board of Avco Financial Services. In a conversation at one of our class reunions, I asked Wally if he would entertain the thought of having our championship cup named after his company. He indicated that there might be some interest. I then asked our energetic and capable director of WHA properties, Max Muhleman, to contact Avco and their marketing director. The rest is history, and the "Avco Cup" was born. The Avco Cup brought our league a lot of help, both financially and in credibility. Avco was a great sponsor and they helped develop our league. At the time of their involvement with the league, Avco Financial was doing a large share of their business in Canada. Thus, the league was a perfect fit for their advertising and promotions.

The WHA's leadership always felt that we could play with the big boys of the NHL, but not until 1977 did we actually arrange inter-league competition with the NHL, and we won most of the games. In our first exhibition games with the NHL, the WHA won 13 games, tied two and lost six. Our position then was that the WHA was competitive and thus justified. In the first six years after the merger, the Edmonton Oilers won the Stanley Cup four times. The clubs, which Glen Sather put together, were awesome. They were led by "Mr. 99," Wayne Gretzky. It became obvious to all that the WHA had great talent and was competitive with the NHL in every aspect of the game. Don Regan, our chief lawyer, put the package together with Avco in legal form. It was a great marriage, and we thank Avco for being first class all the time that they were involved.

WHA Awards

Gary L. Davidson / Gordie Howe Trophy for MVP
1979 – Dave Dryden, Edmonton Oilers
1978 – Marc Tardif, Quebec Nordiques
1977 – Robbie Ftorek, Phoenix Roadrunners
1976 – Marc Tardif, Quebec Nordiques
1975 – Bobby Hull, Winnipeg Jets
1974 – Gordie Howe, Houston Aeros
1973 – Bobby Hull, Winnipeg Jets

Bill Hunter Trophy for Regular-Season Scoring Leader
1979 – Réal Cloutier, Quebec Nordiques
1978 – Marc Tardif, Quebec Nordiques
1977 – Réal Cloutier, Quebec Nordiques
1976 – Marc Tardif, Quebec Nordiques
1975 – André Lacroix, San Diego Mariners
1974 – Mike Walton, Minnesota Fighting Saints
1973 – André Lacroix, Philadelphia Blazers

Dennis A. Murphy Trophy for Best Defenseman
1979 – Rick Ley, New England Whalers
1978 – Lars Sjoberg, Winnipeg Jets
1977 – Ron Plumb, Cincinnati Stingers

1976 – Paul Shmyr, Cleveland Crusaders
1975 – J.C. Tremblay, Quebec Nordiques
1974 – Pat Stapleton, Chicago Cougars
1973 – J.C. Tremblay, Quebec Nordiques

Lou Kaplan Trophy for Rookie of the Year
1979 – Wayne Gretzky, Edmonton Oilers
1978 – Kent Nilsson, Winnipeg Jets
1977 – George Lyle, New England Whalers
1976 – Mark Napier, Toronto Toros
1975 – Anders Hedberg, Winnipeg Jets
1974 – Mark Howe, Houston Aeros
1973 – Terry Caffery, New England Whalers

Howard Baldwin Trophy for Coach of the Year
(Renamed Robert Schmertz Memorial Trophy in 1974-75)

1979 – John Brophy, Birmingham Bulls
1978 – Bill Dineen, Houston Aeros
1977 – Bill Dineen, Houston Aeros
1976 – Bobby Kromm, Winnipeg Jets
1975 – Sandy Hucul, Phoenix Roadrunners
1974 – Billy Harris, Toronto Toros
1973 – Jack Kelley, New England Whalers

Paul Deneau Trophy for Most Gentlemanly Player
1979 – Kent Nilsson, Winnipeg Jets
1978 – Dave Keon, New England Whalers
1977 – Dave Keon, New England Whalers
1976 – Vaclav Nedomansky, Toronto Toros
1975 – Mike Rogers, Edmonton Oilers
1974 – Ralph Backstrom, Chicago Cougars
1973 – Ted Hampson, Minnesota Fighting Saints

Ben Hatskin Trophy for Best Goaltender
1979 – Dave Dryden, Edmonton Oilers
1978 – Al Smith, New England Whalers

1977 – Ron Grahame, Houston Aeros
1976 – Michel Dion, Indianapolis Racers
1975 – Ron Grahame, Houston Aeros
1974 – Don McLeod, Houston Aeros
1973 – Gerry Cheevers, Cleveland Crusaders

The Playoff MVP award for the World Hockey Association was handed out annually from 1975 to 1979 to the most valuable player of the playoffs.

WHA Playoff MVP Winners
1975 – Ron Grahame, Houston Aeros
1976 – Ulf Nilsson, Winnipeg Jets
1977 – Serge Bernier, Quebec Nordiques
1978 – Robert Guindon, Winnipeg Jets
1979 – Rich Preston, Winnipeg Jets

Pat Mulcahy & Associates

Have a successful book.
We wish you the very best.

Cynthia and Pat

Dennis, keep on enjoying
our salad bar.
Good luck on your book.

Your friends from the
Fullerton Sizzler

SECTION IV: WTT (1973-1978)

World Team Tennis

"The right people at the right time do make a difference. The right combination is magic. Larry and Billie Jean King were those kinds of people. They made things happen."
– Dennis Murphy

"As life takes its turns, the winners say, 'Can do!' The losers make excuses.' " – Melissa Haarlammert

World Team Tennis played a major role in the explosion of professional tennis in the 1970s. This wonderful game made great strides with the help of people such as Billie Jean King, Virginia Wade, Chris Evert, Margaret Court, Rod Laver, John Newcombe, Roy Emerson and Rosie Casals leading the way. WTT introduced us to colored floors, yellow balls, colorful team uniforms, and was the forerunner of the tie-breaker. The format featured five complete sets of women's and men's singles, men's and women's doubles and mixed doubles. This format figured in the scoring – the team that had the most points was the winner. WTT allowed cheering, clapping and stomping of feet – much different than the reserved protocol of mainstream tennis.
It was novel in every aspect of the game and allowed the fans to be a part of the contest.

The owners in the league were Jerry Buss, Jerry Fine, Bob Kraft, Walter Kaiser, Don Kelleher, Jerry Saperstein, Dick Butera, E.Z. Jones, Joe Zingale and many more. Not only was it a fun league, it was exciting. We were now on a roll. Gary Davidson, Don Regan, Lee Meade and our crew were hotter than a pistol. Everything we touched seemed to take off and turn to solid gold.

My first meeting with Larry King was indeed different. My associate Carl DiPietro, a flamboyant Italian salesman, met Fred Barman, a professional tennis agent, at a Hollywood party. Carl called me from Beverly Hills and said, "Murph, I got a hot tip from Fred Barman, a women's tennis promoter. He said that the Women's Tennis Association is unhappy with its leadership and are looking for someone to take over."

Carl, in his charming Italian style, told Fred about me and my record of achievements. When Carl was finished, it was a "done certain conclusion."

Apparently, the men's association, headed by Stan Smith and Arthur Ashe, was making great strides in improving prize money, sponsorships, endorsements and benefits. These improvements were done under the watchful eye of the Association of Tennis Professionals and ATP co-founders Donald Dell, Jack Kramer and Cliff Drysdale. Dell was an attorney who headed a promotional company headquartered in Washington, D.C., and Kramer and Drysdale were both former professional tennis stars.

Barman told us that the women were receiving a fraction of what the men were making on the tour of tournaments throughout the world, despite the crowds being equal to what the men had been drawing. He felt that his daughter, Shari, was a perfect example. She was a member of the women's tour and was struggling to make ends meet – yet at the time, she was one of the top 16 female players in the world. This position greatly contrasted from the men's.

The Struggle

World Team Tennis was not only a new league, it was a new concept. We were going to have to do a super selling job to get the tennis purists to accept our format, and we needed to have a united front. The new league was only successful because of the support of Billie Jean King. She was the dominant woman player in the world at the time and had the total support of the other top women players on the tour. She was the most recognizable woman in the world and one who was never at a lack of words when it came time to defending her positions. If she felt strongly about something, she let the world know about it, and, in most cases, we agreed with her stance. With Billie Jean's undivided support, the WTT founders took on the tennis establishment.

Fred Barman and Larry King knew the politics of tennis – they understood the pitfalls that stood in the way of creating a team concept. Shari Barman a fine tennis player in her own right, was also a great help in the trenches. She helped spread the word to her fellow players and was an immense help in getting additional support for our concept.

The Start

Women's tennis in 1966 was under the direction and control of Gladys Heldman. She had been the publisher and editor of Tennis World magazine and was highly respected in the tennis community. At the time she was "establishment prone," and didn't want to stir the pot. Billie Jean King, together with Rosie Casals, Ann Haydon Jones and Francoise Durr, decided it was time for women players to get their fair share of the money being paid for tournament play. With attorney Larry King leading the way, they put together a 10-page proposal for Heldman, suggesting that the women organize their own tour. This set up a battle that taxed the tennis establishment to the hilt.

Our company, D.A.M. Professional Sports, was the answer to the Women's Tennis Association's problems. Carl DiPietro told me that we should get in touch with Larry King, a lawyer and the husband of Billie Jean King. I told DiPietro that our plate was full, but I did have a lot of respect for Billie Jean King. She had a reputation of being not only a great tennis player, but also a good businesswoman and strong leader. I thought about it and told DiPietro to pursue a meeting with Larry King. The purpose of the meeting was to make a presentation to the women's association to be their worldwide promotional organization, similar to what Donald Dell was doing with the men's association.

A few weeks later, DiPietro called and said that he had arranged a meeting with Larry King in Oakland. He felt we should "put on the dog" and go to the meeting in real style. He said that he was going to rent a limo and that John Kanel and I should join him at the meeting. He told us to wear our finest and to be on our best behavior. I asked Carl about the cost of the limo and he said, "Three hundred dollars, but it would be an excellent investment."

I agreed with his suggestion. Kanel, DiPietro and I arrived in Oakland where a limo as big as a boat awaited us. We got in and headed for the Tenderloin District of San Francisco. As we approached Larry King's office, I noticed that the area looked shabby and rundown. I was especially concerned when the limo driver stopped in front of a massage parlor with steps on the side, leading to an office upstairs.

"Carl, you've got the wrong address," I cried.

Carl responded, "No, this is it."

As we exited the huge limo, the curious neighborhood kids gathered around to see the boat-sized vehicle. We walked by the massage parlor to the stairs. We looked up, and there was Larry King, wearing shorts and a baseball cap.

I said, "Larry King, I presume?"

"The one and only," he replied.

Up the stairs we went, and into his office. We found King to be a likeable and friendly person with the mind of a genius. He was extremely bright and knowledgeable. This was the beginning of a long, fruitful friendship that has endured for more than 35 years. Larry and I have made a lot of deals and agreements over those 35 years, and most of the time we closed the agreements with just a handshake.

Professional World Team Tennis actually came to fruition as an accident. We prepared graphs, had a business plan, documented our accomplishments and put together our presentation to King. This was the manner in which Carl DiPietro always did his presentations. They were well organized and effective, as they were prepared by our "detail man," John Kanel.

After making our opening statements with King in his "unusual" office in Oakland, we got down to business. He told us that he and Billie Jean were concerned about the women's tour. The concern was not so much about Billie Jean – she was the best female player in the world – but for the rest of the players, especially those in the lower brackets of competitive professional tennis. It wasn't uncommon for one of the top four seeds in women's play to win the tournaments. At the time those players were Margaret Court, Evonne Goolagong, Chris Evert and Billie Jean King. The rest of the field had it tough because the money was so limited.

Larry King felt that the women needed to expand their horizons and develop their own sponsorship bases. King was always a visionary, and, in my opinion, he did more for women's professional tennis than what he was given credit for. He was the person responsible for getting Virginia Slims into women's tennis as the major sponsor. I feel this alone helped turn the corner for women in tennis.

As the discussions proceeded during the meeting, I became more aware than before that our organization didn't fit the needs of the women's player's association. We were not a sponsorship-oriented company. We had never been involved in tennis and its politics. We didn't know the players, and above all, the representations that Larry King was talking about were out of our influence. I correctly figured that our $300 limo expense was ours to eat at this particular time.

As in many discussions, a slip of the tongue brings out new areas of chance and opportunities. King, in passing, stated that many of the players in the association had come from the college ranks where they played in a team format. This slip in the conversation haunted me as Carl, John and I flew back to Los Angeles. I asked myself the question, "If team competition worked at the college level, why won't it work professionally?"

I called King and said, "Larry, our company has decided not to go forward with representing the Women's Tennis Association because we feel we can't do a good job. We think that they need administrators with experience in securing sponsors. We don't fit that bill. We do feel that we have an idea that we can develop into a winner. We could develop a professional team tennis concept featuring teams made up of both men and women. We don't know enough about the structure, so why don't you talk it over with Billie Jean, come up with a format, and get back to us?"

Larry said that the idea sounded interesting to him and that he would get back to me.

Billie Jean King

Billie Jean King is a beautiful person both inside and out. She is blunt and to the point, and never hesitates to tell you her side of any discussion. She has been a champion for the rights of women worldwide and has done more for women athletes than any other person alive. Her tennis career speaks for itself. She has won more professional tournaments than any person on the planet. In the 1970s, she was the most recognizable woman in the world. When we went into airports, restaurants and hotel lobbies, she would be bombarded by autograph seekers. At times, it was downright scary. Her popularity with the public and her peers was immense.

Billie Jean played tennis with a dedication unparalleled in sports. It was a war when she took the court. Her opposition was the enemy – she played to win. She was a masterful psychologist who used that weapon to the hilt. She won many games before taking the court with the things she said and did prior to the contest. She intimidated her opposition with her game face alone.

Larry and Billie Jean talked over the possibility of putting together a professional tennis league. Billie loved the idea. Larry then formulated the rules and the prize-money formula. He added some special ideas, such as fan participation, colored courts, team uniforms and colored tennis balls. He then called me back and said that we should go for putting together a professional team tennis league. He emphasized that we move quickly – and we did.

Early World Team Tennis

Without Billie Jean and Larry King, Team Tennis would not exist today. World Team Tennis was a joy to form and organize. With my partners, Larry King, Fred Barman and Jordan Kaiser, we put the league together in record time. Larry put together the format, I did the organizational work, Barman took over the properties areas, and Jordan Kaiser put up a minimal amount of money. This was perhaps Kaiser's best short-term investment – and he had many, since he was a successful Chicago banker. I attribute the success of assembling the league owners in such a short fashion to the success we had in putting the ABA and WHA together.

The sporting community understands achievement, so getting groups of potential owners to Miami for our organizational meetings was a piece of cake. We had 32 groups present in Miami, representing 29 cities, including the Pittsburgh people who were trying to start their own league and weren't having much success. We merged with them and gave them a franchise. We reasoned that it would be easier having them join us than to have them out there doing a lot of damage and adding confusion.

The Initial Meeting in Miami

After my first meeting with Larry King, I called one of the WHA team owners, Jordan Kaiser of Chicago, and asked him to join King, Fred Barham and me in forming World Team Tennis. Kaiser was a highly successful Chicago developer who was an avid tennis player and fan. I thought that he would consider being a partner because of his love for the sport. I was right. It took him just 10 seconds to say yes and become part of the venture. In retrospect, we could have asked many others and they would all have said yes, because our organization was a hot ticket. The four of us met in Miami, where we moved World Team Tennis forward.

Having lived in Miami for five years during my ABA days, I was very familiar with the area. There was a very popular resort known as the Jockey Club which was located in the Keystone Point area. It was a hangout for many of the South Florida elite and rich, as well as serving as a watering hole for the Eastern establishment. I often wondered about the origin of its name since it wasn't located near a race track such as Hialeah Gulf Park or Calder. The Jockey Club was a private club that accommodated some of the most famous and beautiful people in the world. Despite the club's name, I never saw a jockey there, although I often ran across Don Shula on many visits. Most visitors only came to Florida during the beautiful winter season and stayed away during the hot, muggy summers. Because of this, I knew the resort could not be booked in the winter, but summer looked wide open.

Immediately, we put the gears into motion. We put together a beautiful brochure, which included the prize money formula. We got on the phone and called people. Our thoughts were to shoot for 12 cities in the inaugural year – it turned out to be a bonanza. Because of our track record of putting together successful leagues, groups from all over North America contacted us.

This was so different than the usual "Murphy Formula," in which we came into a major city and first visited the Chamber of Commerce directors, the mayor and top corporate leaders of the community. We then would have to talk to major-eight accounting executives, college and professional sports executives, while at the same time, contact the local media, sports editors and announcers. We would leave those cities with perhaps two or three qualified potential buyers. In contrast, Team Tennis was a snap. After our initial national press conference, the phones literally rang off the walls, unlike in past years where it seemingly took years to get owner groups involved. With the WTT, it was completed in weeks. We actually had 36 groups at our organizational meeting in Florida.

Part of our success was because of the popularity of tennis throughout the world at that time. Clubs and tennis courts surfaced everywhere. Tennis was in its "Golden Era," with such strong professional tennis personalities as Billie Jean King, Chris Evert, Evonne Goolagong, Rosie Casals, Margaret Wade and

Margaret Court on the women's end, and John Newcombe, Rod Laver, Arthur Ashe, Stan Smith and Ilie Nastase representing the men. Kids were joining tennis organizations all over the place. Women were playing socially. It was so hot that promoters couldn't keep up with the demand for new tennis facilities. Everyone was talking about the sport – our timing couldn't have been more fortuitous.

As with everything worthwhile, there is competition. We were no different – it started at our very first organizational meeting. We decided that we would only give out 18 franchises, but we had 36 groups attend our meeting at the Jockey Club. As was our policy, we interviewed each group individually. By using this method we got to know the people. We weren't necessarily looking for just financially strong people; we were also looking for quality people who would blend well with their teams and fellow owners.

In our other leagues, we had many personality conflicts. Because World Team Tennis was a seller's market, we were in the driver's seat this time, which made our strategy feasible. Because we were meeting with each group individually on a time schedule, we had to make changes in this approach.

Some of the promoters sitting at the watering hole wondered out loud, "What do we need these guys for, let's organize our own league."

Normally I wouldn't have put stock in those threats, but in our meeting we had potential owners who were familiar with professional football, basketball and hockey. In fact, they *were* capable of doing it on their own. One of these groups was led by my Shanghai friend, Bill Putnam, who was the owner of the Atlanta Flames at the Omni Arena. The stinker actually had a league put together during the waiting period. We did a lot of maneuvering to prevent him from putting together a competing league. Never again will I have an "open investors" meeting without some constraints. We just about had our clocks cleaned before we even started.

On June 1-2, 1973, the WTT owners held the first structural meeting in Palm Springs. It was held at Jerry Buss' lodge. I was elected as the league's first president. Jordan Kaiser was selected as vice president, Larry King was chosen as chief administrator and George McCall became the league's first commissioner. At that meeting we set up bylaws, rules, regulations and a format for competition and play. We decided to conduct our first draft in New York City in August of the same year.

The owners determined that it was essential for each team to have identification of stars. The owners' goal was to go after the big names of tennis. In order to help make this a reality, we hired noted agent Steve Arnold of New York to become director of player recruitment. His job was to sign the players by using the argument of better working conditions, a lucrative pension program for players and a firm period of three months that the player could be based in one location, rather than traveling the globe. The players would have a steady paycheck, with incentives for medical insurance and paid road-trip expenses. In addition, by winning on a team basis, the players would not have to rely on individual accomplishments to garner a paycheck. Many of these provisions appealed to the prospective players.

For younger players working their way up the ladder, our concept was to have older players like Ken Rosewall, Tony Roach, Billie Jean King, John Alexander, Marty Riessen and Rod Laver as player-coaches who brought years of experience to the teams. The younger players were thrilled to have the stars help them to develop their skills.

Arnold moved forward to do his job. With this game plan, strong ownership and a dedication to get the job done, Arnold arrived in London during the Wimbledon week. Upon arriving, he discovered that Jack Kramer had gathered his troops in the ATP for a confrontation with this "group of rich crazies" from North America that was trying to change the traditional, long-time heritage of tennis. He built his case strongly and had most of the establishment of the tennis world in his corner.

George McCall, Fred Barman, Larry King, Jordan Kaiser, Billie Jean King and I arrived in London unaware of how the political world of tennis was going to treat us. Larry King felt that we had put together a strong package featuring our Team Tennis format. Larry felt that he would cover the prize money area, with the player's concerns foremost as their equations. He also felt that the women would jump at the program but because of the big money now in place for tournament play, especially for the men and top stars, that resistance against us could be quite strong.

The men were divided into two strong camps. The Americans were entrenched in the favor of the ATP. Not only were they opposed to WTT, they in fact, were hostile. They treated our delegation as if we had the plague. We were making little progress in their ranks. It was obvious that Jack Kramer and Donald Dell ran a tight ship in their organization and they wanted nothing to do with WTT. Kramer was especially upset when he heard that George McCall, another Davis Cup captain, had accepted the position of commissioner of our new league and was a strong promoter of the WTT concept.

Each year at Wimbledon, the tennis world congregates to put together its schedule of tournaments, evaluate its politics, establish new sponsors, formulate new rules and have fun meetings with its peers. It is the premier tennis tournament of the year, much the same magnitude as the World Series or the Super Bowl. Wimbledon is festive, gracious and rich with tradition. Strawberries and cream are plentiful everywhere and the tennis purists were supreme and in control.

After moving around and talking with tennis world shakers, George McCall informed us that we were in for a tough battle. He suggested that we may want to step back and make another charge when the atmosphere was not so charged up against us. Billie Jean King, the consummate fighter, answered with a resounding "No." She wanted to battle them now. Larry King agreed with Billie Jean and decided to go for the whole ball of wax. Larry King felt that in order to get our World Team Tennis program quickly approved by the players, we had to make a strong presence at Wimbledon.

This tournament is the championship of the tennis world. All the top tennis stars point to winning Wimbledon – the jewel of all tournaments held each year. Larry and Billie Jean King, Jordan Kaiser, Fred Barman and I set up our meetings, presentations and discussions with most of the important shakers in the tennis world prior to Wimbledon. We met in London with Arthur Ashe, John Newcombe, Ille Nastase and Stan Smith of the ATP. We found out early that we had our work cut out for us to get their support for our project.

The Pilić Affair

The expected confrontation between Kramer and the tennis establishment against the upstart WTT did not occur. Instead, the "Pilić" affair took center stage in Wimbledon in the summer of 1973 and pushed the expected dogfight into the background. This was a great break for those of us who wanted the WTT to become a reality and to have a place in the tennis structure.

Niki Pilić was a member of the Yugoslavian Davis Cup team. He was suspended by the Yugoslav Tennis Federation for three months when he refused to play in a Davis Cup competition. He appealed the ruling to the International Lawn Tennis Federation (ILTF) with the support of Jack Kramer and Don Dell. This set up a major war between the ATP and the ILTF. The ILTF tried to smooth the waters by reducing Pilić's suspension to one month. However, Kramer said the ATP would have nothing of it. Their reasoning was that the Federation had no authority over the players.

Because of the initial division on the Pilić suspension, the WTT contingent was able to make inroads, especially with the Australian players who resented Jack Kramer's and Don Dell's power grab. The Australians felt that Don Dell and Jack Kramer were attempting to destroy the pro federation. John Newcombe and Rod Laver, along with Ilie Nastase, were in our corner. They reasoned that all types of tennis could only help. They felt that Team Tennis would help some of the emerging stars by giving them a financial base to support their needs while moving up the tennis tournament scale.

The Pilić affair showed the sports world that the tennis establishment was torn within. Arthur Ashe and Stan Smith, the two top leaders of the ATP, were totally opposed to bringing in a new concept, especially into the fast-growing tennis explosion. They felt that all the efforts of the tennis community should be centered on building the tournament structure. Team Tennis would only confuse the issue. Great players such as John Newcombe, Rod Laver, Ken Rosewall and Tony Roach didn't appreciate the high handedness of Kramer and Dell and wanted nothing to do with the ATP. They became very receptive to the WTT pitch. Laver, Rosewall and Roach were in the twilight years of their outstanding careers. Because of this, a steady paycheck and benefits appealed to them. John Newcombe, who was competing for the No.1 men's ranking in the world, was a different story. In his case, he was offered $75,000 to play for Houston. It gave him the opportunity to take a break from the rigors of tournament play, as well as giving him a home for three months. He loved the team concept and became the first "big name" to sign with our fledgling league. The first season was going to be played.

Jack Kramer was furious after the Newcombe signing. He called a meeting of the ATP membership to boot Newcombe out of the organization. He failed, as most of the players reasoned that the purpose of the ATP was to protect the players, rather than to do away with their options. After his rebuke, Kramer became more conciliatory to the WTT. He even offered to help if WTT changed their playing time to October, November and December. Team Tennis didn't change its time slot, playing from May through August, beginning with the completion of Wimbledon. The reasoning was that at that time, baseball was the only other major sport performing. Since baseball played 162 games per season, tennis would break up the monopoly and would have a good opportunity to succeed.

Team Tennis had a great first season despite having to fight off the Kramer-Dell combination. In early February, 1974, the league, with Larry King's connection in the television industry, was able to announce to the world that a mixed doubles tournament was to be held in Dallas. It would be sponsored by the WTT and would be broadcast on national television.

Dell and Kramer quickly threatened to bar ATP players from competing. The WTT legal department, headed by Tim Grandi of the firm of Davidson and Regan, moved into action. Larry King stated that the actions of Kramer and Dell were a case of anti-trust and that the WTT was prepared to go to war over the issue. Lamar Hunt, who was the chief architect and president of World Championship Tennis, took note of the ATP threat and joined forces with the WTT to fight the dominance of the Kramer-Dell axis. The players in the WTT also took notice of the arrogance of the duo and rebelled. They voted to allow its membership to assume a position of neutrality.

This was a huge victory for the success of Team Tennis. Even the elected president of ATP, Cliff Drysdale, signed with the Florida franchise of the new league. At that moment, World Team Tennis had made its mark.

Moving on to the WHA

In November, 1973, I was offered the job as president and commissioner of the World Hockey Association. Because of my great love for hockey, I resigned as president of World Team Tennis. It was a very difficult decision because I was so close to Larry King, Billie Jean King, George McCall and others in the tennis establishment. I also was very fond of their ethics, decency and dedication. It was a tough battle getting to where we were in WTT, but I saw the future as being very bright. Jordan Kaiser assumed my position as president and Larry King became the real force behind the scenes. I knew that WTT was in good hands with King and Kaiser. I did maintain a small piece of the Los Angeles Strings as I moved on in my career.

World Team Tennis was one of my most pleasant experiences. I respected Billie Jean King, George McCall and others in the tennis establishment. I was also very fond of the tennis players' ethics, decency and dedication. It was a tough battle getting to where we were in WTT, and I saw the future as being very, very bright.

Team Tennis is in business today, headquartered in Chicago, Illinois, and New York City. It is a great concept and it helps the young players immensely.

Regency Outdoor Sign Company

Best wishes
my USC Trojan friend,
Dennis Murphy.
Good luck on your book.

Brian Kennedy, President

8820 Sunset Blvd., 2nd Floor
Los Angeles, CA 90069
(310) 657-8883

SECTION V: THE HALLS OF FAME

"You have the ability to attain whatever you seek. Within you is every potential you can imagine. Always aim higher than you believe you can reach." – Dale Brown

Lifetime Achievement Award

In 1994, I was selected to the Orange County Sports Hall of Fame and given a "Lifetime Achievement" award for my accomplishments as an organizer of sports leagues. It was a great honor, and I consider myself very privileged to have been inducted, as I'm with great company – Tommy Lasorda, Gene Autry and Bill Thompson received the same honor. This award was especially gratifying as the sports writers of Orange County made the selection.

The award I received is in a place of distinction in my home and I do appreciate it. I have also been blessed being nominated to both the basketball and hockey halls of fame. In hockey, the great hockey player, Gordie "Mr. Hockey" Howe did me the honor to nominate me, and Jerry Saperstein did the same in basketball. To me, just to be nominated is an honor I will always cherish. We all respect the accomplishment of achievement. I am no different, and I thank God He bestowed the honors He has given me.

Nomination Form by Gordie Howe

United States Hockey Hall of Fame Selection Committee Nomination Form: 1. Nominee's Full Name: Dennis Arthur Murphy 2. Place/Date of Birth: Shanghai/China, September 3, 1925 3. U. S. Citizen and and both parents U.S. citizens. – Nominated by: Colleen and Gordie Howe, Mr. & Mrs. Hockey 4. Hockey Category: Administrator: 6. Dennis Murphy of Anaheim, California is the father and founder of the World Hockey Association known around the sports world as the WHA. In addition, at various times he served as commissioner and President of the revolutionary league. The WHA broadened the overall scope of hockey in the U.S. and Canada and had an everlasting impact on hockey and the entire sports industry.

When one looks at the great names that have helped shape the course of American sports history luminaries such as Pete Rozelle, Roone Arledge, George Halas, Judge Mountain Landis, Bill Veeck, and Walter O'Malley are instantly recognized and revered for their pioneering contributions. All are true originals and giants for changing the course of sports history on the highest level. One humble gentleman, though, who is not so widely known or so universally recognized is Dennis Arthur Murphy. Nevertheless, his impact on sports is huge!

What Dennis did was probably have as much impact on sports as a total and especially hockey than any of the aforementioned immortals. Dennis is the founder of the American Basketball Association (ABA), a league that ultimately merged with the NBA. It is quite a revolutionary accomplishment to be the

founding father of one major sports league that
totally and drastically alters the nature of that
particular sport, but it is even more remarkable
that Dennis was able to pioneer a whole new league,
in a whole new sport, the WHA of the World Hockey
Association.

Founded in 1972 with lawyer Gary Davidson, Dennis
Murphy dreamed of, conceived of, and relentlessly
pursued developing a new hockey entity that would
not only revolutionize hockey history but also have
a dramatic impact on the sports world in general.
For over six decades the National Hockey League had
enjoyed a monopoly on major league hockey and Murphy
decided to embark on an ambitious expansion program
unrivaled in the annals of professional sports. The
task seemed overwhelming. How could this diminutive,
energetic Irishman with little money and little
support but with great passion who concocted the wild
scheme of launching a new major hockey league go
head to head with the NHL and make it work?

Murphy and Davidson were laughed at. The naysay-
ers said it would never work. Doubters universally
far outnumbered the few believers. Others with
passion and enthusiasm had tried before and failed.
Nevertheless, players like Mark Messier, Mike
Gartner and other up and coming greats also saw their
careers launched by the WHA. In fact, the WHA was
the league that challenged and didn't accept the
NHL's underage rule that prohibited players under
age 20 from joining a pro team. The WHA allowed
underage players including the Howe boys, Gretzky,
etc., to begin their pro careers earlier, and the

rest, as they say, is history. Ultimately, the NHL would abolish the underage rule. Furthermore, retired legends such as Maurice Richard, Jacques Plante, Marcel Pronovost and others were also active in coaching in the WHA.

The league began play in Miami in 1972 fielding 12 teams. Many teams were new to various U.S. cities and this helped to foster additional growth and hockey excitement in these uncharted areas. During the leagues stint new teams found homes in the following U.S. locations: Denver, Cincinnati, Chicago, Birmingham, Houston, Indianapolis, Los Angeles, Michigan, St. Paul, New England, New Jersey, Miami, San Diego, Phoenix: Hundreds and hundreds of people secured new positions with the new league. New coaches, referees, trainers, broadcasters, administrators, and all those involved running a successful hockey operation at a major league level were impacted. Thousands and thousands of new fans were able to witness the world's most exciting sport.

Furthermore, fans were able to witness the extended careers of hockey's all-time leading scorers Howe and Hull and see the emergence of hockey's all-time future scoring king Wayne Gretzky.

Consider some of the extraordinary contributions of Dennis Murphy and the WHA.

- The abolishment of the NHL's reserve clause, which bound a player to a team for life. Players were now given freedom and autonomy.
- Issuance of hockey's first multi-million dollar player contract with the signing of Bobby Hull led to a migration of other NHL

stars joining the new league. There were 68 in the first year alone. The WHA attracted Gordie "Mr. Hockey" Howe, and his two sons, Marty and Mark, the first father-and-son tandem to play a pro sport together.

- First family contract. Gordie's all-time dream fulfilled.

- Entered new U .S. and Canadian markets where major league hockey was not being played. This new exposure greatly elevated hockey interest in the U.S. and helped to build and expose hockey to legions of new fans.

- Pioneered having a 10-minute overtime period when the game ended in a tie.

- Increased player salaries nearly fourfold. Sent hockey in the same direction with regard to pay scale as football, baseball, and basketball.

- During matches between WHA teams and NHL teams, the WHA squads won 33 games to 27. When four teams of the WHA merged with the NHL, four of the leading top ten scorers were from the WHA that first year.

Although the WHA expired nearly two decades ago, its influence on the NHL and hockey remains profound both fiscally and culturally. Not only did the WHA offer new avenues for American skaters, but also innovated the European Collection, importing talent from Sweden, Finland and Czechoslovakia. In its first year achieved major league status alongside the 56-year-old NHL. Wayne Gretzky, "The Great One," says, "I don't know where my career would have gone

if I hadn't gone to the WHA. I'd have been in junior
(hockey). I could have been hurt. I could have gotten messed up or gone to the NHL in a bad situation.
I'm very grateful the WHA was around and that I
became a part of it."

Mr. Hockey, Gordie Howe says, "Playing with sons
Mark and Marty was my all-time dream fulfilled.
Colleen and I will forever appreciate that Dennis
Murphy and the WHA allowed the Howe family to live
an incredible dream. We played together for seven
seasons and they were truly among the happiest
times of my life."

Dennis has been married to his wife Elaine for 50
years. He is a former WWII veteran and former Korean
War veteran. They have three children. Although so
many others have claimed the spotlight in sports and
touted their accomplishments, Dennis has remained
humble and has let others take the limelight.
Nevertheless, this dynamo is truly a legend in hockey.
His dreaming, vision, innovation, and perseverance
dramatically altered not only U.S. hockey history
but also sports history the world over. He is a
passionate and kind man. He is quick to thank God for
all his blessings and share his success with others.
Recently Dennis suffered a stroke, but is recovering
very nicely in California.

United States Hockey Hall of Fame.
Thank you… and Howe!

Colleen Howe, Mrs. Hockey
Gordon Howe, Mr. Hockey

Letter from Jerry Saperstein

June 21, 2001

Mr. Dennis Murphy
1037 East Dorothy Lane
Fullerton, California

Dear Dennis:

I am now a member the Nominating Committee for the
Basketball Hall of Fame. My first nomination will
be: Dennis Arthur Murphy as founder of the American
Basketball Association and one of the creators of
modern professional basketball in the United States.
I have asked John Kanel to give me as much printed
informational materials as possible (newspaper stories, printed brochures, etc.) and I will submit
that information in support of your nomination. I
intend to discuss your nomination with David Stern
and Jerry Colangelo of the National Basketball Association and I am sure that they will support your
nomination. This is an honor long delayed and much
deserved; you are a legendary figure in American
professional sports and you deserve the recognition.
Love to Elaine.

Sincerely,

Jerry Saperstein

SECTION VI: PHOTOGRAPHS

The Early Years

(Left) My mother, my brother John, and my father. (Right) Elaine and me in our younger years and happier days.

(Left) I served Uncle Sam proudly, in WWII and the Korean War. (Right) Mayor Dennis Murphy and Councilman Paul Wishek discuss important city business in Buena Park, California.

(Left) ABA Commissioner George Mikan. (Right) Cheerleaders in skimpy outfits attracted fans.

(Left) The ABA's first president, Gary Davidson. (Right) Sharpshooting ABA forward Rick Barry.

(Left) Dr J. dunks the ball. (Right) Mack Calvin on the dribble.

Wilt Chamberlain had planned to play for the San Diego Conquistadors, but a lawsuit filed by the L.A. Lakers forced him into a coaching role only.

(Left) Bill Sharman coached the Los Angeles Stars and the Los Angeles Lakers. (Right) We celebrate the commemoration of the Lakers' memorable 33-game win streak, which took place in 1971-72.

(Left) Lee Meade of the Denver Post did wonders for our ABA publicity department. (Right) Bill Ringsby, owner of the Denver Rockets.

(Left) Pat Boone, gospel singer, author, and owner of the Oakland Oaks. (Right) Dr. Tom Carney, president of the Miami Floridians.

(Left) Coach Bob Bass and player Larry Jones of the Miami Floridians.
(Right) A Miami owner, Sandy Rywell, shows the red, white and blue
ball to Miami resident Archie Stone.

In my younger years.

(Left) Jerry Saperstein and I have been friends for many years. (Right) My
friend Lenny Bloom owned the San Diego Conquistadors of the ABA.

The World Hockey Association

Gordie Howe accepts an award from me in the WHA.

Bobby Hull and his $1 million signing bonus check.

"Wild" Bill Hunter, the former owner of the Edmonton Oilers (left), poses with "The Great One,"Wayne Gretzky.

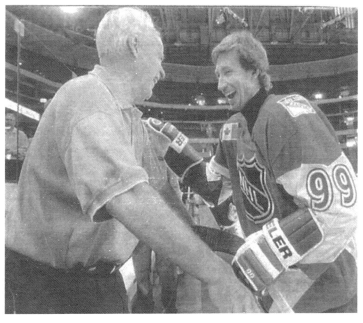

Two legends of hockey – Gordie Howe and Wayne Gretzky.

THEY'VE STRUCK OIl
Edmonton's success pleases founders of the WH

(Left) Gary Davidson, the first president of the WHA. (Right) Jack Stanfield, a great player, later became the GM of the Houston Aeros.
.

Captain Ted McCaskill of the Los Angeles Sharks with baseball star and son, Kirk McCaskill.

The Los Angeles Sharks would have loved to have signed
Bobby Hull. We sure tried!

(Left) Howard Baldwin owned the WHA's New
England Whalers and became league president in
1976. (Right) Don Regan, an attorney, worked on
several of our leagues.

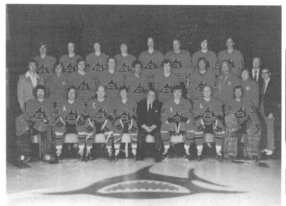

(Left) The Los Angeles Sharks of the WHA. (Right) The great Bernie Parent.

**Ralph Backstrom played for the Chicago Cougars
of the WHA. He later became commissioner of RHI.**

DREAM COME TRUE---Gordie Howe had done it all...except play
professional hockey with his boys Mark and Marty.
The WHA allowed him to do so.

**(Left) Gordie Howe lived his dream of playing pro hockey with
his sons Mark and Marty. (Left) Jack Stanfield and the old man.**

World Team Tennis

(Left) WTT brass: Elaine (third from left), me, Billie Jean King, John Kanel and others. (Right) Dr. Jerry Buss was involved in World Team Tennis before becoming the owner of the NBA's Los Angeles Lakers.

(Left) Larry King and (right) Billie Jean King were both integral to the success of World Team Tennis.

Bjorn Borg (left) and Don Newcombe were also big-name WTT stars.

The victorious Denver Racquets. (Left to right) Francoise Durr,
Jeff Austin, Pam Austin, Tony Roche, Kristen Shaw, Andrew
Pattison and Stephanie Johnson. Ms. Durr's dog Topspin is the
team mascot.

Roller Hockey International

Mark Brown of Roller Hockey Magazine (left) presents the RHI 1993 Playoff MVP trophy to Anaheim Bullfrogs' star Bob McKillop (center) as Robert Dean (right) looks on.

(Left) Jeanie Buss, owner of the Los Angeles Blades.
(Right) David McLane presents me with a USC football helmet.

Larry King, Patrick Mulcahy, me, and CBS' Steve Gigliotti and Jim Hill. Gigliotti, Hill and CBS helped RHI get off the ground by televising our first exhibition event at L.A.'s Great Western Forum.

(Left) Richard Neil Graham always asked me the tough questions at RHI press conferences. I'll get even with him. (Right) Manon Rheaume was the roller hockey league's standout lady goaltender.

Family

A recent family portrait with my son and daughters.

.

(Left) Elaine and I celebrate our 50th wedding anniversary. (Right) Our eight grandchildren: Melissa, Debbie, Mindy, Denise, Sean, Michelle, Danielle and Dina.

My son, Denny, whom I love so, and me at the Orange County Sports Hall of Fame ceremony. He made my introduction very special and I was honored he did so.

(Left) My daughter Dawn and her husband David Mee. (Right) My daughter Doreen and her husband Guy Haarlammert.

(Left) Denny Jr. and his wife Nanci in Hawaii. (Right) My great-grandchildren: Allie and Jake Sexton, Heidi and Taylor Doralde.

Movers & Shakers

(Left) CNN's Larry King and the old man. (Right) Me and
Jeff Buma, a longtime friend and fellow sports promoter.

Elliott Haimoff, me and Sam Oldham. Elliott produced the documentary
on my life in sports, and Sam is his cameraman.

Joe DiMaggio (second from left), Frank Mahovlich (fourth from left) and hockey and baseball friends. John Kanel, my friend and right-hand man, is on the far right.

Randy Friend (second from right), with his wife and parents in this photo, helped to produce the documentary on my life in sports.

SECTION VII: RHI (1992-1999)

ROLLER HOCKEY INTERNATIONAL

"The difference between a realist and a dreamer
is that a realist sees the chance for failure and the
dreamer sees the chance for success." – Author unknown

A Complete Surprise

Roller Hockey International began as a complete surprise. Larry King called me from Kauai, Hawaii, and asked if I would be willing to help WTT commissioner Billie Jean King develop a new international division of Team Tennis.

"I'm getting to be 65 years old," I told Larry King. "I'm ready for Medicare; and I'm tired. But, for you and Billie Jean, I will look into it."

Despite their divorce, the Kings have maintained a cordial relationship. He has since remarried to one of the jewels of the world, his beloved, Nancy. I say that because, not only is she a beautiful woman, but she is a warm and decent human being who is a wonderful wife and good mother to their two children, Sky and Katie.

After Larry flew in from Hawaii, we talked for hours about the possibility of putting an international Team Tennis division together. I sensed from Larry that Team Tennis was on a "downer" and that most of the charismatic stars of the past were fading away. This venture looked as though it might be a tough sell.

On my return from the airport in my car, I remember being delayed on a side street. I saw some kids playing roller hockey and said, 'That's what we ought to be doing." I thought it was a sport that could become a professional league. When I told my brother John what I had seen, he informed me that inline skating was a hot ticket item – people everywhere of all ages and sizes were playing roller hockey in parks and playgrounds. This appealed to me. Imagine hockey being played on concrete rather than ice. Imagine being able to play hockey anywhere in the world, rather than being limited to the ice arenas. Wow! What a way to finish up my life, working to develop a new sport. I was off to the races. I called Larry King to tell him that I wasn't going to do Team Tennis, and I invited him to join me in developing roller hockey at a professional level.

Roller Hockey International was a great challenge. During my long career, RHI was the easiest league to put together and the most difficult to keep together. To begin with, inline roller hockey was a new sport. Though roller hockey has been played for decades, it was always played with a ball and a short stick. The skates were of the four-wheel variety. This brand of hockey is especially popular in Spain and Portugal, Juan Antonio Samaranch, the president of the International Olympic Committee, played the game and was very proficient at it. Needless to say, in that part of the world, it's "roller hockey" period.

When Larry King, Alex Bellehumeur, Ralph Backstrom and I decided to form inline roller hockey as a professional league, people said we would never get it off the ground. They maintained that the purists of the game would never allow our version of the game to succeed.

We were missing one thing – a high-profile hockey man. We convinced my longtime friend, Ralph Backstrom, to join the team. Ralph was the natural person to be commissioner of the league. He had a full and distinguished hockey career, playing 13 years for the Montreal Canadiens. He wears six Stanley Cup rings to prove it.

Ralph also played four years in the WHA and was voted Most Valuable Player of the second Canadian-Russian series, which featured WHA players against the Russians. Ralph's credentials also included a six-year coaching stint at Denver University. Aside from his impressive hockey credentials, more importantly, Ralph is one of the most honorable and decent people on this earth. He is "Mr. Integrity" and a man that all of us can be proud to have been associated with. It was left up to Ralph and me to put the rules of professional roller hockey into place.

To help us with this important task, we visited amateur leagues throughout North America to see how their games were played. Paul Chapey, a dedicated and hard-working roller hockey purist, was the first person we spent time with. Paul is considered, and rightfully so, the American who had the most to do with making amateur roller hockey work. He is the catalyst who has been essential in the sport moving forward. If there ever is a Roller Hockey Hall of Fame, Paul is a shoe-in to be in it because of his efforts of cultivating the popular sport.

Paul and his attorney partner, John Black, gave us a great deal of pointers and ideas for our new professional league. I suspect that at the time that we visited them, they gave us two chances to be successful – slim and none. Nevertheless, they were extremely helpful with their advice and consultation. Ralph and I were looking at developing the league through the eyes of the "paying sports spectator." We knew that we had to incorporate excitement, skilled hockey play and new rules into the sport.

Our first move was to create the hockey puck in place of a rubber ball. We also decided to use hockey sticks rather than the traditional short hockey sticks being used in Europe. We encountered problems with hockey purists who believed the sport should be played wearing traditional "quad" skates, whose wheels were configured like a car's wheels. We were convinced that inline skates, with their wheels all in a line, were the future. I had to utilize my best political skills to get over that hurdle.

I pushed the inline skates at: our tryout camps while allowing the quad skates to be used. I remember our tryout director, Anno Willison, saying in desperation, "I can't wait until we decide to use the inline skates for our league – these quad skaters are driving me up the wall."

Another big issue was the puck and what style it should follow. Alex Bellehumeur, one of the original founders, was given the task of putting the puck into place for our league. Over the years, Alex had been tinkering with new inventive ideas and considered himself to be an inventor of new products. Along with Anno Willison, Matt Dovin and my son-in-law, Guy Haarlammert, they spent hours looking at existing hockey pucks and then coming up with their own version.

From Up to Down

I have always reasoned that there were only two ways to develop a new professional league – start from the bottom up by building a strong youth program – or develop the product and professionalism and move down. It was a "no-brainer" as to which way we needed to go. We had to gamble and go from "up to down."

Roller hockey was played by a lot of people in the United States and around the world, but there were lots of factions, and amateur organizations were very protective of their sport. Roller hockey, at the time, was a well-kept secret. With my experience in putting leagues together, I was confident this would work.

I had worked with Alex Bellehumeur, a Long Beach businessman, for 10 years on various political and sports programs. We had shared an office and he was my boss in his International Football League project. Alex is a decent person. He is stubborn, but I found him to be very creative, as well as being a very hard worker. He had a small office in his business complex which he let me use while we worked on the football project.

I was always able to talk freely with Alex. He was always blunt and to the point, but was also constructive. When I brought up the idea of inline roller hockey, he liked it and wanted in. He said he would allow me the use of his office space and provide us with secretarial help and the use of the telephones. This sounded great to me. The team of Murphy, Bellehumeur and King was on its way.

Alex and I had a corporation already in existence, so we converted WSML, Inc., into the RHI program, retaining 51 percent of the new entity.

The Initial RHI Tour

Roller Hockey International's founders felt that we should kick off the league with a tour. The tour started at the Great Western Forum in Los Angeles. It then moved on to Phoenix, Arizona, where Jerry and Brian Colangelo hosted the event. The tour then went to Vancouver, British Columbia's Pacific National Exhibition Agrodome, where Mike King and Tiger Williams hosted the affair. The crowds on the tour were respectable and the games were accepted by the fans, players and the media. Former NHL coach Chuck Catto led Team Canada and John Black coached Team USA. The games were exciting and competitive. All three games were televised and the response from the public was excellent. Patrick Mulcahy handled the event's marketing. At the conclusion of the tour, we knew that we had a winner.

Roller hockey was a new sport with a fantastic future, and we felt at the time that it was one of the only new sports with a chance to become a successful international sport. Baseball and American football will always be tops in the United States, but their potential to grow internationally is limited. Soccer will always be the most popular sport worldwide; it's a simple game and everyone plays it. Basketball has emerged as an international sport – and someday could rival the popularity of soccer. Ice hockey is limited to cold-weather regions because of its dependency on a limited amount of ice rinks. Roller hockey can be played everywhere, in all temperatures, by athletes of varying sizes. Roller hockey was the fastest growing sport worldwide and its future seemed unlimited.

Larry King, Alex Bellehumeur, Ralph Backstrom and I saw the opportunity for a successful professional roller hockey league, and we jumped on it. We took a calculated chance of succeeding by starting at the top and working down. Usually, it's the other way around – starting with the youth programs, and then after years of development, a professional league will thrive. We started RHI with the hope that once the public is exposed to the sport, especially kids, the league would immediately take off. We were right.

Roller Hockey International would never have made it in the beginning without the financial help of the Bauer company. Their president, Phil Chiarella, and his marketing director Peter Davis, were instrumental in getting us off the ground. The money helped us pay the legal cost of the organization, travel, tryout camps, and limited personal and secretarial help. They indeed helped us, and we founders appreciated their help.

Dennis Murphy – In a League of His Own

by Nancy King, RHI Media Director, 1994

This summer, "A League of Their Own" was one of the biggest box-office hits of the year. If just one league can justify the making of a movie, then you would have to have an entire series of films to document the formation of all the leagues that Dennis Murphy has started.

"A League of Their Own" had an impressive cast of stars, including Tom Hanks, Madonna and Geena Davis. The stars of Dennis Murphy's new leagues have been legends in sports – Rick Barry, Julius Erving, Bobby Hull, Billie Jean King, Jimmy Connors, Gordie Howe and Wayne Gretzky. Murphy has always had the unique ability to take an established product like pro basketball, pro hockey or pro tennis and make it more enjoyable to the fans while offering more players the opportunity to compete and display their skills.

But these leagues have done more than offer jobs to players. They also created positions for executives, coaches, peanut vendors, parking lot attendants and many more. A graduate of USC, Murphy's first notable league formation was the American Basketball Association, with its multicolored red, white and blue basketball, along with an impressive roster of top players. As founder of the ABA, Murphy signed Rick Barry and later convinced Julius Erving, Dr. J, to join the league. Many of the

ABA teams exist today in the NBA and are worth millions of dollars.

Murphy's next venture was to establish the World Hockey Association. He signed the biggest name in hockey, Bobby Hull, to a $1 million deal and the WHA took off in 1973. It opened up new hockey markets in New England, Indianapolis and Cleveland. It was then time for the former major of Buena Park, California, to invade the world of tennis. Tennis had never been organized into a professional league, as it had instead individual tournaments all over the world. The men and women only competed at the same tournaments during the Grand Slams, which took place only four times a year. Murphy, along with tennis promoter Larry King, devised the concept of having the top men and women playing together on a team representing their city during the summer months. The start of World Team Tennis attracted all the top stars, including Bjorn Borg, Jimmy Connors, Martina Navratilova and Billie Jean King. The World Team Tennis concept was a huge success and is still going strong today.

Now Murphy is on the brink of a brilliant new concept. With the inline skating booming and the love for hockey prospering by the minute, Murphy believes the time is right for a new professional sport, roller hockey. Roller Hockey International will debut this summer with a five-game tour featuring Team USA against Team Canada. The tour will kick off at the Great Western Forum in Los Angeles on August 13 and end at the Santa Fe

Hotel & Casino in Las Vegas on August 29. The league will roll out into 16 teams in 1993, playing in two eight-team divisions for more than $2 million in prize money. The league plans to go international in 1994, with the games being played in major arenas all across the U.S. and Canada during the summer months.

Once again, Dennis Murphy has discovered a new and exciting concept in sports. Roller Hockey International will not only attract the hockey fan and player, but will also create a new grassroots program where kids can play the new sport in the streets near their homes. The new league will offer many jobs to players and workers while giving the fans an affordable family price at the gate.

David McLane

David McLane of Indianapolis, Indiana, headed RHI's marketing, sponsorship and licensing division. He came to us after launching his own World Roller Hockey League in Florida in association with ESPN and Walt Disney World. It soon became clear that only one professional roller hockey league should exist for the purpose of building the sport. In our efforts to land a national television deal for RHI, it also became obvious that if we wanted a shot at broadcasting our games on ESPN, we were going to have to make a deal with David McLane.

McLane is a man of vision who knows the television and marketing business. McLane sold his Gorgeous Ladies of Wrestling

(GLOW) for $4 million, while still maintaining an interest in it. From Indiana and an ardent Indiana Pacers fan, McLane, without doubt, is one of the "new breed" of young promoters.

McLane was a great director of properties for RHI. He made all of us in the league a great deal of money, as well as giving the league a solid footing. He did a magnificent job of selling sponsorships, marketing and licensing for the RHI.

By expanding our marketing base with games broadcast on ESPN and espn2, RHI was able to leverage 24 markets in North America in 1994. With ESPN and McLane's marketing knowledge, RHI created instant credibility with national sponsors and licensees. Within a year – and with the assistance of Jay Coleman's EMCI and a New York-based licensing firm headed by Steve Davis – McLane brought in national sponsors like Pepsi, Taco Bell and All-Sport, as well as more than 20 licensees. Over a 12-month period, RHI's sponsorship and licensing division grew from virtually nonexistent to generating millions in revenues. Based on his vision and success heading the marketing of RHI, I envisioned David following me as the next president of the league.

McLane claims – and I agree with him – that interference from the league moguls discouraged his efforts. Had he been left alone, he would have accomplished a great deal more. Unfortunately for RHI, David's efforts were constantly undermined by team owners who simply wouldn't adhere to the equipment manufacturers' supplier pool, sponsors, licensing companies and exclusive provisions. One example, among many, was two teams that sold their jersey logo rights to direct competitors of Taco Bell. Obviously, moves like this by RHI team owners did not sit well with McLane, ESPN, the sponsors or licensees. It was this constant interference and disregard for league marketing policy from a few of the league moguls that discouraged McLane and eventually led to ESPN and David leaving RHI.

David and I remain good friends today. We enjoy having lunch on occasion, talking about his hometown NBA team, the Indiana Pacers, and looking back on the growth of roller hockey. I still have a plaque that David presented to me at one of the RHI league meetings proudly displayed in my home. The plaque reads in part: "To Dennis Murphy, The World's Greatest Promoter." Thanks, David.

Anno Willison

Anno Willison was very instrumental in putting Roller Hockey International together. Anno, along with RHI Commissioner Ralph Backstrom, put on the tryout camps throughout the United States. The players from those camps provided most of the talent in the league. Anno also helped organize our USA-Canada series which was held in several North American cities, and he worked closely with Jeanie Buss and Tim Harris in putting on the very first professional roller hockey game at the Great Western Forum in Los Angeles. It was a great success.

Willison also had a big part of the European Roller Hockey League Tour. It was Anno who did most of the "advance work" in the developing of RHI Europe. Willison is a USC Trojan, and attended a lot of the games with me. He also is a person who loves his horses. Both of us have left a lot of our money at the track. Anno, I do hope that you hit the home run at the track that you have been striving for. Just split it with me, my dear friend.

Bernie Federko, Part Owner, St. Louis Vipers

Synonymous with the NHL as a former player, Bernie Federko was another original RHI team owner.

"Hockey is such a big part of my life," Federko said. "Anything to do with hockey – and roller hockey is just an offshoot of ice hockey. I have three boys that love to play roller hockey in St. Louis, where we don't have enough ice facilities to accommodate all of the kids that want to play. We just thought it was a great idea to get involved with roller hockey; not just at the professional level, but at the amateur level as well. This league is still new. At five years old, it's still relatively early. You see how long other sports leagues have been around. It takes a long time to become successful. I think it's going to come to the point where RHI could become as accepted as ice. I really believe that with all the participation in all the other countries that there is a good possibility that it will become part of the Olympics. I think it's going to take us a long time to get to what the NHL has done. We believe that we do have a sport of the future."

Thomas Adams, Owner, San Diego Barracudas

Our friend Tom Adams was one of the owners of the San Diego Barracudas. I was also one of the owners. Tom helped make the Barracudas a success. We lost money together, but, oh! did we have fun! We loved to beat Maury Silver of the Anaheim Bullfrogs. We didn't do it very often, but when we did, we usually had a celebration.

Adams has a chemical company called Tiodize in Huntington Beach, and he loved the action of roller hockey. You hope that most teams have owners like Tom Adams, as he was active in making sure that the management of the team was doing its job. He was a "hands on" boss and he knew how to watch the pennies. I consider him to be a great partner. In his youth, he signed a baseball contract with Hall of Famer Jimmy Foxx of the Boston Red Sox. He also played with the great Satchel Paige, a baseball icon. He goes to many professional boxing matches with Jerry Buss, the owner of the Los Angeles Lakers.

"I love roller hockey and its constant action," Adams said. "I feel it's the upcoming sport of the 21st century."

E. Burke Ross, Jr., Owner, New Jersey Rockin Rollers

"I'm a lifelong ice hockey nut," said, E. Burke Ross, Jr., the owner of the New Jersey Rockin Rollers. "What attracted me to ownership in Roller Hockey International is that roller hockey is the fastest-growing sport in the U.S. People predict that there will be 30 million participants in the year 2005, and of course, RHI is the major league of roller hockey. My experiences as an owner have been absolutely positive. The Rockin Rollers have had nice increases in attendance every year, and we're looking for another one this year. League wide, attendance has grown about 20 percent a year. I don't know any other leagues that can make that statement."

In addition to the commitment that Ross has had since day one with RHI, he also owned the New Jersey Red Dogs, an Arena Football League team that also played at the Continental Airlines Arena.

Rich Shillington, Owner, San Jose Rhinos

The Rhinos were one of the only five RHI teams to win a league championship.

"I was the second person to commit to taking a franchise in RHI," Shillington said. "I used to be involved with ice hockey in San Diego and I wanted to do San Jose for a number of reasons. I do live in Calgary, Canada, but I don't think roller hockey would work there right now. When I looked around at the various cities, San Jose was the one that interested me, because the Sharks were building a new arena and are doing a very good job. Hockey has done well in the South Bay area. In my opinion, roller hockey is only going to work where there's an ice hockey presence, because roller hockey is simply an extension of ice hockey. I had a bye in the first year, so I traveled around the league and watched games in other cities. What really sold me was a playoff game in Vancouver where 8,500 people witnessed a last-minute victory over Calgary; the people in the crowd were ecstatic! Initially, I had paid a $10,000 deposit on the franchise. The day after witnessing that incredible game, I paid the balance of the franchise fee."

Norton Herrick, Owner, Orlando Jackals

Norton Herrick was a very successful businessman. He bought the Orlando franchise and he did very well with it. In 1998, he won the league championship. He was a power in the league and was one of the movers and shakers. He hosted a party in his home in Boca Raton, Florida, during our annual league meeting. The paintings in his house were the hit of the affair. He was and is a person of high quality.

Maury Silver, Chairman Emeritus, Anaheim Bullfrogs

In 1993, Anaheim was the first team to win a RHI championship in the league's inaugural year.

"Why did I pick roller hockey as a profession?" Silver asked rhetorically. "I didn't. It picked me. In 1992, my friend and co-inventor of the modern inline skate, Ralph Backstrom, brought Dennis Murphy to see me in my L.A. office. They had a plan that became RHI. I thought it was a good idea and wanted to be a part of it. I felt then as I do now that the sport is fantastic and coming to fruition. RHI is entering its fifth year. I honestly believe RHI will have its best year ever in 1997. It has been challenging for us all, but I think the 11 teams we have now are very strong and will ensure that success. We are the fastest-growing sport in the world, especially in North America and Europe. I personally feel that the sport of roller hockey and RHI have every opportunity to become the number-one league in the national as well as the number-one sport."

Al Howell, Owner, Toronto Wave

"Hockey is the biggest sport in Canada," Howell said. "Roller hockey is growing, but there still aren't that many facilities. I've been involved with ice hockey for years and have been working with RHI to obtain a membership since the league started. I am confident that in a hockey mad town such as Toronto, we will do well. When there was a team here in the first year of RHI, they played in a non-air-conditioned building. We will be playing in Maple Leaf Gardens, which will have plenty of room. We may play outside in 1998."

Jerry Diamond, RHI President

We got off to a good start in RHI, but when Jerry Diamond passed away in late 1996, it was a great blow to the league. Jerry was a wonderful organizer, and when he died, RHI just didn't have the leadership it needed for continued success. Jerry had superb fundraising and organizational skills, and when he was gone, the league definitely suffered. We missed Jerry very much.

No One is Beat

No one is beat 'til he quits

No one is through 'til he stops

No matter how often he drops

A fellow is not down 'til he lies

In the dust and refuses to rise

Fate can slam him and bang him around

And batter his frame 'til he's sore

But he never can say that he's downed

While he bobs up serenely for more

A fellow's not down 'til he dies

Nor beat 'til no longer he tries.

– Dale Brown

Dennis,
Don Marshall of Long Beach State
and Ralph Kehoe of Notre Dame,
your Wednesday night pals,
wish you all the best except when it comes
to college sports activities.
Down with your cardinal and gold Trojans.

Dennis,
Jerry and Jeanie Buss
wish you the very best
on your book.
Go Los Angeles Lakers in 2013.

SECTION VIII: ACCORDING TO MURPH

Our International Goals

Those of us in the WHA knew that the international hockey community loved the great game of hockey. With air transportation bringing the world together, we felt it was just a matter of time before the sport would become international. We felt that sooner or later, we would see Barcelona play Montreal. This explosion is going to happen, and I believe it will take place in the early part of this century. The Olympics are already explosive and big time. Who will ever forget when my friend Herb Brooks, coach of Team USA, won the gold medal at 1984 Winter Olympics in Lake Placid when no one gave his team a chance? Young people should pursue this area of international sport – it is the future and it will be big in all areas. There will be positions available as players, coaches, administrators, licensing, sponsorship and ownership. Move on it!

Consider the Fans

Over the years, I have been thanked by many players for helping them during their time of need. We told them that we had a group of lawyers, led by Don Regan and Telly Mercury, and that justice would prevail with the reserve clause. If, indeed, we did help in some way, I'm happy to have been part of it. Today we urge the players to use restraint, as the advantages they have made over the years did not come easily. We also urge them to consider the fans in their negotiations with the owners. Today's ticket prices in the NHL and NBA are getting out of control. Greed, however, can be controlled by men of good faith. We truly hope that leaders on both sides will work together and will come out with a fair solution for both parties. It can be done – and we hope it will be done soon.

The Media

It seems that when anything goes wrong in the sports world, the media always gets blamed. I'm sure that like all other professions, some members of the fourth estate have, at times, fabricated the facts. However, over my career of 40 years, I have found that the media has treated us fairly most of the time.

This is not an unreasonable position – I have always told our owners that when we start getting crowds, and the product is accepted, the media will respond. Over the years I've been fortunate to have had great journalists cover our new leagues. I have the utmost respect for people like Stu Nahan, Ed Arnold, Jim Hill, Bob Costas, Bryant Gumbel, Bob Verdi, Rudy Martske, Wayne Overland, John Hall, Jim Huber and so many others.

In the 1970s, one of my favorite sportscasters, Stu Nahan, claimed he was a great goalie, as well as a sportscaster. One night, during halftime of a Los Angeles Sharks hockey game, he proved his claim by stopping a slap shot by Bobby Hull. Naturally, we never heard the end of that story. For years, Stu Nahan was a broadcaster in the Los Angeles market along with his partner and toastmaster extraordinaire Ed Arnold. Nahan once good-naturedly said that Arnold "wasn't too swift in his thinking – that's why he ended up a sportscaster." On a serious note, both Stu Nahan and Ed Arnold worked actively in the community with zest and dedication. Nahan has passed away, but both men were the best in their profession and were class acts.

I first met sportscaster Jim Hill when he was a beat reporter in San Diego. He was always helpful when we organized our new leagues. In my opinion, Jim Hill could have made the national scene anytime he wanted to. However, he loved Los Angeles so much he made his roots there. We in that market have reaped the benefits of his decision. He is a consummate human being and a good friend.

Rudy Martske got his feet wet as a public relations and media consultant working with us in Miami when I was general manager of the ABA Miami Floridians basketball team. He is, and always will be, a journalist who speaks his mind with dignity and grace. The USA Today people are fortunate to have him in their fold as a key columnist. I am happy that he has made it "big." He is a friend and a man of decency.

Bryant Gumbel, while working as a beat writer in 1972 for Channel 4, would drive from his office in Los Angeles to Newport Beach to cover the WHA. He always treated Gary Davidson and me very fairly. He was a great journalist with his strength being his great interviewing ability. I was so happy and proud to see our Los Angeles journalist become so successful on the national television scene.

Terry Pluto's best-selling chronicle of the ABA, "Loose Balls," was a collection of anecdotes that captured the league's qualities and history wonderfully.

Bob Costas began his career as a play-by-play announcer in St. Louis during the ABA days. He has always reminded everyone of his love of those days. He is one of our alumni who made it to the big time, and we're so proud of his achievements.

Wayne Overland was a major sports columnist from Edmonton, Alberta, Canada. I believe that he helped to make our WHA league. He was critical at times, but as an acknowledged hockey writer and hockey columnist, he always called it as he saw it, and he gave our league a great deal of credibility. He was very fair and honest. His epic "discussions" at press conferences with Bill Hunter will always stand out in my recollections; he was a person who gave you hell on one occasion and embraced you on another. Wayne was one of a kind. I have articles written by Wayne which tore Bill Hunter and me apart; I also have stories written the following week that had a very positive note. I will always cherish and keep those stories in my scrapbook. Wayne was one of a kind – he was also a great friend.

Jim Huber was a reporter in Miami who covered the Miami Floridians. Since those days he moved on to become a featured tured reporter for CNN. He then covered golf for Turner Sports'

TNT network, continuing his quality top-notch job . He always loved his golf – I'm sure he was in love with his work.

Peter Young was the voice of the Winnipeg Jets and also worked with many newspapers and radio stations in the Winnipeg area. He aided the WHA Reunion Committee with his video skills.

Bob Verdi has been a featured columnist in Chicago for more than 30 years. He was very apprehensive of the WHA and WTT in our early years, but as time went on, he was a frequent visitor at our games. Bob did his homework, and I credit this for much of his success. He finds out what is going on, and he does it better than anyone I know. Bob became a good friend of the WHA and WTT. We always used him as a bellwether in our projects; we always got an honest view of things from Bob.

John Hall covered the sports world for the Los Angeles Times and the Orange County Register. John was a writer who was an honest, decent and loyal friend. He was objective and a USC supporter as well as being a topnotch columnist.

Stan Fischler is the major hockey columnist in the United States. He has his own company and does his writing on hockey on an international basis. Without a doubt, he is one of the nicest people in the industry. It is a badge of success to be mentioned in one of his columns in The Hockey News.

We were always treated fairly and objectively by Lee Hamilton of San Diego; Terry Jones, Wayne Overland and Jim Matheson of the Edmonton Journal; Wayne Lockwood of the

San Diego Union; Vic Grant of the Winnipeg Tribune; Al Carr of the Los Angeles Times; Bob Mellor of the Ottawa Citizen; George Gross of the Toronto Sun; Tim Burke and Milt Dunnell of the Toronto Gazette; Hugh Delano of the New York Post; Roy Storey of San Diego radio; Dick Beddoes, Allen Abel and Jim Proudfoot of the Toronto Globe and Mail; Frank Orr and Jim Kernaghan of the Toronto Star; John Robertson and Red Fisher of the Montreal Star; Dave Overpeck of the Indianapolis Star; Dick Denny of the Indianapolis News; Eric Whitehead and Tony Gallagher of the Vancouver Province; Reyn Davis of the Winnipeg Free Press.

Many of the writers and newscasters named above have since retired, but without them and their stories, the "Great WHA" would not have remained on the sports pages. Thank you, gentlemen, for your wonderful coverage. We know we missed many others, but please accept our thanks. There have been many hockey journalists who covered the WHA. They were friends and, at times, critics, but they always managed to spell our names correctly.

Make it a Team Effort

Steve Arnold of New York was selected as the player agent for the league. He did a great job and got us Julius Erving (Dr. J) and George McGinnis of Indiana. Both were superb additions and Julius Erving will go down in history as the man who made the ABA. Erving was not only a great basketball player, but he was class all the way. McGinnis also was superb, and he became a city commissioner in Indianapolis after retiring from basketball. The average salary for an NBA player at that time (in 1965) was $12,000 to $15,000 a year prior to our start. This was a ridiculous wage scale and the NBA knew it, but they had complete control and their attitude was, "Why should we pay them more when we've got a chance to make real money?"

This was a selfish act and if David Stern had been the commissioner then, it would not have happened. He is a man of understanding. Today the pendulum has turned and the players should be more understanding as they make great money and be more compassionate to the fans, as they are the ones in the final analysis who will pay the freight. The players must learn to work together with the owners and the fans to have a winning formula.

The sports fan should understand that businessmen who suffer losses in sports can usually write them off against profits in their other businesses. This is a real aid to the owners. A major reason some owners buy a sports team is that they can depreciate some of the players' salary! It is a fact, however, that no team in the operation of the ABA in its first season made any money. Most lost. Some broke close to even. I truly believe that in today's market of TV and the Internet, the teams can make money, but everyone needs to give a bit so that the economics can work out. It has to be a team effort. Management, owners, the player's unions, the agents, the players and the fans should work together.

It's to everybody's interest. As a business opportunity, professional sports ownership is an iffy investment. Many of the owners could bring a far greater profit in other businesses than investing in sports, but then they would not have as much fun.

Look on the Sunny Side

The path that we had blazed already was a tough go and proved to be taxing on us all. While serving as mayor of Buena Park, I was a member of the Optimist International Club. The club has a creed which has served as a lifelong guide for me:

"An optimist is one who sees an opportunity in every difficulty. A pessimist is one who sees difficulty in every opportunity. Be so strong that nothing can disturb your peace of mind. Talk health, happiness and prosperity to each person you meet. Make your friends feel that there is something worthwhile in them. Look at the sunny side of life and make your optimism come true. Think only of the best, work only for the best, and expect only the best. Be just as enthusiastic about the success of others as you are about yourself."

I've found that those profound words have worked very well in my life. I believed that in the late '60s, the sports world was dominated by a professional establishment whose purpose was to keep professional sports teams to a limit and under their control. Expansion was at a minimum and many deserving cities were overlooked. Television was in its infancy, confining professional sports to the major markets. Because of this, emerging cities were stifled. That attitude allowed the "second league," the ABA, to emerge.

The Professional Agents

Professional sports hasn't been hurt by players' unions, owners or management – the greatest damage has been done by some of the unethical and greedy agents, who for the most part don't give a damn about their clients. There are some exceptions, such as Leigh Steinberg, Bob Wolfe, Charles Abrahams and Bob Erhlich. In the early years of professional sports, negotiations were done by the lawyer and the general manager of the club. The process worked for a while, but then it became obvious that the owners and management were taking unfair advantage of the players. The pendulum started to swing toward the players when the agents began to be involved.

In normal negotiations between labor and management, the two sides meet in bargaining sessions with the intention of reaching an agreement that is amicable for both sides. In sports, it's done much the same way, with players' unions and management, but the negotiations begin all over again between the player and his agent with management.

In essence, there are two sets of negotiations. That's why I believe the public is getting the "business" in the long haul by paying the freight with higher prices for tickets, merchandising, beer and parking. As a young general manager, when I started negotiations with a player, it was generally done in a pleasant and decent manner. Usually, the player would handle his own negotiations, but sometimes he would bring his wife or a parent with him. Today a player has an agent, accountant and financial adviser. Management is often represented by lawyers well trained in negotiation. Now when a deal is done, the first thing an agent does is run to his media friends, who tell the whole world how much his client is making. This is mainly done for cosmetic purposes – an attempt to get other clients to choose him. Naturally, after each deal is completed, the prices continue to soar: "Player one got two million to play and my guy has better stats; therefore, he should receive three million."

This is a common approach by many agents, and this is how agents have helped to destroy sports. Some say that management doesn't have to come across. However, if a team doesn't give in and keep him, the player agent demands that his client be traded or sits out the next season. The same media person raises heck with management. It is a no-win situation for owners, management and, eventually, the fans.

Today it costs an arm and a leg to see professional sports events. Tickets are now selling for $40 or $50 per seat. For a family of four to attend a game it amounts to $200 for tickets, at least $7 for parking, and perhaps $6 per person for concession items. To see a professional game will cost a family of four over $300. That explains why there are so many business executives at games and so few kids. It's a disgrace.

Women in Sports

To me, the leading woman in the sports world is the fabulous Billie Jean King. She is a born athlete who was the premiere woman's tennis player of the 20th century. She holds more Wimbledon championships than anyone else and is a terrific spokeswoman for women's sports. I truly believe that she could have been a great golfer and a more than adequate softball and basketball player. "BJK" as she is fondly known, comes from Long Beach, California.

I enjoyed the many discussions we had about women's sports. She has always been a champion for developing woman's sports, and is a strong advocate of equality between men and women in sports. She took on Bobby Riggs and beat him in a famous confrontation in Texas. It was a fun match and both participants gave it their all. Her former husband Larry King and "BJK" have stayed friends even after their divorce, and she, as always, has remained a classy lady.

The other great woman athlete, to me, is the superb Joan Joyce, who many agree is the top woman softball pitcher of the 20th century. Joan is a terrific athlete who also played golf on the LPGA Tour. She is a wonderful human being as well as an unbelievable pitcher. She was on the first professional women's softball championship team and, as always, she was the humblest person on the diamond. She and Rosie Beard had a strong but respectful competition going, but in most people's minds, Joan Joyce was the foremost pitcher of all time. I'm sure there will be others who will claim that title, but to me, Joan Joyce will always be the ultimate professional pitcher.

The Woman's Professional Softball League was very competitive – but the timing was wrong. Many fans did love the sport, however, and I hope someday it will achieve great success. Joan Joyce would have to be given credit for leading the way.

Our Generation

Tom Brokaw, the noted commentator, has written a book on the "Greatest Generation." I am proud of my generation and that we were picked as the greatest one. This is a credit to all of us that were part of that era. We were the World War II group of Americans and we were a group of men and women who lived in that era with pride and the red, white and blue! Our music was exceptional. Maybe it was because we lived through the war years, and our composers were living their dreams with song.

Our generation returned from war and we entered civilian life with dedication and passion. We had Joe DiMaggio, Ted Williams, Willie Mays, Johnny Unitas, Joe Namath, Rosie Casals, and Billie Jean King in the sports world. In the movies, we had stars like Humphrey Bogart, Spencer Tracy, John "Duke" Wayne, Rosalind Russell, Marilyn Monroe and Doris Day grace our screens. As for singers, we had the likes of Frank Sinatra, Bing Crosby, Doris Day, and Francis Langford.

In the political field, men like Franklin Roosevelt, Harry Truman, and "Ike" led us. Yes, we did have a group of men and women who were a credit to this nation. On behalf of our generation, we thank Tom Brokaw, Tom Hanks and their peers for selecting us and we are indeed a proud group. Our generation believed in marriage and family. We loved our children, always with respect and discipline. We had our problems but on the whole, we toed the line. We sometimes did not give our kids a lot of attention, but we gave them our love. Our generation did it the way that our moms and dads showed us. "Discipline with Love" was our motto.

Sports in General

Professional sports have been my life. I never was a great athlete, but I loved the action in sports. Gary Davidson, Don Regan and I created a lot of jobs and we played by the rules. I don't think any of us ever wanted to hurt anyone, and we loved the camaraderie of starting new ventures. I grew up in a normal California atmosphere. My mom and dad were firm but loving parents. I did not have any hang ups and I was a normal kid who loved the ball games and USC football.

Congress had granted an antitrust provision and exemption to the NFL in football. Basketball attempted to do the same thing, but Larry Fleischer and his players' union had become powerful with the passing years and lobbied bitterly against the total bargaining ability with the U.S. Congress. The NBA owners also helped in the battle, because they thought our ABA would fold, and if so, they could handle the labor unions and finish on top. This attitude proved incorrect, as the player labor unions, rather than getting weaker after the mergers, actually got stronger.

Today, the owners must get the support of the labor unions almost on every major decision. This adds an equation to the total concept, and things have at times become difficult, leading to strikes that have cost both sides. I truly blame the owners, for again being selfish and not looking objectively on the problems. They all want to build on their egos by winning, rather than by being intelligent businessmen.

Accomplishments of Our Leagues

The history and accomplishments of the WHA, ABA and World Team Tennis were many. All three leagues were essential in changing the world of professional sports. One of the most influential changes was the elimination of the reserve clause, which bound a player to a professional team for life. The elimination of this clause has allowed players in hockey, basketball and tennis to be given the right to choose which team they wanted to play for.

In today's game, the sports industry has imposed salary caps. I believe that if this system were to be tested in the courts, it wouldn't stand up. We should allow the free market to work. Players who deserve the higher salaries as determined by their high level of play should benefit. The remainder of players should fit into the marketplace at their own levels. Some say that the continuity of the teams would suffer under this system, but I say "baloney."

In today's market, those players that don't achieve are protected by the player's unions as witnessed by the minimum salary structure that has gone "bonkers." The player's union maintains that the present system, which allows average players to receive such high minimum salaries, which is a direct cause of increased ticket prices for the fans. I really feel that there are a great number of borderline players receiving millions of dollars today. They are entitled to a decent income, but not the outrageous salaries that they are receiving in today's market.

The moguls will try to say that parity will be destroyed under the free market system. I disagree. Those who perform on the field and court would receive their just dues – those that don't can go elsewhere or to other professions. I have often said that one of the greatest powers we have is the power to choose. I believe that players should have the right to decide what team they want to play for.

William James once said: "Compared with what we ought to be, we are only half awake. The human individual usually lives far beyond his means. He possesses powers of various sorts, which we habitually fail to use. We all have the power to choose to go after a lifelong goal or be intent to remain at the same level. In the face of the test, it is up to us to do what we will with our power to choose, which in the end will determine our lives."

I sincerely do hope in the future that the moguls, unions and athletes will have the right to pursue their own destiny. This is how it should be.

Putting Together a League – the Outlines and Criteria

A lot of wonderful people have asked me over the years to help outline the necessary steps of putting a league together. I have always believed that what works for one person may not necessarily work for another, thus I kept my formula to myself. Our leagues were formed before the Internet. With today's Internet, one can get the information needed quickly. We did not have that luxury in those days. We had to use the libraries, the city Chamber of Commerce and our own past experiences and extensive contacts.

The Sports Owners

Overall, sports owners are a good lot. Sure, most of them have large egos; many have had their way in their own business world and are ruthless and overpowering. However, most are compassionate, community-oriented and dedicated to improving the image of their cities. When professional sports were in its infancy, those in the trenches either moved on to a higher level or left the sports business.

In 1998, Peter O'Malley, a member of one of the true pioneer families in professional sports, decided it was time for his family to sell the Dodgers and look elsewhere for other business ventures. This turned out to be a tragedy in the sports community; people like the O'Malleys have been great for the ownership image of professional sports.

Those of us who have been involved with the ABA, WHA, Team Tennis and Roller Hockey International have been fortunate to have been blessed with decent human beings as owners in our leagues. People like Jerry Buss, Burke Ross, Norton Herrick, Murray Simkin, Jim Patterson, John Bassett, Bill DeWitt, Nick Mileti, Paul Racine, Howard Baldwin, Ben Hatskin, Bill Hunter and Bob Kraft all have supported the development of respective leagues with their hard-earned dollars. In so doing, they have created thousands of well-paying jobs and opportunities for many people. As a whole, the owners have enjoyed their time as owners in one of the fastest growing industries today. The limelight and attention they receive is overwhelming.

Bill Ringsby, owner of Ringsby Trucking line and once owner of the ABA Denver team, once told me: "Murphy, I make millions of dollars in my line of business and I belong to the finest country clubs. I have the best of everything in life. I could go into any restaurant in the Denver area and no one would recognize me. I buy a professional sports franchise and today everyone knows who I am after making a trade. I get praise, as well as holy heck from all over the place. It's truly amazing, especially when things do go bad on a trade or where a team finishes in the standings."

It's a fact that sports owners do have more exposure than in any other type of business; it's also true that they can't handle the exposure very well. The Marge Shotts of the world get in trouble by making unfortunate statements which get published worldwide in a speedy manner.

From Politics to Sports

In the course of life, a lot of strange things happen. When I was in politics, a strong young city attorney ran against me in the Democratic primary. I was then considered the odds-on favorite, but Bill Dannemeyer didn't believe any of it, and he won a hard-earned victory. This defeat changed my path of life. I went into the professional sports business. Bill, on the other hand, switched political parties and his beliefs and became a Republican congressman from Orange County. As fate would have it, we became close friends over the years and I came to respect him both as a congressman and as a person. Elaine, Rocky Kalish and I had the honor of having Congressman Dannemeyer and his beautiful wife, Evie, join us on one of our trips to the Philippines. Congressman Toby Roth of Iowa also joined us. It was a special trip, and we all got to see Rocky actually fly a chartered plane. Boy, were we nervous! In fairness, though, Rocky did a great job, and without too many bumps or a crash landing. We all have commented on the trip on many occasions, as our friend Eduardo Cojuangco, Jr. of the

Philippines hosted it. We got to meet a log of high dignitaries of the Philippine government, including General Ramos, who subsequently became the country's president.

Shakers

Over the years, I have had the privilege and pleasure of associating with some of the "shakers" of this world. Some of those include Jerry Saperstein of the Harlem Globetrotters; Jerry and Jeanie Buss of the Los Angeles Lakers; actor Pat Boone and his daughter Debbie Boone; actor Tony Danza; singer Dionne Warwick; financier Lamar Hunt, Governor Pat Brown of California; President John F. Kennedy; announcers Frank Gifford and Bob Costas; sports owners Charley Finley of the Oakland A's, Ray Kroc of McDonald's and San Diego Padres, Bill Dewitt of the Cincinnati Stingers and St. Louis Cardinals, and Bob Kraft of the Boston Patriots. These are just a few of the associations I have made over the years, and I thank them all. I found them to be classy individuals, with a strong love for their fellow men and women.

Cousin Sarah
and hubby Brian Chisick
hope the book
becomes a bestseller.

Jerry Saperstein
of the original Harlem Globetrotters
wishes his friend of 50 years,
Dennis Murphy,
terrific success on his book.

SECTION IX: ANECDOTES

"The first and worst of all frauds is to cheat yourself."
– Pearl Bailey

Loyal Fans

In London, on one of our trips to Wimbledon, Larry King invited my family to sit in the contestant's box. My daughters, Dawn and Doreen, did not know that in tennis the decorum was, and is, not to cheer for your favorite player. Clap politely, but no yelling or screaming. Being teenage girls, my daughters didn't conform to the ruling – they let the world know that they were rooting for Billie Jean – and so what? In the box that day were Chris Evert's mother and father. They are a class act all the way. After the match they told my girls that they would love to have them in their daughter's corner at a future match. They felt that the girls were loyal fans. Billie Jean was the type of player that could capture that type of enthusiasm from the public – she was competition all the way.

Dr. Jerry Buss – The Winning Owner

Jerry Buss, the owner of the Los Angeles Lakers, is the consummate owner. He places his trust in his management team and backs them with support and guidance. Jerry West and Bill Sharman have stated that they could not have had a better owner and boss. Buss is compassionate, fair and innovative. He is the one who has used the "deferred" payment plan with such great success. This practice gives players money for a given future time, allowing the players the opportunity to plan their future in their golden years off the court.

He works very well with people and it shows. He's a winner in every way. I have known Dr. Buss since he and his lawyer, Jerry Fine, were my partners with the L.A. Strings of the World Team Tennis. Jerry told me he was going to buy the Forum, Kings and Lakers, and he did. His involvement with the Strings helped him learn the ropes of sports business and ownership on a small scale so he would know what to do when he was ready for "the big time." Jerry is a quick learner. The first thing he did was to put together a loyal, knowledgeable and strong staff. He chose Jerry West and Bill Sharman to lead his basketball activities. As it turned out, he couldn't have picked a better team. He also believed in order for a team to be successful it needed a superstar. He scored with Kareem Abdul Jabbar, Magic Johnson, Shaquille O'Neal and Kobe Bryant.

I will always remember the phone call that he made to me asking my opinion of having a special floor-seat section and charging $200 for them. I told him that he was nuts and that nobody would pay $200 for those seats. Again, he was right and I was wrong. He didn't tell me that he had planned on having Jack Nicholson, Dyan Cannon and Angie Dickerson sit in those very seats. Today those seats sell for $1,500 and are the first sold each season.

Jerry Buss has been a great help to Larry King and I. He has always been there for us. He let us play our first Roller Hockey International game at the Forum. His daughter, Jeanie, was in charge of that first game. Her wonderful effort allowed us to kick off our product in great style, and we received positive reviews and raves. It was a gamble on their part, and without their support, roller hockey would have taken a lot longer to get off the ground. Sadly, Dr. Buss passed away on February 18 of this year. His son Jim and daughter Jeanie now run the Lakers. Tim Harris is the vice president in charge of operations. Phil Jackson, who retired in 2011 as the Lakers' coach, headed a great cast of winners.

Talk about Feelings!

It was indeed a special evening. I was at that beautiful edifice called Staples Center in Los Angeles at the sixth game of the 2000 NBA playoffs. On one side of the court was the colors and players of the Los Angeles Lakers, the "purple Gang" who are owned by a friend, Jerry Buss, a fellow USC Trojan, and on the other side were the Indiana Pacers, a team that was part of my ABA heritage.

What a setting, and talk about feelings! It was the last year of the 20th century, and the NBA's San Antonio Spurs, a former ABA team, had won the championship in 1999. In 2000, the Eastern Division Champion Indiana Pacers were another former ABA team playing in the finals. As I watched, I thought that it would indeed be ironic to have back-to-back champs from a league that I helped put together with my former partner and friend Gary Davidson. That feat would have meant that former ABA teams were champions in the last year of the 20th century as well as the first year of the 21st!

My feelings went deeper than that because I was also a part of the beginning of the sports career of one of the best owners that any professional sports team has ever had – my friend, Jerry Buss. I reflected back to 1973 when I received a call from a Los Angeles attorney by the name of Jerry Fine. He said he was representing a client who wanted to buy a World Team Tennis franchise in the new professional league that Billie Jean King and I created – Jerry Buss. Fine said that Buss wanted to get into professional sports in a big way. The purchase of the tennis franchise for Los Angeles would help give Buss a feeling of being an owner and help him to experience the strategies needed to be a successful one.

At that time, professional sport was just beginning to take hold; what foresight Jerry Buss had. He built a dynasty in his sports career. Together with his hired guns Bill Sharman and Jerry West, the Los Angeles Lakers have become the dominant professional basketball team of our lifetime. Red Auerbach did wonders with his Boston Celtics, but Buss, West and Sharman created the dominant team of our times. I was torn in my loyalty – one part of me was to a friend and the other to a piece of basketball history. As I predicted to some of my friends, it would be a great series, and lo and behold, I was correct. What a life I've been blessed with. To think that in a small way I was part of a championship contest is indeed very humbling. (The Lakers won.)

Rocky Kalish

One of the jewels on this planet is my good friend, Rocky Kalish. Throughout this book, you will often see his name mentioned in some capacity. He is one of the best and most humorous writers in the world. His credits are absolutely mind-boggling. He has written for many icons of Hollywood, among them Milton Berle, Jack Carter, Carroll O'Connor, Sid Caesar and many more.

He has produced, directed and written many screenplays and TV shows, including All in the Family, Good Times, Gilligan's Island and Carter Country. Rocky and his wife Irma live in Encino, California, with a second home in Palm Springs. He was the original founder of the 6′4″ and Under International Basketball Association and the person who picked Bob Cousy to be its commissioner. Achievers discover their vocations and their specialties. That means they find something worth doing. Rocky fits this mold well.

Mugged the Wrong Guy

One of the first events that Rocky Kalish took me to was the press conference of Hector Comacho and Boom Boom Mancini announcing their fight in 1989. Comacho loved Rocky, and half of the press conference was devoted to the exploits of Kalish.

The event was delightful as Comacho was one of the most colorful boxers in the game. His costumes were absurd and he tried to intimidate his opponents with his psychological games. Boom Boom wasn't bad himself – making the press conference even more delightful to attend.

Rocky was in his glory, as he was a part owner of Comacho. Rocky also really loved the fight game. Rocky's wife, Erma, has a fight promoter's license in California; she, too, is a great fight fan and matchmaker. Not only does Rocky know the fight game very well, he also knows how to dispatch a left hook as well as anyone. In Amsterdam in 1996, a mugger picked on the wrong guy. Rocky decked him and will show you where his hand was broken to prove it.

Rocky also tells of his heavyweight boxer, Truth Williams. Williams, too, had a great left hook, but also a "glass jaw." Rocky always claims that if Williams had a good chin, he could have been champion of the world and would have held the title for many years. Rocky wrote for some of the legends of Hollywood. At his social functions, the boys would tell jokes – one after another – until early in the morning. One day in Munich, Rocky told his stories to Ron Byrne and me for five straight hours. He kept us in stitches as we laughed the entire time.

Advice Heeded

Fred Comrie, the former owner of the San Diego Gulls of the International Hockey League, asked me to help make the IHL a major league. He said that the IHL had some very strong owners with a lot of money behind them and that they were positioning themselves into major markets. He specifically stated that Chicago was in the fold and that he was going to move his Gulls from San Diego to Los Angeles and play at the Sports Arena. He also stated that he had a Donald Trump-type owner to snare New York and thus the three big markets. Once they did, the group was ready to take on the NHL. He stated that the IHL was going to add a European division and that it was already in the works.

I remember telling Fred, "There is no way in hell you can make it go. The climate is not right and the obstacles too great."

Even though Gary Bettman was new on the job, he is a brilliant tactician and learned from the great master of the NBA, David Stern. It was absolutely foolish to go to war with the NHL. Fred was receptive to my point of view and the IHL never went up against the NHL. It was a good decision by Fred Comrie and friends.

Fred and his brothers have built a terrific furniture business in his native Canada. He is a man of purpose and high integrity.

Fans Rights

The fans of North America have, on many occasions, had very little to say in decisions made by the owners and the players' unions. However, the WHA/NHL merger can be attributed to the fact that the fans forced the issue by their economic boycott and protests, especially against the Montreal Canadiens' Molson

Beer ownership. I have often felt that in some of the ridiculous labor disputes between ownership groups and the labor lawyers during the '80s and '90s, fan action could have conceivably played a major part in inserting sense into the negotiations. In the final breakdown, the fans always pay the freight and yet have no say. Maybe that could change for the better if fans banded together and had their say. Negotiations would certainly be expedited!

Stand-up Guys

I have had the privilege of knowing some great athletes and people in my life. All of then hold a special niche in my heart. The hockey greats, however, have always been a little closer to my heart and salvation. On the whole, they are very honest, genuine and sincere. They are upfront people with whom you always know where you stand.

I got to know Bobby Hull, Ralph Backstrom and Gordie Howe as friends. I never had the opportunity of knowing Wayne Gretzky in the same manner, but from what people say, he fits into the same mold. When you saw Wayne Gretzky, Gordie Howe, Bobby Hull and Ralph Backstrom signing autographs for kids, it was because they genuinely wanted to. They did so because they knew what it meant to those kids who, in many cases, waited in the cold for hours to get their autographs and a kind word from their heroes.

When I was around Bobby, Gordie and Ralph, I felt that their answers to questions would be to the point and without malice. I heard that Wayne was the same way. To think that Gordie Howe would play alongside his two talented sons in the toughest sport in the world is mind-boggling. To add to Bobby's honor, he is father to future Hall of Famer Brett Hull. This is unbelievable. Just imagine; father and son as Hall of Famers.

The brothers Gretzky aren't doing too bad themselves. Keith Gretzky is moving up in the coaching ranks, while Glenn Gretzky has served as a general manager of some of the professional roller hockey clubs. I guess "genes" do have their place in this world.

A Matter of Perspective

The ownership of the six WHA teams standing at the end of the battle was again divided. Cincinnati and Birmingham did not like the terms of the merger and agreed to be paid off rather than join the NHL. Their four fellow owners paid them over $7 million to close up shop and fade away. In 1979, it looked like the remaining WHA team owners were shafted, but when one considers that 20 years later those teams (now in the NHL) are valued at more than $150 million each, one has a different perspective.

Talking Turkey

My brother John and his partner Frank Koch owned a race horse called Pager. It was going to run a six-furlong race in Pomona. At the time of the race, the two turkeys were attempting to get me to buy into the partnership. I initially told John that I might buy in, but after seeing the horse go from first place to last in less than three seconds, I begged off. Needless to say, the following week, Pager won a race in San Francisco and paid $99 for $2. When I asked if I could buy back in, both my brother and Frank told me to "get lost." It just shows you – winning one stinking race can completely change a man's perspective.

Tin Ear

During the formation of the WHA, Ben Hatskin owned, along with other businesses, a "watering hole" in Winnipeg. He needed a female singer to perform at his establishment. An agent in New York sent a singer to Winnipeg who had a beautiful voice. After her first performance she was let go. As fate would have it, that singer later turned out to be one of the icons of the music industry – Barbra Streisand. Ben knew hockey talent, but came up a little short when it came to music. Maybe if Barbra had worn a Winnipeg Jets jersey, it would have made her voice sound a little better to Ben.

Class Act

One of the most bruising fights at a WHA game was between Paul Shmyr of Cleveland and Ted McCaskill of the Los Angeles Sharks. Both men displayed a lot of courage in their head butting and fist-throwing contest. I thought it would never stop. Ted McCaskill urged all of his friends to say an extra prayer for Paul Shmyr when Paul was recovering from a bout with a severe illness. That's the kind of spirit we had in the WHA. Play hard, but keep the spirit of compassion in your hearts. Ted McCaskill was class then, and he remains that way today.

"Howe" Perceptive

In Russia during the Canada-Russia 1974 Series, Gordie Howe and his wife Colleen stayed at the Russia Hotel in Moscow. There were two very old chairs in the room. Gordie, in his charming style, went to the chandelier and said, "My good Russian friends, you have a superstar in this room and the chairs go back to the 5th century. Please replace them." After practice, Gordie and Colleen came back to their room and lo and behold, two beautiful 20th century chairs had replaced the old. Gordie then went back to the chandelier and said, "Thank you, my Russian hosts." Bugs of all kinds were featured on this trip.

Upstaged

Jerry Saperstein was responsible for putting on a press conference for World Team Tennis that was held at the Sports Illustrated-Time Building in New York City in 1974. He had a great turnout of media present and he hired 20 New York beauties to serve sandwiches and drinks to the freeloaders. My brother John Murphy was not going to be upstaged, so he brought along to the event Miss Pirelli Tires and Miss Maryland. After strutting his beautiful ladies around the room, he passed Jerry Saperstein's table for the fifth time, and that's when Jerry yelled out, "John, I got your message!" My brother felt great about this acknowledgement and Jerry and I have laughed about it now for 30 years.

The Red Puck

Gary Davidson, co-founder of the WHA, had originally lobbied for a subtle fire-engine red puck for our new WHA to use. The notion, however, was angrily shot down by Wild Bill Hunter, the general manager and president of the Edmonton Oilers. "That is the most ridiculous thing I've ever seen," said Hunter, when he was first shown the proposed crimson puck. "Our goaltenders will never be able to see that puck." Davidson asked Hunter why they wouldn't be able to see the red puck. Hunter replied: "Because they will be looking for a black one!"

Hockey Highlight

A major highlight occurred during the 1977 WHA season, when Wayne Gretzky, Gordie Howe and Mark Howe played on the same line against the Soviet Union All-Stars. The Summit Series with the Russians took place in Edmonton, Alberta, Canada. Jacques Demers of Quebec coached the WHA All-Stars and said, "I still have a picture from those games. I will always cherish that I coached two of the greatest players to have ever played hockey." Wayne Gretzky was quoted at the time as saying, "I didn't think I was going to make the All-Stars as an 18 year old. What a great honor it was to share the same line as Gordie and Mark Howe. I will always be grateful to Coach Demers for giving me that opportunity."

The one and only Gordie Howe said, "That skinny little bugger (Gretzky) is more mature mentally than physically. He has some beautiful moves. It was a joy for me to play with him and my son, Mark." The WHA ended up winning all three games against the talented Soviet team. Those three great stars had a great time together, and the superstar WHA line seemed to click as if they had been teammates forever.

On Second Thought

In 1998, together with real-estate developer Lenny Bloom and attorney Ron Mix of Southern California, we attempted to start an International Football League. We were able to get 12 teams organized, but because we did not have a television package finalized, we decided to forego our plans. That turned out to be a good decision and saved our principals a lot of money.

Penny Wise

During the merger talks between the ABA and the NBA, Senator Tom Kuchel of California, Dick Tinkham of the ABA and Sam Shulman of the NBA were exploring different options. One option agreed to by all parties was that all 11 ABA teams would join the NBA for $1 million each, payable over a 10-year period with no interest. The stumbling block was that both boards of directors would have to agree to the terms. The ABA board of directors, for reasons of their own, did not endorse the agreement. It was a bad decision, as an NBA franchise today cannot be purchased for less than $200 million. Dick Tinkham was mystified by this decision.

Music Man

During our trip to Asia to play a series of games for the 6′4″ and under basketball league, Rocky Kalish and I sent out Carl DiPietro to organize the various arrangements in advance. Our "Italian Stallion" sometimes liked to "embroider" the truth, and on this trip he excelled in that department. When our tour part arrived in the Philippines, we were greeted by a seven-piece band. This was very impressive to our players, coaches and managers, and Carl said he had arranged the great welcome that included PBA officials, city dignitaries and media. "I really worked hard on it, especially the band," Carl told us. Rocky and I were highly impressed. Two weeks later, when I returned to Manila to clean up the final arrangements, I took the same exit from the plane. I walked up the same corridor at the airport and again saw the same band performing their tunes. This seemed a bit strange to me. I later found out that this same band met all plane arrivals in Manila. Our friend Carl had put one over on us again.

Musical Chairs

Dick Tinkham and Mike Storen formed a strong team. They were the "backroom boys" of the ABA. In most cases, they controlled the commissioner's office. The commissioner's office became a "musical chairs" structure during the ABA's existence, as we had six commissioners over the league's 10-year span. It seemed that no matter who wore the title of commissioner, it was Tinkham and Storen who were the final authority.

Top Teammates

Some of the hard-working secretaries who have worked for me included Sandra Lee, Elsie Hill, Dawn Mee, Cathy Turner, Marilyn Lathrop and Ruth Jones. They all did a terrific job.

Lingering Influence

During matches between the WHA teams and NHL teams, the WHA squads won 33 games to 27. When four teams of the WHA merged with the NHL, four of the top-10 scorers were from the WHA that first year. Although the WHA merged into the NHL more than 30 years ago, its influence on the NHL and hockey remains profound, both fiscally and culturally. Not only did the WHA offer new avenues for American skaters, it also became a conduit for players from all over Europe.

Top Guns

The American Basketball Association was known as a fighting league with a cadre of characters like Warren Armstrong and John Brisker. Armstrong was in his second year in the league when he changed his name to Warren Jabali to reflect his African roots. Jabali does not have any religious connotations – it is a Swahili word for "rock." Neither Jabali nor Brisker were big men as basketball players go, but they were tough and very intimidating. Their reputations seemed to precede them. Both players loved to fight and did so at the drop of a hat. Brisker averaged 26 points while pulling down nine rebounds a game in the three years he played in the league. He did this with a 6′5″ frame. Jabali was 6′2″ and averaged 17 points per game over the course of his seven-year ABA career. Brisker also played in the NBA for Seattle in 1972. When his basketball career was over, he became a mercenary involved in the Uganda revolution. Brisker gave his allegiance to Idi Amin, the ruthless, cold-blooded African leader, and it was rumored that he was killed defending Amin.

As tough as Jabali and Brisker were, they never got into it themselves. Every time their respective teams met, the league became concerned they would tangle to see who was the best. That battle never took place, because each man had a great deal of respect for the other. Dick Tinkham relates a legendary story about Brisker that describes Brisker's inner thinking. Brisker played for Pittsburgh, and the Pipers management decided to bring in a tough, 6'7" football player to the team's training camp. The two men had an encounter, and after a few punches were exchanged, Brisker told his opponent that he would show him. Off he went to get his gun. The football player headed in the opposite direction, shouting, "While you get yours, I'll get mine." Needless to say, practice was quickly canceled and the football player was discharged. With pay, of course.

Expensive Gifts

Gary Davidson and I decided to give our charter owners and trustees of the WHA an official founder's ring. The rings were inset with rubies, not diamonds. Ben Hatskin complained at one of our meetings, saying, "I'd like to thank Davidson and Murphy for these rings. In order for us to wear them, we had to lose a million dollars. What a deal." At least Gary and I gave the owners some consideration.

A Bunch of Stiffs

Gary Davidson worked part time at a mortuary while he was attending UCLA Law School. "It was a fine job," he said. "I went to school by day and worked at night. I slept in between shifts. Many a night, while I was studying, I would receive a phone call requesting that I pick up a body. Figuratively speaking, those were not the only stiffs that I encountered in my life. There were also some in the early years of the WHA and ABA."

A Rare Breed

Howard Baldwin, the former owner of the Pittsburgh Penguins, founded the New England Whalers and was the WHA's last president. "Anytime you win a championship, there's a feeling no one can express," Baldwin said. After winning the Avco Cup, Baldwin called Bob Schmertz, the principal owner of the club to say, "Bob, even though we won the championship, we lost $300,000, and your share is '$150,000.' 'Aw, that's nothing, kid,' answered Schmertz. 'You guys did a great job for the first year. The championship will always be a part of history.' That was Schmertzy. There were so many things he did above and beyond the call of duty. Bob was truly a sportsman, an entrepreneur in every sense of the word. You don't find people like him today in pro sports. If it wasn't for Bob Schmertz, I can honestly tell you that the Whalers would never have survived," Baldwin said. Partners like Bob Schmertz are hard to find indeed.

Fan Favorite

Jerry Saperstein loved his Harlem Globetrotters, and Meadowlark Lemon was a great fan favorite. Meadowlark and Jerry would often visit famous restaurants in their tours. Jerry says that while dining, there were long lines of people, including lots of kids, coming up to get Meadowlark's autograph. He always gracefully obliged.

Dialing for Dollars

T.C. Morrow was one of the richest men in Texas. He was in the oil business and had struck black gold. Slater Martin talked him into buying the Houston franchise of the ABA. Martin was a longtime friend of Morrow, and after talking Morrow into buying the team, he promised that he would do everything – all Morrow had to do was go to the games. This seemed fine to Morrow, but a crazy thing happened in Anaheim at one of our league meetings, which Morrow attended. While checking into the Disneyland Hotel, he struck up a conversation with the registration girl. They hit it off, and within a month, they were married. A few months later, George Mikan called me and said, "You won't believe this, Murph, but Morrow just sent me a telegram. He wants out of the league. His new wife isn't a basketball fan and he feels that they could spend their time together doing other things. He said that he would finish the season, but would need a buyer for the next season."

Over the summer, we tried to sell the Mavericks without success. At a pre-season meeting in Indianapolis, Morrow said that he was going to fold the team and take back his performance bond of $150,000. This caused a debate. Dick Tinkham, who was the league's attorney at the time, knew a connection at Morrow's bank, and he said that we had two chances of getting that $150,000, slim and none. As things often happened in the ABA, a new owner appeared out of the blue. It was Jim Gardner, who was a former congressman and founder of the Hardee's restaurant chain. He and a group of North Carolina businessmen wanted an expansion team in his state. Tinkham told our board of directors that they would sell them the Houston club rather than an expansion team. This was a great solution. Gardner bought the Mavericks, and the team finished the season in Houston and later moved to North Carolina. Once again, a crisis had been averted.

Caring Coach

Slick Leonard, the Indiana Pacers coach, believed in getting along. He instilled that spirit after replacing Larry Stoverman 10 games into the 1969 season with Indiana struggling with a 1-9 record. Slick had coached in the NBA with Chicago and Baltimore, but in both cases, he had little player talent and produced losing records. With the Pacers, he knew he had talent and that it was his job to make things happen. He immediately took charge. He initiated a postgame get-together to discuss what happened in the game. Some of the players drank orange juice, others relaxed with a beer. They were together, and it formed strong bonds within the player ranks. When the team won, the practices were easy. When they lost, especially games that they should have won, the practices were brutal sessions with much huffing and puffing. Leonard treated his players like men, letting them do as they pleased. There were no curfews and very few rules when they were off the court. On the court, it was all business. Leonard was born in Terre Haute, Indiana. He came from a poor family, but they understood togetherness and life. Leonard believed in emotion and was the first coach from Indiana who kicked chairs, bottles of resin and floor furniture. He often claimed that Bobby Knight followed in his footsteps regarding his behavior on the basketball court. This always got a response from Knight, often not so friendly.

Slick always maintained that coaches in sports are a special breed and often a little goofy. He stated that most good coaches, like Bear Bryant, Red Auerbach, Vince Lombardi, Bill Sharman, Lou Holtz and John McKay all believed in one thing – winning. Leonard also believed in togetherness, as well as being physically and mentally tougher than opponents. He also felt that his team consisted of a special group of athletes and he cared for them greatly. He also cared about children, taking his team to hospitals, especially those for crippled children. He made it clear to those who played for him that they were not only blessed with the ability to play, but that they were fortunate to be able to walk and run. He instilled a feeling of compassion in his players and they loved him for that. Leonard was a master of psychology, but above all, he was a decent human being who loved his fellow man. The Indiana Pacers were the Boston Celtics of the ABA, and it didn't happen by chance. The team, from top management to the ball boy, were instilled with that special feeling of being on top and daring others to change it.

An Integral Role

Don Anderson, one of the top public relations men in the world, orchestrated much of the positive press that the WFL and Gary Davidson received. Don was the PR director for the WFL and played an integral role in the formation of the league. He also once served as the sports information director at USC. He had great credentials, knew all of the major media players, and most importantly, had their confidence. People like Frank Gifford, Jim Hill, Stu Nahan, Bryant Gumbel, John Hall, Braven Dyer and Jim Murray. He was a great addition to Gary Davidson's organization, creating a positive image for Gary and the WFL in its infancy.

Timing is Everything

The International Football League was organized and ready to go when the XFL, led by Vince McMahon and NBC Television, emerged onto the scene. The IFL board of governors decided that it would be suicidal to go head to head with the XFL, so we dropped out of the picture. The XFL moved ahead, but unfortunately, it was a total disaster for both McMahon and NBC. New leagues are difficult to get off the ground, and timing is all important. Ed Litwak, Leon Fulton, Art Blackwell, Craig Fertig and I made the right decision not to move forward in this case.

The Doctor is In

In Roller Hockey International, Dr. Richard Commentucci owned the Edmonton Sled Dogs. In addition to his general practice, Richard was the doctor "on" call for the New Jersey Devils. On many occasions, he'd take a red-eye flight to see his beloved team play in Edmonton, and then fly across the continent to be with his clients. Doc Richard was a real hockey fan and owner, with dedication and a love for the game.

Round Table

Every morning, those of us in St. Julian's Men's Club have our daily breakfast at Coco's Restaurant. We talk sports, politics and church matters. Our group consists generally of Sandie Mattie, Ed Marrier, Dom Ferrante, Pierre Nicolas, Father Jude, Father Luke and me. The Dodgers, Angels, Trojans and Irish get a lot of attention in our discussions. It's a great way to start the day.

Gone Globe-Ball

The innovative red, white and blue ABA basketball made a startling impact in the media and further separated the ABA from the NBA. It also gave the basketball industry a jolt and made Wilson a bundle of money. That gave Rocky Kalish an idea. The new IBA (International Basketball Association) also needed to further separate itself from the NBA, so Rocky bought an ordinary brown basketball and then paid a Disney animator he knew to turn the ball into a global map of the world. The ball was now mostly ocean blue, with every country a bright and eye-catching color. We took the new ball to a manufacturer in Renton, Washington (Baden), who put it into production in their plant in Taiwan. The global ball looked great on TV. We don't know how much money Baden made on the ball, but we do know that we never saw a nickel of it.

David Stern and Gary Bettman

People have told me over the years, "With what you've accomplished for both hockey and basketball, and especially for the players, you should be considered for the Hall of Fame."

I have responded that I had no chance, because the old-time hierarchy of both leagues would have no part of it. The fact is, the timeworn establishment of the NHL and NBA had always wanted to keep their leagues under their control. This was to aid in furthering their own greed. The backward-looking owners of those leagues were men who knew they had a good thing going for them and they wanted it all. Thank God, the modern leaders of both leagues, under the leadership of David Stern and Gary Bettman, are up with the times. They have moved both of their leagues into the 21st century.

There are always problems to work out, but then, no more so than the corporate presidents have to deal with at General Motors or Westinghouse. The only difference is that Stern and Bettman have their decisions out in the public domain. Every time they act, the media notes it, and they are constantly in the limelight and on the hot seat. The World Hockey Association was nurtured by a lot of dedicated men and women. The league was blessed with strong owners like Nick Mileti, Howard Baldwin, Jim Pattison, John Bassett, Paul Racine, Leonard Bloom and Bill Hunter, and was especially blessed to have Ben Hatskin and Gary Davidson there to lead the ship.

These men remind me of the quote by an unknown author. It states that excellence "comes from striving, maintaining the highest standards, looking after the smallest detail, and going the extra mile. Excellence means doing your very best."

A Point of View

Unfortunately, in our society, a slip of the tongue creates trouble for the rest of our lives. In my climb to the top of the line in my professional sports career, I often have stated at various sports seminars and university guest appearances that most people associated with professional sports are honorable and decent human beings. However, much like today's society, we have some "bad apples." It's that small minority that seems to draw the most attention to themselves and their problems. I believe that a great majority of our athletes, management and owners are good citizens, who in fact, do more than their share of good deeds in their communities. I have great disdain for those athletes who have disgraced themselves, their teams and fellow man. They were blessed by our Lord with wonderful athletic bodies as tools, and therefore, should be ashamed of themselves and look toward making their own restitution.

I choose to talk about the thousands of men and women who have distinguished themselves in life by doing the right things for others in sports. The only true "role models" are generally your parents, which I believe is only appropriate.

With our hyperactive lifestyles, those who attain distinction in sports should realize their God-given good fortune. They should always be conscious that others do look up to them because of their athletic accomplishments and act accordingly. Sports are a common denominator in our lives and they should be cast in that light.

In my life, I have had the great privilege of meeting some of the world's greatest athletes and achievers – Joe DiMaggio, Gordie Howe, Julius Erving, Ralph Backstrom, Bob Cousy, Bill Sharman, Chris Evert, Rod Laver, John McKay and Billie Jean King. They are good people with sound morals and are humble and understanding of their fellow man. They realize that our God has been good to them, and they prefer to give back. This to me is admirable.

Red Rush, Mr. Announcer

One of my dearest friends in life was the "Old Redhead," Red Rush, of the Chicago White Sox, Oakland A's Loyola of Chicago and Chicago Cougars fame. He was indeed a renowned announcer. I often kidded Red about his distinctive moniker. Can you imagine being called "Red" when he didn't have one strand of red hair on his head? He received that nickname back in his White Sox days with Bob Elston and it stuck with him ever since.

Red had a "hand game" that he played for years where he invited you to grab a dime out of his palm. He has, without a doubt; the quickest hands in the universe, which has helped him "burn" quite a few of the top athletes playing it with him. Rocky Kalish tells of a time when the 6'4" and Under Basketball League was touring China. Instead of the teams, Red was the hit of the show. He would get the top Chinese players and literally keep the fans in awe while he played his "hand game" with them at center court. He especially did a lot of kidding with the big fellas; the crowd loved it.

I knew Red for more than 50 years. We went back to our college days at USC where he was a "second rate" linebacker and I was the team's manager. Neither of us distinguished ourselves, but we loved it at USC and we were loyal alumni since. That shared love for USC football cost us a lot of money over the years, especially during the 13-game run the Irish had over us. Nevertheless, "cardinal and gold" has stuck with us through the ensuing years.

Red was our radio and television announcer every time that I put on a special event. First, he was good at what he did. Second, and maybe most important, I was always able to afford him. He especially enjoyed telling a story about me that usually got an audience to laugh. While we were on tour in the Pacific, we were supposed to play Korea, Taiwan, the Philippines and mainland China. The tour was going great but I had a major dilemma of not wanting to miss the Trojan-Irish football game in South Bend. My associate detail man, John Kanel, was with me on tour, along with Rocky Kalish. I knew the tour was in good hands, so I excused myself from continuing on to China, saying that I had a major television meeting with Bob Wussler of CBS.

My friend, Red, and his beautiful Nancy, went along to China with the tour. As it worked out, Red and Nancy spent the night at the "royal suite" at a YMCA the night before I left to return to the States. Because of those sleeping accommodations, I have had to listen to the fallout for years. Red continues to tell how they got very friendly with the mosquitoes and roaches, how the hot and cold water didn't work, and how the beds were falling down.

I met Red and Nancy at 6 a.m. in the hotel lobby and they both sported looks that could kill. I gingerly asked, "How was your night?" and quickly proceeded to disappear. The Rush's survived the first night at the YMCA, but rest assured, they will never let me make hotel arrangements for them again. (By chance, Red and Wussler later met in Chicago and the truth came out. Since that time, Red constantly gave me the business about it.)

Red was the announcer for all of our tours as well as being "the life of the party." He had the ability to make people feel at ease at all times. If you couldn't get along with Red, it's you that had the problem. He and his wife, Nancy, were delightful and decent people who loved people, especially their family.

Don Marshall, Pilot and Friend

One of the more decent men I know is my friend, Irishman Don Marshall. We have had great times together. He claims that Marshalls are better than Murphys. This naturally causes a major debate. He roots for UCLA and I am a Trojan of USC! Our mutual "turkey" friend, Ralph Kehoe, is Notre Dame. We meet each other on Wednesdays, we wear our school colors, and we lie to each other for two hours while we have dinner. Don is a proficient pilot, but I won't let him fly me, as he can't find himself on the road, let alone in the air. He is a very dedicated man with passion for his fellow man. He is a true friend.

Richard Neil Graham, Editor

We were both involved with Roller Hockey International. Richard was a reporter and I was one of the founders. We struck up a friendship that has lasted for more than 20 years. He and I have kidded each other about the questions that he asked me at the league's press conferences. He was a terrific reporter and he loved to see me dance over some of his questions. I told him that I would get even with him one of these days, and I have been working on it ever since. We both realized that I would have to clean up my initial autobiography, and Graham, in his nice manner, offered to do so. Thank you, Richard! We have spent many hours working on cleaning up the original book; we hope that have done a good job and that you will enjoy it. I thank Richard for his efforts.

Rick Torres, My Friend from Fresno State

I have been going to the Food Connection restaurant in Grand Terrace, California, for more than four years. During that time, I kidded a man who wore a Fresno State T-shirt about football. One day, I went to my car, and lo and behold, I had a flat tire. Rick, the man from Fresno State, offered to change the tire. A friendship developed between us – a Trojan of USC and a Fresno State fan. For more than three years now, Rick has helped me in driving the freeways. He has been a true friend and has helped me out a lot. Thank you, Rick.

The Hawaiian Leis

My friend Lenny Bloom sold his World Team Tennis franchise to Bill Schoen, a Honolulu lawyer, and Diana Plotts, a real-estate executive headquartered out of the Honolulu Hyatt Hotel. Since I helped in making the sale, Lenny gave me 15 percent interest in the team. The Hawaiian Leis featured the exciting European star, Ilie Nastase. Not only was Nastase a colorful character on and off the court, he was respected by his peers. My small percentage in the team gave me the excuse to visit Hawaii on a periodic basis. The Leis played their home games at the Honolulu Convention Center, which seated upwards of 8,000 tennis fans.

Of course, Hawaii proved to be a beautiful and popular place for our visiting tennis teams. The players loved the location and many of the players made Hawaii a resting stop and vacation spot from their busy schedule. Larry and Billie Jean King had a place in Kauai, which featured a tennis court on site. Many of their friends made frequent visits for relaxation and some on-court tennis time. Larry and Bill Schoen were business partners in a local Honolulu magazine called Spotlight. Through the years they did very well with their magazine, however the team lost money. As time passed, and with the support of the locals, the Leis almost broke even.

I drove a rental car in the islands and had a hard time negotiating "one-way" streets. I frequently got lost. My kids gave me the "business" over those indiscretions. We loved the Kahala Hotel and its close proximity to the golf course. I was lousy golfer, but I tried. I did manage to talk a good game. We loved Pearl Harbor, the Pele and the Mauna Kea Hotel. The swimming and food were terrific. The residents were very friendly and special to us during our visits. I hope our good friend, Bob Peyton, gets those great shows going again – they were a highlight to our stay on the islands.

Another special time was the early morning, when my wife and I would look over the majestic Pacific Ocean, watching the beautiful waves roll in with the surfers gracefully gliding across as they made their way to the shore.

In 2001, Elaine and I celebrated my 75th birthday and our 50th wedding anniversary in Hawaii at the Mauna Kea. They have a show that begins at 5:30 in the evening and lasts until 8:30 p.m., featuring a trio that plays Hawaiian music and hula girls dancing. It was a wonderful time. It was a time that I hope all of you may someday experience. Since I had my stroke, I look at times like those in Hawaii much more preciously than I did in the past. I realize just how lucky we were to be able to enjoy the beauty of the Hawaiian Islands. My son, Denny, has his National Junior Basketball program flourishing on the islands. This, too, gives him the opportunity, like his dad, to visit the islands on a regular basis. He will keep up the tradition.

Memories

There is a beautiful song named "Memories." Those of us of Irish-American descent have long been sentimentalists. Whenever that song plays, I think back to my younger days. In 2002, I was at the Anaheim Convention Center, when lo and behold, this great song was played over the loudspeakers. I reflected back to 1967 when the Anaheim Amigos, and ABA team, was playing their first game ever in the same center. There were about 4,000 people in attendance at that game, and the teams were in their nice and shiny uniforms. Owners Art Kim and Jim Ackerman were floating around the facility saying hello to their friends, and Ed Mikan, the league's chief referee, was making the rounds. Tom Liegler, the facility's manager, was meeting many of the dignitaries and it was a glorious night.

Gary Davidson, Don Regan, Sarah Regan, Elaine and I were talking to the guests and politicians, and it was indeed exciting. At the "ABA 2000" opener at the same convention center 35 years later, the same scenario played out, only this time, the faces were changed. Mike Carroll and Ed Litwak were the owners. Jack Armstrong and Bob Gottlieb, two of my friends, were waltzing around me saying hello to our friends. The players were warming up in their new uniforms, and Scott Brooks, the coach of the Los Angeles Stars, was discussing the upcoming game with the media. Kirk Watanabe, the team's GM, was rushing around putting the final touches together for the evening's activities, and Greg Smith, the arena manager, was making sure that the event staff was all in place. It was 35 years of history, yet very little had changed in substance. The game of basketball with some changes is the same. The players seemed taller, the cheers louder. Oh, what memories!

Affordable Prices

Americans have always believed in having an alternative – if you don't want to buy a Ford, you can buy a Chevrolet – and vice versa. Every day I hear from fans saying that they are tired of spoiled athletes and their million-dollar contracts. They are weary of scandals and are disgusted with the drugs, drinking and some of the players' mistreatment of women. That is why I believe that fans are finding a "breath of fresh air" in the minor leagues and are responding at the box office.

I have been very involved in the "other sports." It is here that I find a wealth of fans that support these sports and love the dedication of the athletes involved. The average family enjoys the entertainment that they receive, however, these sports are limited to a solid few and they remain a big secret. The media and fans that complain about high ticket prices do not come in droves to support "other sports." In reality, these very fans continue to support the four giants, namely the NBA, NFL, MLB and NHL.

A perfect point of contention is that fans didn't know how great and talented the ABA and WHA players were until the mergers took place and the "second league" started playing head-to-head with the so-called biggies. The indoor soccer leagues, Arena Football League, Roller Hockey International, lacrosse leagues and outdoor soccer leagues all offer the fan an alternative choice of sports venues. You'd be surprised at the level of talent, dedication and effort that these owners, management groups and especially the players expend to gain fan support. They desire the fans to come and watch them play and enjoy the experience. Unlike the mainstream athlete for the four major sports, these athletes are very fan accessible and enjoy signing autographs. By no means are they spoiled. You and your family are able to attend one of these sports, have fun, and in so doing, not go broke. I urge you to seek such teams and support them. You will be surprised at how much fun you will have at an affordable price.

A Strong-Willed Group

In the ABA, Don Regan and I had a difficult time with some of our leadership. It seems like we were constantly appeasing someone. It was not because of any personal feelings, but usually over what to do on issues. Points of contention usually ran rampant and we did have strong-willed people. A prime example was the usage of the red, white and blue basketball. Boy, was that a battle. George Mikan insisted on it, but Gary Davidson was against it along with Dick Tinkham, and they formed strong opposition. Lucky for those of us in favor, Mike Storen of Indiana changed his vote.

Some Feelings about the Sports World

The sports world is special. The people involved make the difference. I have found that in most cases, people in sport give others a sense of dedication and understanding. It's like in competition; one wins and one loses. It seems to be a matter of respect for each other's sacrifice, and the knowledge that a handshake is genuine and respectful. In my life in sports, I have found that most participants and owners were people of honesty, feelings and decency. Let's hope that it will stay that way.

I have observed that the bigger the star, the more humble and understanding they are in competition. They seem more down to earth. The sports world is a close fraternity; most people in it enjoy the profession and generally know what they're doing. It's often a tough life, but the rewards can be great. Many people think it's a glamorous life, but in reality, athletes, owners and administrators work hard to improve their skills and abilities. Agents and lawyers usually represent their clients well. There are a few exceptions to this rule, and in those cases, the media generally make a big issue over the results, often giving the agents too much attention. I have felt that many agents and lawyers use the media to benefit themselves to the detriment of the industry. Each player representative has his or her favorite media person and uses them to the hilt. I hope this practice will be controlled and not allowed to escalate, as it hurts all of us in sports.

The Documentary on My Life in Sports

In the final years of my life, I got to meet Hollywood producer Dr. Elliott Haimoff. My friend Don Marshall introduced us at a California restaurant. It so happened that I had also scheduled a meeting with Randy Friend, a 25-year friend, to the same restaurant. It was one of the best mistakes I ever made, as the two of them subsequently got together and created the outstanding documentary on my life in sports. This is very humbling.

Together with their associates Gordy McKenzie, Joanne Fox, Sam Oldham and Jose Sanchez, they put together a terrific history of our leagues. Our God surely honored me with the documentary: "Game Changer: The Dennis Murphy Story." We have since made a trip to Canada where my longtime friend Peter Young arranged a night out with the Edmonton Oilers, an original WHA team. It was a dream come true. The event was especially great as I had my granddaughter Melissa and her husband Chris along with us.

There were many reporters and friends at the game. The original captain, Al Hamilton, was there, and he and two cheerleaders escorted me to center ice, where I dropped the puck. The only thing missing was my friend Bill Hunter, the original owner of the Oilers, who is now resting in heaven. It was a night filled with memories.

Producer Dr. Elliott Haimoff has done more than 300 documentaries and is considered one of the best in Hollywood. Randy Friend has his own real estate business. They are both compassionate and decent human beings. I thank them both from the bottom of my heart. To order the documentary, please call (310) 553-4904, or email Elliott Haimoff at globalscience@sbcglobal.net.

Producer Elliott Haimoff and
Eagle Real Estate owner Randy Friend
are proud owners of the
Dennis Murphy documentaries.

DVD copies of the documentaries can be
purchased by calling (310) 553-4904.

Tom Adams of Tiodize Inc.,
wishes the Trojans of USC
and the Miami Hurricanes
future football success.

SECTION X: FAMILY

Elaine, My Wife of 58 Years

I first laid my eyes on her at the University of Southern California. She was a pretty blonde with a "10" figure. She had brown eyes that were gorgeous, further enhanced by her beautiful smile. As the years have gone by, I can honestly say that she has never once embarrassed me with her appearance or decorum. She always dressed with class and has always been a lady, conducting herself with grace and style.

Elaine has three college degrees. One of her favorite pastimes has been visiting the finest museums in the world. She is also an accomplished oil-based painter. We had three children and she was a terrific mom, but we are now unfortunately separated. Although at times our life was a bit turbulent, I wish her much love and happiness.

John Murphy – My Brother

Most basketball teams arrive two hours before game time so that they can relax with some conversation, get dressed and taped and then do some pre-game shooting. Don Sidle, a 6-foot-8 forward from Oklahoma, and Miami's second-round draft selection, was sitting in one of the arena box seats, when my brother John, our friend George Tommasino and I joined him. We chatted for a couple of minutes in conversation and I introduced John as "my little brother."

After John and I left, Sidle remarked to Tommasino, "Mr. Murphy's little brother is the biggest little brother I have ever seen."

He was referring to the fact that my brother stood 6′ 2″ and weighed 400 pounds. What he should have included with that statement was that my brother had a giant of a heart and could easily charm a snake. For 62 years, John brought happiness to most of the people he was associated with. He loved life and food, almost to a fault. He was Notre Dame and I was USC. We truly carried out that rivalry to the fullest. Just before John's death we gathered family and friends together at my daughter Doreen's home. It was a great time. We received wonderful letters from his beloved coach, Lou Holtz of Notre Dame, and from Mike Garrett, the athletic director of USC, urging John to continue his courageous battle against cancer. He cherished those classy letters until the day he died.

Lou Holtz later said in a letter to me, "It was such a meaningless letter to write." Yet my brother loved and cherished each word. I will forever be grateful to Mr. Holtz for his kindness and wonderful gesture.

My brother John was always thinking. He never got credit for a lot of the things he did, but he was always there for me and my family. John was the one who came up with the idea of getting Rick Barry to join the ABA by going through his father-in-law, Bruce Hale. He was also the one who suggested that we get Bill Sharman to join the ABA with a team. It was also John Murphy who constantly rescued me from trouble when my Irish temper would flare up.

Our Daughter, Dawn

In the later years of my business career, I made the decision to hire my daughter Dawn to help all of us in our office. She did a remarkable job. In addition to helping her "old man" in our everyday business activities, she was a great help in our endeavors. Dawn is a very moral and ethical person. She brought her sense of decency into all of our lives on a daily basis. Dawn is one of the foremost clogging instructors in the world. She enjoys clogging, and her husband, Dave Mee, enjoys square dancing. Dave is a financial planner for the Disney Corp. The Mees have three daughters: Denise, Debbie and Danielle. They too are involved in clogging. Our daughter is a blessing to me and she has been my "right arm" in the business world. Dawn has also greatly helped me in putting this book together. I thank her for her patience with me.

Our Son, Denny Jr.

My son, Dennis Murphy, Jr., was a fine athlete in his own right. He grew up with a bat on his shoulder and a ball in his hand. He loved sports and was blessed with great athleticism. He was very proficient at baseball and basketball and I was the typical father – I pushed him to be Mickey Mantle... Ted Williams... Joe DiMaggio. Dennis was 5'9", had good hands and was a good contact hitter. On the basketball court he was a fine point guard and a good shooter. Dennis was always with me as a youth. And, I must say, I loved it. Now he has his own son, Sean Michael Murphy, and, of course, I have him slated for quarterback or PAT kicker for the USC Trojans. He and his wife Nanci also have a daughter, Dina, who is now married to Matt Grubb. They are a terrific couple.

During Denny's senior year at Norland High School and my third year in Miami as the general manager of the Miami Floridians, Denny was named to the Miami All-City Baseball Team and was a third team all-city basketball team pick as a point guard. He was also voted Norland High School's Athlete of the Year. Needless to say, I was very proud of him.

Prior to his graduation from Norland High School, he called me at my office asking for a family meeting. The Murphy's have always had one special trait, saying our piece at all times. We were also very stubborn and still remain that way. At the gathering Dennis spoke up.

"Dad, we love you very much, but we need, especially for the girls, to settle in one place. We've traveled from Fullerton to Denver, to Long Beach, back to Fullerton and then Miami, all in five years. Dawn and Doreen (Dennis' sisters) are getting ready to enter high school and it wouldn't be fair to them to move again. I'm getting ready for college and I'm confused as to where to go."

He ended up attending Cal State University Fullerton. It was obvious to me that he was correct. In my years of developing leagues, I always attempted to fulfill my family responsibilities by attending my children's special events. However, if I had the opportunity to do it all over again, and I think I speak for most parents, I would have changed my priorities and spent more time with them during those critical developmental years. This especially applies to my two daughters. After the family "pow wow," I was convinced that Denny was correct. We owed it to the girls to spend their high school years in one place. My wife and I decided that we would go back home to California. It was the proper thing to do, and thankfully, circumstances made it easy to accomplish.

Our Daughter, Doreen

Doreen is a housewife and she is married to Guy Haarlammert, who has his own company in Placentia, California. They have three children, Melissa, Mindy and Michelle. The family lives in Chino Hills, California. They were extremely helpful to me in my recovery from a stroke in 2000.

Guy and Doreen are a giving and sharing couple. They help their family at all times. In our world, all families should be as blessed as our family has been. The Haarlammerts now have four beautiful grandchildren, Jake, Heidi, Allie and Taylor. Naturally, the great grandpa is blessed with their youthful activities.

Doreen and Guy spend a lot of time with their kids Melissa, Mindy and Michelle. The family is fortunate to have great in-laws in Ben and Chris. Michelle is single. As president of his company, Guy does a lot of work. He has more than 70 employees and Doreen helps him constantly.

Late-Breaking News

As we were doing the final proofreading of this book, our family was blessed with a new addition, Jonathan Robert Williams. He was born on March 24, 2013, to his parents Debbie and Michael Williams. My daughter Dawn and her husband David Mee are proud grandparents. Thank you, Lord.

POSTSCRIPT

And Finally

As we all move on, it is apparent that all of us did have a part in history. Some will say we hurt the progression of sports, and others will give us credit in developing new markets and new interest in the development of our profession. I like to think that we helped in making the sports world better, and I am happy that we played in cities that might otherwise never have had a professional team. I am pleased that the players, administration, coaches and management prospered. I also like to think that, in our small way, we were able to get new blood and new ideas into pro sports.

As for me personally, in my retirement I have found that there are other things in life than sports. I take my walks each day at the Tri-City Park here in California, feed the ducks at the park, and spend as much time as I can with the kids and grandkids and new friends who have come into our life. We spend a lot of time with our God, reading his words, and we find it rewarding.

Thank you for reading this book about those of us who tried to create new leagues and new venues for athletes to shine; our motives were always good and our hearts were in the right place.

Long live the field of professional sports. If we helped, so be it. God bless all of you!